Points of Resistance

Points of Resistance

Women, Power & Politics in
the New York Avant-garde Cinema,
1943-71

Lauren Rabinovitz

UNIVERSITY OF ILLINOIS PRESS
Urbana and Chicago

This book is printed on acid-free paper.

Earlier versions of portions of chapters 6 and 7 appeared as "The Films of Joyce
Wieland," in *Joyce Wieland*, ed. Philip Monk (Toronto: Key Porter Books, 1987),
117-79. An earlier version of portions of chapter 7 appeared as "*The Far Shore:*
Feminist Family Melodrama," *Jump Cut,* no. 32 (Apr. 1986): 29–31.

Library of Congress Cataloging-in-Publication Data

Rabinovitz, Lauren, 1950–
  Points of resistance : women, power and politics in the New York
avant-garde cinema, 1943–71 / Lauren Rabinovitz.
      p.   cm.
  Filmography:
  Includes bibliographical references.
      ISBN 0-252-01744-7 (cloth : alk. paper). — ISBN 0-252-06139-X (paper :
  alk. paper)
      1. Experimental films—New York (N.Y.)—History and criticism.
  2. Feminism and motion pictures—New York (N.Y.) 3. Women motion picture
  producers and directors—New York (N.Y.)—Biography.
  4. Deren, Maya. 5. Clarke, Shirley. 6. Wieland, Joyce, 1931-
  I. Title.
  PN1995.9.E96R34   1991
  791.43'082—dc20   90-10897
                                                                CIP

In Memory of Ed Lowry

And, in order to understand what power relations are about, perhaps we should investigate the forms of resistance and attempts made to dissociate these relations.

Michel Foucault, "The Subject and Power"

Contents

Acknowledgments

The research for this book began a decade ago as part of my doctoral dissertation at the University of Texas at Austin. It was at that time that I first met and interviewed Joyce Wieland and Shirley Clarke. Shirley Clarke generously gave her time, personal recollections, and candid thoughts despite the heavy demands and pressing deadlines of her schedule. Joyce Wieland opened up her heart and home to me and, over the ten years that I have been writing on her films and career, she has become a dear friend and source of professional support. Clarke's and Wieland's confidence in my efforts to discuss and analyze fairly their lives and films has been overwhelmingly generous, and without their trust and candor, this book could not have assumed its present shape. Despite many scholars' cautions about getting too close to living subjects, I am happy to say that the single greatest pleasure of this project has been my growing friendship with these two women.

My oldest debts are to those who guided this research as a dissertation and suggested directions in which to develop it into a book: William H. Goetzmann, Robert M. Crunden, Thomas Schatz, Suzanne Shelton-Buckley, and George Wead, all of whom worked with me at the University of Texas at Austin. The American Association of University Women and the University of Texas at Austin awarded me doctoral fellowships that allowed me uninterrupted time in which to work.

I wish to thank everyone—too many to list individually—who assisted my research trips over the last ten years. I do wish, however, to acknowledge Sandra Harris, Jason and Ruth Monas, Leila Sujir, Betty Ferguson, Lea Jacobs, and Leslie Midkiffe-DeBauche for their hospitality and ideas on repeated occasions. I am also grateful to the staff of the Special Collections at Mugar Memorial Library, Boston University; Richard Peña, Barbara Scharres, and the staff at the Midwest Film Center of the School of the Art Institute of Chicago; Maxine Fleckner-Ducey and the staff of the Wisconsin Center for Film and Theater

Research; the staff of the National Gallery of Canada; and the staff of the Art Gallery of Ontario. In addition, my cousin Hana Moll of Stratford, Ontario, voluntarily became my Canadian newspaper and magazine "clipping service," which quickly and easily afforded me materials not generally available in the United States. I am sad that she died before she could see how her labors aided mine and before I could publicly acknowledge my thanks.

Other individuals provided support and assistance during the book's preparation. My former colleagues in the History of Architecture and Art Department at the University of Illinois–Chicago and my Chicago community—Richard deCordova, Mimi White, and Stan Hughes—listened to many of my ideas in their various stages of development and helped me sort out what I should keep and what I should discard.

Ed Lowry read the first chapters that I wrote, and out of our daily discussions during the summer of 1985 the final structure and shape of this book took hold. Ed's enthusiasm and support for my work—perhaps even at the expense of his own—are the source of whatever original contributions this book is able to make. His death in the fall of 1985 was a devastating personal loss and deprived film studies of one of the freshest intellects of my generation.

I could not have finished this book were it not for the intellectual sustenance and unwavering support of everyone with whom I have worked at the University of Iowa. My department chairs in American Studies and Communication Studies, Rich Horwitz and Bruce Gronbeck respectively, backed up their enthusiasm for my work with release time off and assistance for manuscript preparation. The Graduate College underwrote photographic expenses. University House afforded me the scholar's retreat of which I have always dreamed; my thanks to Jay Semel and Lorna Olsen for making my stay there so pleasant and productive.

My extraordinary students in film studies at Iowa have consistently rewarded me with their curiosity and excitement about my ideas; they have shared many resources, criticisms, and insights of their own that have sharpened and polished what is here. Steve Wurtzler and Hanley Kanar assisted me in manuscript preparation. I feel especially grateful for my colleagues who welcomed me into their intellectual community, who read portions or all of my manuscript, and who have shared their insights, comments, and friendship: Leighton Pierce, Dudley Andrew, Rick Altman, Franklin Miller, Michael McGee, Albert Stone, Wayne Franklin, and Sam Becker.

Don Crafton's and Lucy Fischer's thoughtful comments, gentle criticisms, and advice were enormously beneficial, and I owe them a great deal. My editors, Larry Malley and Judith McCulloh, were patient and good-humored even when I was not.

My parents, William and Jeanette Rabinovitz, encouraged my passion for intellectual endeavors long before this project but have maintained an unflagging excitement and cheerful enthusiasm (even when I did not) throughout the duration of this particular effort.

My deepest debt, however, is to Greg Easley, who discussed and contributed to the ideas and materials at every stage of this book's development. He counseled and consoled me through the number of life's changes encountered during this book's progress.

1

Introduction:
The Woman Filmmaker
in the New York Avant-garde

One autumn afternoon in 1961, a dozen women assembled in a Greenwich Village apartment in New York City. The hostess welcomed her guests and served them tea. The guest of honor unwrapped colorful boxes and held up for view a succession of tiny infant's garments. The women's overlapping voices responded in harmonious, conversational rhythms that framed the visual display of gifts. The baby shower, like countless others across the country in the 1950s and 1960s, celebrated women's bonding while it affirmed the traditional importance of motherhood and childbirth in a woman's life.

But this baby shower, conventional enough in practice, also strained some of the social conventions to which it appeared to adhere. Amidst the clutter of wrapping paper, the women sat cross-legged on the floor of a Greenwich Village apartment filled with cat odor and Haitian music. Rather than an array of ready-to-wear fashions, the guests presented an odd visual assortment of bohemian costumes.

These women were known not for their support but for their renunciation of women's traditional sex roles and their celebrations of women's sexuality. Among them was author Anaïs Nin, who wrote erotic stories and flaunted her sensual lifestyle to a degree that would have appalled most bourgeois matrons. Another of the guests, independent filmmaker Shirley Clarke, had just completed a feature-length movie about a group of "junkies," and her fourteen-year marriage to Bert Clarke was in the divorce courts while she lived with an African-American actor several years her junior. Marie Menken was well known in New York City for her experimental films, and she soon acquired a different kind of notoriety as one of the regulars at Andy Warhol's Factory. The guest of honor, Bebe Barron, was a composer working in the male-dominated area of electronic music. Barron and the other guests (who included filmmakers Storm De Hirsch and Betty Ferguson and film organization activists Marcia Vogel and Cecile Starr) were all artists who were part of Greenwich Village's avant-garde.

The one, perhaps, who looked and played her part as a bohemian artist to the fullest was the hostess, filmmaker Maya Deren. More often than not, she appeared colorfully dressed for her parties wearing a peasant blouse, hoop earrings, jangling bracelets, and a long flowing skirt so that she could easily break into impromptu dancing. Deren was a beautiful woman whose curly dark hair formed a mane around her face. She was charismatic, opinionated, and outspoken—a leader in the avant-garde who championed filmmaking as an art form that was the equal of painting, modern dance, or poetry.

Deren frequently invited all sorts of people to the Greenwich Village apartment that she shared with her husband, composer Teiji Ito. She collected dancers, choreographers, filmmakers, poets, writers, art critics, and musicians in what could be considered a bohemian salon. Amidst her sizable collections of Haitian drums, Caribbean masks, primitive figures, contemporary paintings, and eighteen cats whose odor permeated the room no matter how filled with cigarette smoke it became, Deren held court.

If Deren and her parties were well known in Greenwich Village, her baby shower for Bebe Barron became legendary. For one thing, it was the last time many of her friends saw Deren; she died shortly afterward, at forty-four. A baby shower, overripe with associations of the conventional female roles of motherhood and housewifery, may not have been the one last party for which Deren would have wanted to be remembered. But this humorous irony may have strengthened the event's image as a Greenwich Village legend, making this baby shower a romantic remembrance of women artists banding together and supporting each other.

The Deren-Barron baby shower was simplified into a protofeminist gathering as it was retold to succeeding generations of women film-makers. Filmmaker Joyce Wieland recalled hearing about it as early as 1963, and she later thought about it as an example of the way that Deren led the women artists in a mutual support group.[1] However much dramatic and political color the occasion later offered artists as well as historians in the 1970s and 1980s, such contemporary depictions of the event project feminist concerns onto the meaning of the gathering. Once the discovery of available women models and mentors spurred new women's histories in the 1970s and 1980s, artists and critics alike made this baby shower a political metaphor removed from its social and cultural context.

The image of the baby shower, however, seems to illustrate more fully the cultural contradictions that Deren and the other women experienced. The baby shower evolved within the American ideology of the 1950s that idealized an all-consuming motherhood, linking childbearing and child-rearing to women's fulfillment. At the same time, white bourgeois women who increasingly entered the job market faced both their inability to live up to notions of the ideal mother and the possibility of individual fulfillment outside home and family.

The baby shower is more appropriately a female ritual that reconciles a woman's desire for independence from the family with her belief that she be selflessly devoted to familial needs. The shower itself represents a woman's leisure time selfishly devoted to socializing with other women primarily for her individual pleasure. At the same time, it allows her to fulfill a familial role of selfless devotion to home and children as she prepares for a new baby by receiving gifts and advice that will aid her in the future. Thirdly, the baby shower serves an important economic function, providing the woman and her family with material goods that will lessen the financial burden of infant care. One may further claim that such collective celebration of economic consumption associated with impending motherhood has an ideological value as a means for valorizing a woman's traditional role as the primary consumer in the family. As a ritual—the function of which is to resolve symbolically those beliefs that cannot actually be reconciled—the baby shower gives outward visible form to these contradictory impulses.

Deren's and her friends' psychic lives as artists might seem to have required little need for the baby shower's ritualistic function. Their actions outwardly opposed the dominant ideology of the 1950s. They were the exceptional women who balked enough at the conventions that they achieved a measure of success in artistic areas usually considered "masculine"—the erotic novel, electronic music, and filmmaking. But they did so without entirely understanding how the cultural institutions, including the family, constructed and organized women's social subordination.

Whereas the women may have individually prided themselves on the ways that their bohemian lifestyles and artistic pursuits subverted bourgeois appearances, they were also identifiable, as a group, as the wives of highly respected artists. In several instances, their relation to male filmmakers or artists was a condition of their entrance into the arts.[2] Deren had learned filmmaking from her second husband, Alexander Hammid. Bebe Barron's career began as a collaborator with her husband, composer Louis Barron. Marcia Vogel, likewise, was a film activist largely in collaborative efforts with Amos Vogel. Anaïs Nin's initial literary successes were intertwined with those of her celebrated husband, Henry Miller. Even Shirley Clarke, who became a filmmaker through both her financial and professional independence from her husband, still depended upon her marriage as a psychological precondition to a professional career as an artist. She married Bert Clarke because he supported her desire and calmed her fears about an artistic career.[3]

The stereotypical woman artist whose success depends upon her relationship to a male artist has a historical basis. Rozsika Parker and Griselda Pollock argue that only in the last two hundred years have women been so systematically denied access to the social institutions necessary for an arts career that they have had to depend more regularly upon familial relationships to overcome institutional restraints.[4] In addition, Parker's and Pollock's argument also suggests that modern art histories have implicitly perpetuated the stereotype by either omitting the existence of working women artists or dismissing as insignificant those they do acknowledge.

Such histories themselves are part of the modern definition of the artist that, since the nineteenth century, has equated artistic creativity with masculinity and male social roles so that Woman becomes excluded as a subject from this domain. Responding to Linda Nochlin's 1972 essay, "Why Have There Been No Great Women Artists?" and its query from a defensive, negative point of view, Parker and Pollock demand a reformulation for inquiries about women artists, "Each woman's work is different, determined by the specific factors of sex, class and place in particular historical periods. . . . But because of the economic, social and ideological effects of sexual difference in a western, patriarchal culture, women have spoken and acted from a different place within that society and culture."[5]

Constructed as synonymous with structures of femininity, Woman is a social category. As Simone de Beauvoir said in the heralded statement that has become a slogan for contemporary radical feminism, "One is not born a woman, but becomes one." Women occupy particular positions—economic, social, and ideological—within patriarchy, positions marked by unequal relations to the structures of power. As Parker and Pollock note, "Power is not only a matter of coercive forces. It operates through exclusions from access to those institutions and practices through which dominance is exercised. One of these is lan-

guage, by which we mean . . . positions from which to speak."[6] Art is
a language in these terms of representations and sign systems as well
as a cultural, ideological practice. As such, it constitutes a discourse by
which power relations are sustained on several cultural levels, and it
reproduces those relations in language and in images. In short, art
presents the world from points of view that represent positions of and
relations to power of sexes, classes, and races.

As female pioneers in their "masculine" fields of endeavor, women
artists remained prisoners of an ideology that even constructed their
positions of resistance within traditional social roles. As Parker and
Pollock assert, "The phrase 'woman artist' does not describe an artist
of the female sex, but a kind of artist that is distinct and clearly
different from the great artist."[7] The bohemian realm of the Greenwich Village scene in the 1940s through the 1960s celebrated the male
artist as a Romantic hero while configuring women's roles only in
relation to the male artist's greatness—as either wives or lovers. The
large, familial atmosphere typically describing Greenwich Village's
legendary artists' parties was structurally an enclave consisting of artists, wives, and mistresses. In this environment, bohemian male artists
were exempt from the bourgeois morals and demands of marriage
but women were not.

If the woman artist's dilemma was as simple as radical feminist
theorist Shulamith Firestone's belief that women's oppression stems
from the "natural handicap" of pregnancy, then one could easily claim
that Deren and her friends unwittingly celebrated at the baby shower
the source of their oppression.[8] But from a materialist point of view
that identifies a social—rather than biological—source for women's
oppression, the position of the shower guests was more contradictory.
As French feminist Christine Delphy points out, "Society does much
to make us think that the material conditions of periods [menstruation]
or motherhood derive from the physical event: that these *socially constructed* conditions are *natural* conditions. . . . There are thus not one
but *two* cultural interventions: 1—the devaluation of women's bodies
and physiology; 2—the material handicap created by the social conditions."[9] The baby shower—itself a ritual that eased women's conflicting
tensions without erasing them—encapsulated the complex web of
emotions associated with women's class and status while it affirmed
their dependency upon the family for their social identity and position.

Indeed, the whole issue of childbirth and motherhood as a material
condition of women's cultural worth raised conflicts and contradictory
desires among women artists seeking measures of professional value.
Maya Deren never had a child, although she began to express a desire

for one in the late 1950s when she was past forty. Shirley Clarke had a daughter early in her adult life, but suffered recurring bouts of guilt over her ambivalence toward motherhood, over an abortion in the late 1940s, and over her decision to pursue a professional career rather than to be a full-time mother. Even among the next generation of women filmmakers, Joyce Wieland was resolutely silent about her inability to bear children, and her silence on the subject itself may be a mark of the degree to which society has equated a socially constructed condition with a biological one.

Acknowledging the contradictory state of relations that these women represent provides the means by which one may begin to understand women's impact on the art world after World War II. Women filmmakers played an especially significant role in shaping the film avant-garde. Avant-garde, or independent, cinema offered women greater opportunities for artistic success because arts institutions initially accorded cinema only marginal status. Feminist film scholar Annette Kuhn explains, "Low investments of money and 'professionalism' have meant that avant-garde cinema has historically been much more open than the film industry to women."[10] The independent filmmaker individually or with a small group controlled the production process using inexpensive technology in what has become known as an artisanal mode of production. Pam Cook has noted that this cinema, concerned as it is with personal expression (the autobiographical, the intimate, the domestic), was especially appealing to women.[11]

Three women in particular explored cinema as a means for personal expression, and they successively represent the woman filmmaker's evolving function in the American avant-garde. Maya Deren, Shirley Clarke, and Joyce Wieland made films that ranged from psychonarration to social realism to feminist polemic—a progression that establishes the dominant direction of independent cinema after World War II. They supported their films through unifying their activities in movie production, distribution, and exhibition. Through lectures, printed interviews, published articles, and books, they shaped the receptions for their films and for independent cinema and identified the avant-garde cinema as an important contemporary means of self-expression.

It is perhaps significant that each woman had decided to become an artist and had already made a personal commitment to a career as an artist before she became a filmmaker. Maya Deren moved to film in 1943 from involvement in the New York dance theater and in writing poetry; Shirley Clarke moved from modern dance to film in the early 1950s; and Joyce Wieland gradually turned from drawing and painting to filmmaking in the late 1950s and early 1960s. The fact that each was already active in the avant-garde arts and had already become identified with an unconventional, even socially unacceptable position for a woman in the 1940s and 1950s may explain the ease with which all three achieved visibility in a medium that frequently intimidated young women unaccustomed and unacculturated to working with movie technology.[12] Because the three had already faced social pressures regarding the propriety of their chosen careers, their transitions to a newer medium may have presented fewer challenges to them than to other women who have embarked on filmmaking careers.

Maya Deren made her first film, *Meshes of the Afternoon* (1943), with documentary filmmaker Alexander Hammid. Deren's initial cinematic interest was in an individual woman's psychological experiences and in presenting a female subjective voice. But she expanded her interest from the individual woman to women's collective experience and its celebration in myths and rituals. Her short, modernist films both adapted strategies from other art forms and rhetorically challenged the aesthetic ideology of Hollywood filmmaking.

Since she was unable to secure continued financial backing for her films, Deren assumed the roles of lecturer, teacher, publicist, and organizational administrator to create and promote a more sympathetic climate for independent filmmaking. She developed organized economic bases for the production and reception of a radical film aesthetic. In the decade following World War II, Deren argued for artist-controlled organizations as a means for achieving a discourse of cinema art that would promote and celebrate independent films. Against the norms of New York City practice, she insisted that the contemporary artist must be more than a specialist in artistic production and must assume social and economic responsibility for artistic reception.

Deren set an example for many young filmmakers and, for Shirley Clarke in particular, she was a role model. The two women became friendly in the early 1950s when Clarke was an aspiring dancer studying with the renowned modern dancer and choreographer Hanya Holm. When it became clear to Clarke that her career as a dancer had limited possibilities for individual success, she began making dance films.[13] Clarke's first effort, *Dance in the Sun* (1953), reminded her friends of Deren's work, so they suggested that the two meet. After visiting Deren and seeing her films, Clarke applied Deren's ideas of poetic editing to short films that used nondance subjects.

Deren's strong sense of identity as a woman artist and her filmic philosophy shaped Clarke's political commitment to the independent cinema. Clarke's fierce campaigns for the independent cinema paid off in the New American Cinema movement of the 1960s. The New American Cinema advocated low-budget, starkly realistic films that addressed social rather than psychological issues, and it emerged temporarily in the 1960s as an alternative to Hollywood cinema. As a leader of the New American Cinema, Clarke made feature movies that critiqued patriarchal structures of knowledge—*The Connection* (1961), *The Cool World* (1963), *Portrait of Jason* (1967). She also applied and adapted Deren's model of economic organization and artist-participation. She preserved Deren's vision of an alternative cinema in the 1960s but extended it to a commercial cinematic system that included more diverse types of filmmaking than those envisioned by Deren.

Clarke met Joyce Wieland in 1963 when Clarke was at the height of her career in the New American Cinema and Wieland was a newly arrived painter-filmmaker in New York City. Wieland approached the independent, or underground, film community rather than any of the established art institutions because she was intimidated by the intensely competitive nature of the more prestigious art gallery system. After being encouraged by the filmmakers' open, friendly atmosphere, Wieland concentrated more on her filmmaking. Wieland admired Clarke's artist-defined role as an advocate for independent economic practices as well as for politically informed aesthetics. She, too, addressed culturally constructed ways of seeing in such experimental films as *Water Sark* (1965), *Hand Tinting* (1967), and *Rat Life and Diet in North America* (1968). Wieland emulated Clarke's move from experimental to documentary films, seeking a more politically expedient format for social critiques and, in the early 1970s, she introduced an explicitly feminist identification in such films as *Solidarity* (1973) and her feature-length melodrama, *The Far Shore* (1976).

Each woman worked under constant social and psychological constraints because of her status as a woman. For example, male art critics from Wieland's hometown of Toronto angrily dismissed Wieland's explicit psychosexual art solely because they felt women should not publicly address sexual pleasure. Deren's male peers made fun of a woman having intellectual theories regarding film as an art form. Clarke's business associates only invested in her films when she found male producers. The social relations that shaped the women's lives encouraged their trivialization or marginalization as artists as a means for containing them within dominant ideology.

Deren, Clarke, and Wieland were aware of their problematic position among filmmakers and artists. Clarke announced to an interviewer in 1967, "I have to deal with myself as a woman, then as a director."[14] In the same year, Wieland said, "I looked at a lot of men's art . . . but I thought: where is my tradition, where is my life? . . . I still had to look into the lives of women who had made independent statements."[15] Clarke also remembered Deren's words: "We [women] get everything we want by raising hell except what we want most."[16]

But, more than other women filmmakers working throughout the 1950s and 1960s in New York City, each of these women achieved public acclaim that went beyond the independent cinema community. The popular discourses about each woman focus on the female artist's body in a way that they might not for a man. Deren is represented as the embodiment of the exotic, Romantic woman, a mysterious and much talked about figure among the Greenwich Village art crowd. A decade later, Clarke delighted the popular press because she represented to them the eccentric Beat girl. Descriptions portray her as a diminutive, pixielike woman whose sleek dancer's body dramatically contrasted her intensity and spoken strings of profanities; she embodied the cool, hip attitude associated with the Beat generation of the early 1960s. A generation younger, Wieland came of age as an artist and political activist during the height of the counterculture in the middle and late 1960s. Journalists represented her as a plump woman with a round Madonna face, and they often photographed her wearing fashionably long, flowing cotton dresses that gave her an earth mother appearance.

Whether the women knowingly or unknowingly manipulated such poses is not the issue. They may have individually discovered that they were successful publicity ploys, or they may have wanted to protect the privacy of their identities, but their respective images fit the fashionable myths of femininity of their times, rendering the women culturally acceptable stereotypes within dominant ideology. Whereas these images helped to draw popular attention to artists and their causes as points of resistance, they also contradictorily popularized the idea that such women artists were still feminine.

The public construction of these three filmmakers may or may not be representative of public discourses surrounding women filmmakers and artists as a group in the 1940s through the 1960s. These women were certainly not the only individual artists contained by feminine stereotyping and language. In the same city in the 1950s, Helen Frankenthaler's stain-and-soak paintings were either dismissed or discussed in relation to metaphors, historical references, and literary analogies of the "eternal feminine."[17] Parker and Pollock describe such critical discourse surrounding Frankenthaler as "oozing notions of femininity from every pore."[18]

In the case of the three women filmmakers, it is especially important that they were contained and categorized because the films that they made consistently articulated positions for a *refusal* of the male gaze. The fact that, in the course of promoting their films and art practices, the filmmakers themselves were repetitively positioned as the sexual objects and stereotypes of male reporters' gazes is significant for telling what can and cannot be said about women artists and their work in the postwar era. Unable to discuss the women simply as artists and their films as breaking new ground within existing film movements, the discourse shifts the terms and focuses rhetorically on the filmmakers as women. It is an important condition for the reception of their films, always prefiguring the possibility for containment of their more radical filmic practices.

The troubled and troublesome nature of the woman filmmaker's continuing position in the American avant-garde was ultimately ruptured in the late 1960s when the art establishment noticed the independent cinema because of its successful programs. Museums and universities began carving out whole territories for independent cinema as a part of their institutional programs. Film production grants, filmmaking curricula taught by newly appointed filmmaker-professors, art journal coverage of film, collection development, and exhibition—the entire support system that Deren originally had envisioned—became inscribed within visual arts institutions. As institutional support for independent film increased, a rigid hierarchy concerning economic practices and political goals developed within the institutions that excluded women artists from the positions of authority and privileged their male counterparts. Women filmmakers—including Clarke and Wieland—lost their voices in the discursive and economic systems they helped establish. Such exclusion radicalized them, and they identified their experience in political terms of sexual and social power.

Clarke and Wieland felt so keenly betrayed that they both dropped out of the New York scene. Clarke first resumed work on private, short 8mm films, and then she turned to the newer medium of video. She subsequently moved to California and worked as a film instructor. She has only recently renewed her ties to documentary and feature film practices. Wieland returned to Toronto in 1971, where she became an important leader in feminist and nationalist artists' groups. She continued to experiment with the creation of an alternative cinema system and, learning from her New York City experiences, she attempted to create a more politically radical cinema for popular audiences. But after the commercial failure of her feminist feature film, *The Far Shore,* Wieland quit cinema and returned primarily to painting and drawing. She, too, has lately pursued filmmaking interests concentrating on the kind of short, intimate, artisanal films with which she began her film career.

As Deren, Clarke, and Wieland created an avant-garde cinema, their conflicting successes and failures forged connections among women, women's films and art, and women's lives in social institutions. Each one encouraged another to build upon the same strategies, creating a continuous chain of alternative film practices in spite of the frequency with which their efforts flagged and their films publicly failed. Constantly challenged in their attempts to control production and dissemination, they demonstrated that the means by which they financed, marketed, and exhibited their films were politically crucial to stopping their suppression. Deren's, Clarke's, and Wieland's struggles demonstrate that relationships among women's sexuality, power, and economics were important both to independent cinema's position as a subversive program of American cinema and to independent cinema's institutional implantation in dominant arts organizations.

NOTES

1. Joyce Wieland, interview with author, Toronto, Ontario, 15 Nov. 1979.

2. Several scholars, including Germaine Greer and Eleanor Munro, have identified women painters' relations as daughters or lovers of famous male artists as a social condition for their success. Many New York City painters in the 1950s who became acknowledged as leading artists only in the 1970s and 1980s were more likely to be known in the 1950s as the wives of major painters. More recent accounts of the professional careers of Lee Krasner (married to Jackson Pollock), Elaine de Kooning (married to Wilhelm de Kooning), and Helen Frankenthaler (married to Robert Motherwell) are replete with anecdotes and examples of how their marriages exacerbated the contradictory position of a woman as a professional artist. For general historical examples, see Germaine Greer, *The Obstacle Race: The Fortunes of Women Painters and Their Work* (New York: Farrar, Straus, and Giroux, 1979). For a discussion of American women painters in the 1950s, see Eleanor Munro, *Originals: American Women Artists* (New York: Simon and Schuster, 1979).

3. Shirley Clarke, interview with author, Chicago, Illinois, 24 Sept. 1981.

4. Rozsika Parker and Griselda Pollock, *Old Mistresses: Women, Art and Ideology* (New York: Pantheon, 1981), 82–113.

5. Ibid., 49; Linda Nochlin, "Why Have There Been No Great Women Artists?" *Art News* 69, no. 9 (Jan. 1971): 22–39, 67–71.

6. Ibid.

7. Ibid., 114.

8. Shulamith Firestone, *The Dialectics of Sex: The Case for Feminist Revolution* (New York: Morrow, 1970).

9. Christine Delphy, *Close to Home: Materialist Analysis of Women's Oppression,* trans. and ed. Diana Leonard (London: Hutchinson, 1984), 195.

10. Annette Kuhn, *Women's Pictures: Feminism and Cinema* (Boston: Routledge and Kegan Paul, 1982), 185.

11. Pam Cook, "The Point of Self-expression in Avant-garde Film" in *Theories of Authorship: A Reader,* ed. John Caughie (Boston: Routledge and Kegan Paul, 1981), 271–81.

12. As Deren said to an interviewer in 1947, "[It] always comes as a little bit of a shock to men when a woman is doing something in a field that has to do with machinery and with creating in terms of inventing with a machine." "Interview with Maya Deren," WGXR-Radio, New York City, 1947, Audio tape collection, School of the Art Institute of Chicago, Chicago, Illinois.

13. Shirley Clarke, interview with author.

14. Albert Bermel, "Young Lady with a Camera," *Escapade* 10, no. 5 (May 1967): 78.

15. Barrie Hale, "Joyce Wieland: Artist, Canadian, Soft, Tough, Woman!" *Toronto Telegram,* 11 Mar. 1967.

16. Maya Deren, as quoted in "Maya Deren," Shirley Clarke TS, November 1966, Shirley Clarke papers, Wisconsin Center for Film and Theater Research, University of Wisconsin-Madison, and the State Historical Society of Wisconsin, Madison. Quoted with the permission of Shirley Clarke.

17. Parker and Pollock, *Old Mistresses,* 149.

18. Ibid.

2

The Meanings
of the Avant-garde

What was the avant-garde in which Maya Deren, Shirley Clarke, and Joyce Wieland worked? The most consistently offered definition couples what the avant-garde is not with what it might be. Film textbooks generally claim that an avant-garde cinema both rejects the cause-and-effect relationships that are the primary moving force in Hollywood cinema and attempts to explore the spatial and temporal possibilities of the medium.[1] David Bordwell and Janet Staiger echo such an accepted notion in *The Classical Hollywood Cinema: Film Style and Mode of Production to 1960.*[2] But rather than defining the avant-garde solely by its oppositional style of filmmaking, they argue for the necessity of thinking about style in relation to mode of production. If Hollywood cinema is characterized by its studio system division of labor, then avant-garde cinema may be further identified by its particular conditions of production in individual filmmaking or small group collaborations.[3] Because numerous factors—such as economics and technology—affect production and production conditions, any definition of an avant-garde cinema must therefore be broader than a matter of aesthetics. A definition of avant-garde cinema must incorporate its inclusion in specific institutions that identify its practices as well as its aesthetics.

But even as Bordwell and Staiger foster new terms, the neat categorizations they encourage do not work in practice. Several kinds of cinema—avant-garde, modernist, art, and occasionally Hollywood—borrow styles across categories. At one time or another, films identified with each category have rejected narrative causality and emphasized spatial-temporal formal exploration. Differences between individual or collaborative artisanal productions and large group divisions of labor are often more dependent on the format (16mm vs. 35mm), length (short or feature), or size of budget than on aesthetic programs. When a film is marketed and exhibited with other so-called avant-garde films, audiences may associate that work with the avant-garde no matter how it was made. Even Bordwell and Staiger provide cinematic examples that cut across the very categories they delineate.[4] The existing confusion over what constitutes an avant-garde cinema demonstrates the inadequacy of joining style to mode of production as the means for understanding any cinema.

The Term *Avant-garde* in Culture

The term *avant-garde* itself has a long history among cinema, theatrical, visual, and literary arts. It has been used to describe various art movements since the mid-nineteenth century when it was first applied to a faction of the highly stratified Parisian art world. Since then, it has been used to identify the members and tenets of schools whose chief recognition comes from their opposition to current artistic standards and practices. Avant-garde literally means the "advanced guard" or "vanguard," a term originating in military usage and still connoting a militant, even macho purpose. Thus the words themselves transparently signify that the avant-garde has a fundamental charge to oppose and even to overthrow existing art practices.[5] But by designating something as avant-garde, the critic or historian assigns such historical struggle a binary pattern of opposition and confrontation. Used in this way, the avant-garde has all too often devolved into a convenient label stuck on each successive movement in modern art at the moment that it simultaneously confronts the dominant culture and is championed by an elite, intellectual class.

The term *avant-garde* then historically carries with it the ideological assumption that history is a tradition of regular disruption and continuous, progressive productivity. It encourages the historian to examine only those events and moments that fit the paradigm, disallowing other traditions that do not resolve in the prescribed way. It fosters a narrow, static view of history that cannot account for pluralism in a society and for simultaneous multiple points of view. In the past, such a historiographic approach has privileged the dominant tradition, inscribing other possibilities only insofar as they provide momentary alternatives to what is dominant or conflicts that are eventually diffused into the mainstream. History practiced in this fashion valorizes the status quo defining anything "other" only by its relation to what has been culturally dominant.

Furthermore, the emphasis on avant-garde as a continuous opposition does not answer the questions: to what is it in opposition and why? It cannot take into account the fact that the objects of its oppositions have changed with time and that such changes animate the avant-garde. In his efforts to situate the avant-garde historically, art historian T. J. Clark has argued that the important issue is not simply whether an avant-garde was progressive or vanguard but how it functioned socially as a political response to particular conditions of conflict.[6] He has demonstrated that the first group named avant-garde in mid-nineteenth century Paris expressed itself as vanguard to recoup power and to dominate the artistic world, "The aim of the avant-garde was to snatch a transitory and essentially false identity from the unity of the artistic world. . . . In such a world, being avant-garde was just an institutionalized variant of everyone's gambit. It was a kind of initiation rite."[7] In this context, the avant-garde may be understood as a social phenomenon rather than as a purely aesthetic one. It is the locus for unified aesthetic, social, economic, and political practices and representations only insofar as it is constructed in relation to conflicts in the art world and to the larger culture.

The term *avant-garde* has been especially problematic when applied to the cinema because its meaning has often changed with the writer and the occasion, depending on whether the context is literary, cinematic, or painterly. It is sometimes semantically interchangeable with the concept of an independent cinema (independent from Hollywood production) or an experimental cinema (emphasis on time, space, and lack of narrative causality). Avant-garde cinemas have been identified as auxiliaries of an avant-garde of painting and sculpture (e.g., Dada and Surrealism); they have been defined independently from any set of relations and identifications in the art world (e.g., underground film of the 1960s); and they have been tied to or overlapped with an avant-garde in the visual arts (e.g., structural film/minimal art). One may more broadly view each of these historical configurations as avant-garde so long as the object of study is the complex framework of practices—dependent on technology, aesthetic context (both cinematic and noncinematic), economic conditions, and the cultural or social milieu—that mark and organize such activities.[8] The term *avant-garde cinema* will hereafter refer to historically specific moments in which individuals, groups, and institutions produced and were produced by a system of artistic meaning from interrelationships among political, aesthetic, and economic practices.

Auteurism and the Avant-garde Cinema

Histories of American avant-garde cinema have traditionally been concerned only with close analysis of the films themselves. Tracing the cinematic lines of inquiry into intellectual, perceptual, and aesthetic matters, they chronicle an evolution of vanguard filmmaking after World War II that paralleled the dominant aesthetic direction of American contemporary art. The result has been the critical elevation or canonization of films that most closely and most overtly are relevant in these terms.

The promotion of such an American avant-garde cinema originated from a historiographic impulse in the late 1960s to legitimate American cinema as an art form. Historians and critics identified *auteurs* (film artists or "authors") whose films and styles transcended the lowly aesthetic levels of representation in which they generally placed the popular commercial cinema. Although many such studies—evolving from the direction established by the French *Cahiers du Cinéma* critics in the 1950s—focused on the extraordinary Hollywood director, auteurism also offered a way to historicize the independent practices of a cluster of filmmakers in New York City. The dominant film histories canonized a cinematic avant-garde that summarily linked Maya Deren to such successors as Stan Brakhage, Jonas Mekas, Kenneth Anger, Andy Warhol, Michael Snow, and Hollis Frampton.

The New York configuration provided a particularly good site for locating auteurs. New York City was the international center for both publishing houses and art galleries, which established it as the economic and critical center of the arts. As a result, independent film distribution, screenings, and written criticism consolidated there in the 1960s. A large, coherent discourse on New York independent filmmaking represented artisanal film as expressions of art. In the late 1960s and early 1970s, books dominated by the Manhattan filmmakers entered into the art and film book market. Gregory Battcock's *The New American Cinema: A Critical Anthology*, Sheldon Renan's *An Introduction to the American Underground Film*, Parker Tyler's *Underground Film: A Critical History*, David Curtis's *Experimental Cinema*, and Jonas Mekas's *Movie Journal: The Rise of the New American Cinema, 1959–1971* all set forth an American independent cinema constituted by the personal artistry of the New York City filmmakers.[9] The culmination of this trend was P. Adams Sitney's *Visionary Film: The American Avant-garde, 1943–1978.*[10]

Sitney characterized the film styles of the canonized avant-garde by the ways each infused independent cinema with the formal aesthetics of Surrealism, Abstract Expressionism, Pop Art, and Minimalism. He identified a veritable potpourri of vanguard art movements in a New York avant-garde cinema that perpetuated the Modernist tradition established in the 1920s by Marcel Duchamp, Fernand Léger, Man Ray, Luis Buñuel and Jean Cocteau. Sitney promoted cinema aesthetics as a Romantic quest for self-knowledge set within a Modernist conception of film history as groups of "film objects" inside a closed system of formal practices.[11]

Sitney's influential book not only secured the myth of an independent cinema grounded in the same Modernist formalism as contemporary American art, but it also established an agenda for filmmakers, critics, and curators alike into the 1970s and 1980s. Generally ignoring the Marxist theories that dominated film studies in the 1970s, American avant-garde cinema studies either continued in the auteurist tradition (Amos Vogel's *Film as a Subversive Art,* John Hanhardt's *A History of the American Avant-garde Cinema,* and Robert Russett's and Cecile Starr's *Experimental Animation*) or incorporated semiotic or phenomenological approaches into more rigidly formal analyses (Annette Michelson's *New Forms in Film,* Dennis Wheeler's *Forms and Structures in Recent Film,* Peter Gidal's *Structural Film Anthology,* and Regina Cornwell's *Snow Seen: The Films and Photography of Michael Snow*).[12] Such studies maintained their orientation in formal textual valorization while being marginalized in a professional discipline of film scholarship less focused on American cinema's artistic value than dominated by the ways that Hollywood functions as a culture industry commodifying and circulating itself as an ideological expression of a post-industrial society.

During the 1970s, Peter Wollen's 1975 essay "The Two Avant-gardes" became a model for historicizing the New York avant-garde cinema. Differentiating between the contemporary avant-gardes of New York, London, and Paris, Wollen claims for the New York movement that "in North America there is only one avant-garde centered on the various Co-ops. There are no obvious equivalents of [Jean-Luc] Godard or [Jean-Marie] Straub-Huillet [and Danièle Huillet]."[13] Wollen not only ties conditions of distribution to specific aesthetic and political programs but to an implicit "lack" of an exemplary-styled cinematic practice, "I think the absence of any avant-garde of the Godard type in North America could ultimately prove a severe limitation on the development of the New American Cinema itself, narrowing its horizons and tying it unnecessarily closely to the future of the other visual arts, condemning it to a secondary status within the art world."[14] Because Wollen develops his ideas about North American production and aesthetics from the reduced handful of films canonized as the American avant-garde, he is able to set up North American avant-garde cinema as "Modernist cinema" and as a lesser cousin of European avant-gardism.[15] He then decries Modernist cinema as a politically uncommitted extension of self-reflexive tendencies in contemporary painting, "This way of thinking about art has remained one that filmmakers have in common with painters and other visual

artists. . . . Thus the impact of avant-garde ideas from the world of
visual arts has ended up pushing filmmakers into a position of extreme
'purism' or 'essentialism.' "[16] Wollen sees this cinema as the dead-end
result of what he and others have frequently labeled, in deference
to critic Clement Greenberg's advocacy for such a program, "post-
Greenberg 'modernism.' "[17]

Wollen's "true" avant-garde deconstructs its subjects or investigates
its materials, symbol structures, and meaning processes in relation to
their political significance in the world. For Wollen, Soviet filmmaker
Dziga Vertov's *Man with a Movie Camera,* Sergei Eisenstein's films, Jean-
Luc Godard's post-1968 films, and, in painting, Pablo Picasso's *Les
demoiselles d'Avignon* are all exemplary avant-garde texts because they
generate new meanings and understandings of our relationships to
reality. Instead of being merely formal contemplation, they have a
social mission, a project that, for Wollen, is the essential goal of art.

Wollen's essay creates a simplistic bifurcation between North American and European cinemas so as to make the study of Modernist/North
American cinema appear irrelevant to those interested in relations
between politics and art, art and ideology, ideology and practice. A
few scholars have criticized Wollen's assumptions regarding film and
literary theory or his privileging of individual texts as the means
for reading off the effects of an entire production and consumption
system.[18] Others have pointed to the way that Wollen's theory of film
language even ignores Eisenstein's, Vertov's, and Godard's writings
that call for their filmic languages within a new system of practices.[19]

But the central problem is Wollen's critical presumption that one
can only understand the New York independent cinema as a whole by
adopting and being faithful to the same aesthetic approach that the
dominant filmmakers themselves advocated. Such a historiographic
blunder precludes the possibility of understanding the formal and
political dynamics of such independent, feature-length American narratives as John Cassavetes's *Shadows* (1959), Shirley Clarke's *The Connection* (1961), Adolfas Mekas's *Hallelujah the Hills* (1963), Shirley
Clarke's *The Cool World* (1963), Jonas Mekas's *The Brig* (1964), Andy
Warhol's *Lonesome Cowboys* (1967), or Emile de Antonio's *In the Year of
the Pig* (1969), all of which tackled the social and political issues of the
1960s from an avant-garde position of alternative representation and
production practices. It negates the possibility that the avant-garde,
even as Wollen defines the constituent texts, could also function as a
critique of contemporary society. Short, experimental films such as Stan
Vanderbeek's *Science Friction* (1959), Bruce Conner's *A Movie* (1957),
Kenneth Anger's *Scorpio Rising* (1963), or George Kuchar's *Hold Me*

while I'm Naked (1966) did protest social reality by investigating, deconstructing, and subverting dominant forms of mass culture representation.[20]

Wollen's argument is significant here because it frames the dominant attitude toward New York independent cinema in the 1960s and 1970s. The principal historians of New York independent cinema were also the histories' chief objects, thus conflating their intentions and their interpretations. For example, authors Jonas Mekas and Peter Gidal were primarily independent filmmakers; Amos Vogel organized and ran Cinema 16, one of the first postwar independent film societies and distributors, and he directed the first New York Film Festivals. In addition, such filmmakers as Stan Brakhage, Maya Deren, Hollis Frampton, Gregory Markopoulos, Michael Snow, Sidney Peterson, and Stan Vanderbeek frequently described their ideas and intentions to shape their films' critical receptions.[21] Although such a practice may not be exceptional within the history of the arts where the professional functions of the artist, critic, and curator are often intertwined, the ways that this practice contributes to constructing meanings of any historically constituted avant-garde is important. As Constance Penley and Janet Bergstrom have said about the significance of such critical practice in the 1960s, "The discourse about the object becomes (is the same thing as) the discourse of the object."[22]

Whether through personal appearances with the films or through published articles and books, the filmmakers and historians supported an artist-centered system that placed textual meaning in the author's statements. They considered the artist the central primary source for historical interpretation. Patricia Mellencamp has suggested, "The resultant interpretive translations are nostalgic documentations, circumscribed by intention, remembrance and anecdote. . . . [They] risk an individualism of 'secret singularities,' outside history, without politics, and thus without effect."[23] In other words, much of the history of American postwar independent film has been a discourse of personal interests forwarding points of view that enhanced individual historical roles as well as the overall importance of the individual artist.

The emphasis on authorship that coalesced in the 1960s as the means for valorizing an entire system of filmmaking grew out of a discourse already circulating that privileged the identity of the author as the mark of artistic value. The function of the author as an indication of artistic merit has dominated twentieth-century criticism. The important task of Modern criticism became the reestablishment of the ties between an individual and a work, an individual and a body of works, offering the evidence of this relationship from the internal forms and relationships of the works. Implicit in author-centered criticism is the philosophy that the author as an individual is a free agent who accomplishes a design and endows an object with meaning. The author becomes a means for classifying a unified subjective voice acting directly on an audience.

But the name of the author more accurately unites a number of speaking voices in one ego. Michel Foucault describes the name of the author as a "second self" whose similarity to the individual bearing the name is never fixed and undergoes considerable alteration within the course of artistic production, circulation, and reception, "It would be as false to seek the author in relation to the actual writer as to the fictional narrator; the 'author-function' arises out of their scission—in the division and distance of the two."[24] Although he discusses the "author-function" in literature, the concept is equally applicable to other arts, including painting, music, theater, and cinema. To discuss "Jackson Pollock" in painting or "Alfred Hitchcock" in the movies is to open a discourse uniting aesthetic, economic, and ideological practices under the rubric of an individual who bears a relationship to the discourse but cannot be equated with it. (One might even say, using popular lingo, that the name of the author or filmmaker represents a "brand name," and as such, it acquires an economic value all its own that can be traded upon in the "name" of art.)

This concept of the "author" does not deny that works of art may bear the imprint of an individual who participated in the work's production. But authorship itself participates in a more complex cultural operation than the simple attribution of a product to an individual producer. In the case of Hollywood classical cinema, it may be easy to see how the studio mode of production and division of labor involve many people who finance, make, market, and distribute the product. All of their labor contributes to what we know of as cinema and how we consume and interpret individual films, even though auteurism assigns authorship to the film director.

In book publishing, it may not be so obvious that a manuscript is likewise the site of multiple discourses and practices (the "credits" are hidden in the text or made invisible). Before a book is actually sold as a commodity (including this book), it is rewritten and edited (often more than once and sometimes by different individuals), packaged under headlines or titles, juxtaposed with visuals, and marketed according to the publisher's need to achieve sales. All the components of this process draw upon cultural conventions of "meanings" already in circulation that are activated as meaningful statements before, as well as during, the work's reception in the reading process. As Walter

Benjamin points out in his essay "The Author as Producer," the interests of institutions that produce written literature are not necessarily the same as those of any individual who labors as the signatory "author" while the institution itself works to convince individual participants and the public that they are united in the book's "consciousness" displayed and displaced as that of an individual author.[25] It is the discourse of authorship that addresses only a single identity as a speaking subject and it ultimately disguises the program and process of meaning construction.

Two books demonstrate with varying success the way the entire historiographic project of an avant-garde is reframed when the avant-garde is defined as discursive practices rather than as a series of individually constituted creative acts. Dana B. Polan's *The Political Language of Film and the Avant-Garde* lays the groundwork by theorizing an artisanal culture of discursive practices.[26] He draws heavily upon Benjamin's Marxist writings that deal with the social and economic position of avant-garde practices. Polan argues that the social reformulation of the avant-garde is required to explain how meaning is achieved when the artistic act of addressing experience is itself historically conditioned.

Designed for an audience less knowledgeable in film theory and history than Polan's, J. Hoberman's and Jonathan Rosenbaum's *Midnight Movies* addresses authorship in avant-garde practices.[27] It situates the appearance and identity of the auteur within audience expectation and reception (e.g., *The Rocky Horror Picture Show*), within the economics of distribution and exhibition in "midnight time slots" (e.g., Kenneth Anger's *Scorpio Rising,* Andy Warhol's films), and within competing discourses of drug culture, avant-garde art, and mysticism (e.g., *El Topo*). Hoberman and Rosenbaum demonstrate that all the above films were posed discursively as oppositional along the fringes of the commercial movie industry in a midnight exhibition time slot. Whereas Hoberman's and Rosenbaum's book is not so cogent as is Polan's regarding its historiographic project, *Midnight Movies* refocuses attention on the issues of economic power and reception in film interpretation.

By overturning the notion of authorship as one of "pure" creativity, the historian abandons the Modern critical project of excavating themes and concepts in a work of art whose meaning is already constituted and predetermined by a godlike creator. Foucault proposes instead that authorship be understood as the basis of social relationships that enact the text and allow the reader to construct a unified subjective voice across it.[28] Authorship is a discourse of the text as well as one circulating outside it, and what Foucault calls the "author-function" is an ideological web of textual practices, social discourses, and subject relationships.[29] Foucault outlines the new questions that the historian must address: "Under what conditions and through what forms can an entity like the subject appear in the order of discourse; what position does it occupy; what functions does it exhibit; and what rules does it follow in each type of discourse?"[30] Instead of looking for a transhistorical and singularly fixed meaning in a work of art, the critic's task is to find out how *meanings* are constructed among different groups and at different moments. The implications of Foucault's argument are monumental for studies of avant-garde practices in general and for women's positions as both social and textual subjects in avant-garde practices.

Developing Foucault's critical model becomes especially important for a feminist theoretical practice that, guided previously by ontological questions about women's art and literature, style, etc., could only approach the knowledge of its topic from the humanist point of view that informs auteurism as a free subject endowing objects with meaning. Feminist film critic Kaja Silverman is one of the first to point out the special relevancy of this model for feminist theory and experimental cinema,

> The author often emerges within the context of discussions [on women's experimental cinema] as a largely untheorized category, placed definitively "outside" the text, and assumed to be the punctual source of its sounds and images. . . . There is no sense in which the feminist author, like her phallic counterpart, might be constructed in and through discourse—that she might be inseparable from the desire that circulates within her texts, investing itself not only in their formal articulation, but in recurring diegetic elements.[31]

Although Foucault does not address the role of sexual difference in the discursive formation of the text's subject, the discourse of the "author-function" is all the more important when the name of the author is a woman's, because it signifies and empowers a gendered social subject as an index of a female textual subject. As Nancy K. Miller said in an insightful critique of Foucault's position on the relative unimportance of the name of the author, "What matter who's speaking? I would answer it matters, for example, to women who have lost and still routinely lose their proper name in marriage, and whose signature—not merely their voice—has not been worth the paper it was written on. . . . Only those who have [power] can play with not having it. . . . If feminists decide that the signature is a matter of indifference . . . the real end of women in the institution will not be far off."[32] Miller's critique is especially helpful here because it does not circumvent Foucault's position through the admission of a psychoanalytic subject that has preoccupied so much of contemporary feminist critical theory, but rather through the very terms of subjectivity that Foucault engages. Miller as well as Silverman rightly asserts that the "author-function" is important as such for feminist theory because it marks critical sites for understanding the cultural underpinnings and enunciation of any specifically female discourse.[33] For feminist critics, whose goal is not detached academic observation but intervention in the institutional structures that sustain oppression, it is particularly crucial to map out such historical instances and to understand their constructions.

The Discourse of Women in the American Avant-garde Cinema

If Deren, Clarke, and Wieland represent the expressions of women's discourse in an artisanal culture, the questions of their auteurism or themes and styles must likewise defer to the more important questions regarding their formations as discursive subjects, their individual functions as social subjects among independent film practices, and the political systems of their constructions. But studies of women's cinema, of independent cinema, and of individual women artists have not addressed them in this way; the implications of their "author-functions" have been ignored. Although the independent cinema histories previously mentioned do occasionally discuss Deren, Clarke, or Wieland, all three have not been considered together as a continuous, connected woman's discourse affecting the directions and expressions of American independent cinema.

Deren, Clarke, and Wieland achieved positions of visibility in a system of practices that admitted few women. Although fewer women filmmakers than men participated in the emerging artisanal culture of New York City in the 1960s, there were other women besides these three who made movies, worked together, or helped effect the discursive system so frequently chronicled in the existing histories. Marie Menken, Storm De Hirsch, Barbara Rubin, Naomi Levine, Carolee Schneemann, Linda Talbot, and Amy Taubin made and showed films; Marcia Vogel and Barbara Rubin were effective organizers; Cecile Starr wrote about experimental film for national as well as local publications. But none express the attempt to unify practices among filmmaking, organization administration, and public discourse so well as Deren, Clarke, and Wieland.

Critics have noted that all these women were marginalized by contemporary film histories and institutional film collections. In 1974, two *Velvet Light Trap* essays asserted that historiographic practices of the New York independent cinema contributed to the women's critical neglect or marginalization. Russell Campbell's "Eight Notes on the Underground" said that inherent sexist and elitist attitudes were the basis for the New York independent cinema's preoccupation with formal novelty.[34] Ellen Freyer's "Formalist Cinema: Artistic Suicide in the Avant-Garde" argued that this formalist sensibility masked a conformist practice that denied expression to anything or anyone that did not celebrate the same values as the white male leaders of the so-called avant-garde.[35] Both Campbell and Freyer concluded that a handful of male filmmakers and critics maintained control over independent cinema for their own self-glorification and inscription into history.

In 1978, Constance Penley and Janet Bergstrom provided a more extensive critique of the New York cinema. Published in *Screen*, the influential British journal of film theory, Penley's and Bergstrom's "The Avant-Garde: Histories and Theories" was an explicitly feminist analysis of the New York formalist discourse usually named "avant-garde."[36] It is significant that they wrote as representatives of the feminist collective editorial board of *Camera Obscura*, outlining as their journal's goal the investigation of discourses and the ways that the interplay of discourses is controlled. By pitting themselves against the ideological project of the New York discourse in the most influential international film theory journal, Penley and Bergstrom started a debate that insured no one could again take for granted the power elite of the New York independent cinema while they squarely placed *Camera Obscura* in an important discursive position of opposition.

Penley and Bergstrom examined the politics behind a canonization of films and filmmakers in the New York independent cinema. The specific discourse that they examined cohered in the late 1960s and early 1970s in the practices of Anthology Film Archives, Sitney's publication of *Visionary Cinema* as well as *The Essential Cinema: Essays on the Films in the Collection of Anthology Film Archives*, and John G. Hanhardt's museum catalogue *A History of the American Avant-garde Cinema*.[37] Echoing Freyer and Campbell, Penley and Bergstrom asserted that the critical ideology forming the consensus was a formalist one steeped in the philosophy of the dominant contemporary art world. According to Penley and Bergstrom, New York University professor Annette Michelson's representation of cinema as a grand metaphor of vision or as an analogue for consciousness became the philosophical basis for the books' critical discourse. Penley and Bergstrom first took issue with Michelson's phenomenological approach to cinema and then claimed that her ideas infused Sitney as well as the authors of essays in Hanhardt's catalogue because all of them were her students or colleagues.[38]

The three books explicate films largely in the collection of Anthology Film Archives, an institution whose self-proclaimed goal was to collect masterpieces of cinema according to the standards of its five-man selection committee. Films that adopted Michelson's model of cinema became institutionally inscribed—that is, critically celebrated and bought for collections as masterpieces—whereas films and film critics that did not conform were denied a place for expression. Penley and Bergstrom argued that such a policy contrasts with that of most film archives, which attempt to collect as diverse a group of films as possible on the assumption that present critical standards will, in time, give way to others. They said that the standardization among volumes based on Anthology's collection was particularly insidious because it caused other institutions to believe that an official canon existed, "The fact that there is such a consensus on the 'sublime achievements' (Anthology's phrase) of the American avant-garde . . . suggests that a particular corpus and a particular interpretation of its development are quickly becoming standardised, thus threatening the critical recognition of those films which are not included."[39] Other museums and universities (e.g., the Centre Georges Pompidou in Paris) began basing their own collection foundations on the "avowedly idiosyncratic" one (Penley's and Bergstrom's words) of Anthology.[40]

Penley's and Bergstrom's argument is important for the way it defined a discursive process. It identified the mid-1970s publication of three books as a point of consolidation for intellectual discourse that had begun in the late 1960s with film's entrance into the academy. The analysis demonstrates how the process functions politically, sustaining particular power relations and determining ideology. But Bergstrom and Penley neglect how well placed and consolidated such a discursive practice was before it became further valorized within professional discourse. Penley and Bergstrom failed to examine the discursive roles played by the battery of nonacademic books published in the years (1967–72) preceding Sitney's *Visionary Cinema*. The books on independent cinema by Battcock, Curtis, Mekas, Renan, and Tyler rarely apply rigorous film theory to the objects of their fascination, but they nevertheless single out the same films for a canon of experimental cinema. Their canon is the same one that Sitney adopted for his two books, and Hanhardt for his.

Penley and Bergstrom attributed too much power to academia itself in the establishment of a unified critical voice and institutional command over avant-garde cinema. At best, they overgeneralized the new role that university film studies began to play in the late 1960s for regularizing the discourse. At worst, they made Michelson (who, as one of the few established women in academia, had a reputation for not supporting either feminist film criticism or young women scholars) the patriarchal villain.

Feminist Film Theory and Avant-garde Cinema

Since Penley's and Bergstrom's landmark article, few feminists have accepted the challenge to rewrite American avant-garde film history. Even *Camera Obscura*, the journal on which Penley and Bergstrom continued as editors, has devoted only occasional space to this activity. But, inspired by both the collectivist political goals of *Camera Obscura* and the sense that women independent filmmakers have been neglected, one group of women began to attempt a redress even before Penley's and Bergstrom's article appeared. *The Legend of Maya Deren* Project, a Berkeley feminist collective composed of the *Camera Obscura* editorial board's colleagues, began a documentary biography on Maya Deren in 1973.[41]

The Legend of Maya Deren Project aimed to unite feminist goals and methods in a biography that would analyze a woman's life within historical forces. In a 1979 group interview in *Camera Obscura*, the Project outlined its collaborative effort as a feminist attempt to create "a cumulative and multiple telling" through documents and interviews so that no one authoritative voice would unify and direct the narrative.[42] Relying upon extensive documentation that would offer alternative points of view, the Project promised to demythologize American independent film history.

But in the fifteen years since it began, the Project has produced only one (in two parts) of three projected volumes, and it represents a validation of, rather than a challenge to, traditional independent film studies. *The Legend of Maya Deren: A Documentary Biography and Collected Works. Volume I, Part One: Signatures (1917–1942)* is a five-hundred-page book consisting of autobiographical documents, interviews, photographs, and an astrological chart that examine the details of Deren's life and thought only up to the point where she was about to embark on her first film.[43] Schoolgirl letters, samples of handwriting and drawings, adolescent poetry and stories, school transcripts and report cards, and family album photos are extensively reproduced. Arranged within the Project's organization and analysis of Deren's life and personality according to astrology and an African philosophical schema, the artifacts function as material traces of meanings in Maya Deren, but more important—through their sheer numbers and scale—to assume mysterious significance in their own rights.

The Legend of Maya Deren: A Documentary Biography and Collected Works. Volume I, Part Two: Chambers (1942–1947) reproduces the same kinds of materials—interviews, photographs, letters, autobiographical notes, published writings—that were made available in the first publication.[44] But because the focus here is on the period for which Deren is best known, the scrupulous attention to biographical detail and the new availability of unpublished or out-of-print sources are more explicitly relevant to Deren's individual film productions. The Project, however, has continued to reproduce auteurism's basic assumption that an artist's life (and particularly early life) is the best source of evidence for understanding the themes and meaning of her *oeuvre*. The result is that so far the redress of women filmmakers' neglect has been to counter silence with an overwhelming amount of information on one woman filmmaker.

It is, perhaps, not coincidental that the filmmaker chosen was the only one of two women initially represented in the Anthology Film Archives collection. It is certainly not merely circumstantial that although the Project's own history began intertwined with that of *Camera Obscura*'s at the University of California, the Project's current project and program are supported and being published by Anthology Film Archives, the very institution that the *Camera Obscura* editors originally singled out as the prime perpetrator of a rigorously narrow auteurist cinema. The point is not that there is a political conspiracy of institutions or individuals at work here, but that the discursive practice as well as its social politics are not unified and without contradiction.

In direct counterpoint to *The Legend of Maya Deren* Project's efforts to excavate the reputation of one woman filmmaker, others approached women's cinemas as a means for understanding how women have activated their own language of self-discovery as well as a critique of dominant cinema. Feminist film criticism that shared this purpose flourished in the early 1980s. Sandy Flitterman's and Wendy Dozoretz's articles on French filmmaker Germaine Dulac and Anne Friedberg's work on the film activities of the poet H. D. (Hilda Doolittle) express ways in which reworked terms of experience and knowledge result in women's language that asserts a new experience of culture.[45] Both E. Ann Kaplan's *Women and Film: Both Sides of the Camera* and Annette Kuhn's *Women's Pictures: Feminism and Cinema* concentrate on the cinematic apparatus as a signifying practice, the female spectator's position, the role of pleasure, the notions of Hollywood and avant-garde as oppositional categories, and documentary and fiction as dualistic cinematic strategies.[46]

But neither Kuhn's nor Kaplan's landmark book addresses how extratextual practices and, particularly, avant-garde as oppositional or resistant practices condition reception and the social functions of the films. Only as an afterthought does Kuhn list organizations that participate in independent distribution and exhibition.[47] Without analyzing the roles that institutional practices and feminist practices play in producing meaning, she admits their importance,

> The institutional practices of film production, distribution and exhibition intersect at the point of meaning construction, operating in specific ways in individual film texts. . . . These formations and interrelations are often contradictory, and are certainly constantly changing. In this situation, meanings generated by films are conditioned by a series of textual and contextual operations . . . [that] may both condition the reception of feminist film texts and govern the construction of feminist film practice.[48]

Kaplan agrees with Kuhn's observation, but she, too, merely calls for further studies that will examine the strategies of reception as well as the economic base for film production and distribution.[49] Kuhn's and Kaplan's call for uniting context and filmic text is an important starting point, even though it is a social relationship they were theoretically unable to address. They elaborate the dominant positions of feminist film criticism and theory in the 1970s and 1980s, basing arguments in a fragile balance between psychoanalytic feminism's attention to the sexual subject created through cinematic language and materialist feminism's focus on divisions of gender maintained in such social institutions as family, school, and church. Although one need not see such orientations as theoretically oppositional, the ways in which each troubles and may even subvert the other can provide a dialogic from which to begin in feminist film studies. Rather than pursue one unified line of inquiry, we might do better to examine the gaps, fissures, and contradictions within our own discourse.

More recently, Lucy Fischer has persuasively demonstrated that women's cinematic expression is a practice of resistance even while recognizing that women's sexual identities are constituted and cast inside patriarchal institutions. *Shot/Countershot: Film Tradition and Women's Cinema* argues that women filmmakers adapt the language of dominant cinema so as to remake the position of Woman, a practice that has an extensive range of historical instances.[50] She states that gender is fixed not only through the construction of sexual difference in the individual subject but through institutional conditions, "Women's art [especially within the avant-garde] is engaged in an oppositional struggle with the patriarchal tradition—not out of some personalized Oedipal or Electral desire to replace the parent but, rather, out of a wish simply to speak *at all*. For the canon/cannon has functioned aggressively to intimidate and silence women."[51] To "speak at all" or "to utter" here implies not simply a psychoanalytic definition of subjectivity constructed through language, but the material constraints that grant one cultural access to the means of address.

Fischer's argument rests in her case studies; she argues that, for example, Chantal Akerman's *The Eighties* (1985) parodies and deconstructs both the Hollywood musical of the 1930s and the family melodrama. Akerman's film demonstrates how gender, notions of femininity, and the denial of female pleasure are inscribed within the traditional conventions of the musical.[52] Akerman's deconstruction further attempts to reinvent a "musical" whereby woman's pleasure is a controlling factor. Fischer finds other examples of women filmmakers "rewriting" dominant forms in other times and cultures; for example, Gunvor Nelson's *Take Off* (1973) rewrites the porn film's striptease; Anja Breien's *Wives* (1975) rewrites John Cassavetes's *Husbands* (1970); Mai Zetterling's *The Girls* (1969) rewrites Ingmar Bergman's modernist fantasy about women's interior states (*Persona*, 1966); Sally Potter's *Thriller* (1979) rewrites the Hollywood detective *noir*; even Germaine Dulac's *The Smiling Madame Beudet* (1927) rewrites the conventions of domestic melodrama of the 1920s.

A woman's discourse here suggests more of an intertextual debate in which women reconstruct a cinematic language by confronting the cinematic norms rather than by specific self-originating language as argued through Luce Irigaray's and Hélène Cixous's adoption of the term.[53] While such a definition may keep women in a position of marginality since it acknowledges a woman's discourse only through confrontation and subversion of the dominant, it is useful here to help categorize a set of historical practices rather than to posit a textual theory working from the industrial margins or "other" artisanal arena of cinemas. The point is that women filmmakers have consistently articulated and defined themselves as women by confronting their position as "other" in dominant cinemas.

Fischer's, Kuhn's, and Kaplan's efforts to engage a feminist theoretical and critical discourse that encompasses women's avant-garde cinema owe much to a larger body of feminist critical theory that has dominated professional film scholarship in the 1980s. Since Claire Johnston's 1973 "Women's Cinema as Counter-cinema" article and Laura Mulvey's 1975 touchstone essay "Visual Pleasure and Narrative Cinema," feminist film criticism has continuously confronted and addressed the dilemma of woman's position in cinematic representation.[54]

Mulvey's essay on the centrality of the male look or "gaze" and woman's image as the object of that gaze introduced psychoanalysis as the critical foundation for feminist inquiries into the nature of the cinema and the spectator's experience. Since then, discussion has been configured largely around the issues of woman's spectacular fetishization, defining her "Otherness" as the site of male-identified pleasure/threat. The well-known arguments derive their intellectual drive (no Freudian pun intended) from the systems of Freudian and Lacanian psychoanalysis. French psychoanalyst Jacques Lacan reinterpreted Sigmund Freud's theories of the unconscious and infant personality development through the acquisition of language. An individual's newly found ability to speak and to distinguish oneself as speaking marks not only one's entrance into the social realm of Culture but also his or her sense of identity as a gendered being.[55] The intersection of Lacanian psychoanalysis and feminist film criticism has been the most significant theoretical discourse in the establishment of academic film studies during the 1980s, as well as the most frequently debated issue among feminist critics and historians.

French feminist psychoanalysis has progressed even further in these matters by deconstructing the centrality of male sexuality that is fundamental to both Freud and Lacan. Luce Irigaray and Hélène Cixous theorize femininity in relation to female desire, female desire in relation to female sexuality. Female sexuality is not constituted by a lack of the penis, as in Freud, but by its fundamental "otherness" to male sexuality and, as such, it has been repressed by the phallocentric patriarchal order. Arguing for a fundamental and integral relationship between sexuality and language, they have introduced a theory of feminine identity through *l'écriture féminine,* or feminine writing. *L'écriture féminine* occurs through signifying pleasures of the female body and is not so much an escape from patriarchy (since there is no escape) but a return of the repressed feminine aspects of language. For many psychoanalytic feminists, the celebration and pleasure (*jouissance*) of the feminine may be authentic in those forms of discourse where the female subjects have been historically suppressed or marginalized; these historical discourses may be read as attempts to defy patriarchy and to reinstate the feminine.

When specific examples of women's independent cinema have been interpreted in this light, the dominant objects for discussion have been

American and Western European feminist films made during the last two decades. Marguerite Duras's *Nathalie Granger* (1973), Yvonne Rainer's *Film about a Woman Who . . .* (1974), Chantal Akerman's *Jeanne Dielman, 23 Quai du Commerce, 1080 Bruxelles* (1975), Laura Mulvey's and Peter Wollen's *Riddles of the Sphinx* (1976), Sally Potter's *Thriller* (1979), and *The Gold Diggers* (1984) have been the privileged examples of woman's cinema as a feminist practice engaged in an extended dialogue with critical theory.[56] These are admittedly rich films for feminist critical practice. But their valorization to the exclusion of others smacks of a new essentializing, albeit feminist, canon. Critical preoccupations with their refusals of conventional aesthetic categories and Western cultural values tend to place the films outside contemporary history and culture while denying both a voice and the possible admission of less homogeneity to other rebellions and subversions waged by women in other cultures and times.

It is important in this context then that feminist theories of social relations also be brought to bear on cinema's positions among discourse, power and resistance, and the subject. In this regard, Michel Foucault's ideas have figured prominently in theorizing how the plurality of meanings and the structures of subjectivity have been integrated into a theory of language and social power that specifically focuses on the ways in which power is exercised and individuals governed through institutional discourses and social practices of everyday life.[57] Discourses and social practices are ways of constituting cultural knowledge, forms of subjectivity, and power relations. In application, Foucault analyzes how the body as a site, the centrality of sexuality as a locus of power, and the special relations between power and the gaze in modern societies frame contemporary subjective identity. Looking in detailed fashion at specific instances—the penal system, the medical clinic—he analyzes how discourses (always more than abstracted thought and the production of meaning) constitute the very being of those they seek to govern, and the process by which they do so is always part of a wider network of power relations as well as a specific historical formation. The importance of Foucault's attempts to understand power in all its forms is crucial for feminists because, as Chris Weedon explains,

> The failure to understand the multiplicity of power relations focused in sexuality will render an analysis blind to the range of points of resistance inherent in the network of power relations. . . . Foucault insists that 'points of resistance are present everywhere in the power network' and revolt or revolution have likewise no one reference point. . . . What Foucault's work offers feminists [then] . . . is a contextualization of experience and an analysis of its constitution and ideological power.[58]

Foucault's work offers feminist film critics a model for analyzing women's discursive formations as filmmakers and for investigating how such processes of singularization are constituted within an active and conflictual network of power relations. It provides a model of analysis for Deren's, Clarke's, and Wieland's discursive formations as women filmmakers and their activation as such within a New York avant-garde cinema of the postwar period. It is a theoretical model that makes the focus for analysis the following kinds of questions: How were their voices singularized among the many—both male and female—of the New York avant-garde? Did their assaults on art industries resist or reconfigure women's positions in arts institutions and in art discourse? Can their relationships as individual women and as discursive subjects of alternative film practices be read as a women's cultural site in patriarchy?

My goal then is to confront a kind of institutional cinematic activity—avant-garde—and the ways women have been engaged in that cinema with biography and theories about the sexual difference of the woman artist and a woman's discourse. My interest lies in examining both the films and the material evidence of production and circulation as cotextual discursive sites that participate in meaning construction and activation at the social level. I am interested not only in the relationships of the filmic text with historically specific discursive practices but also in the way that accrued meanings may be dispersed across these texts in the present. I am interested in the "author-functions" of a certain kind of filmmaking and in the individual women (designated the authors) whose labor functioned within the films as well as in cinematic discourse itself. I am interested in the troubled and troubling relationships among women, the institutions of our lives, and the construction of political power. I am interested in the power of (my) critical interpretation and how that power may be activated both as a means to dissociate other histories, and to circulate feminist goals for resisting forms of cultural oppression.

NOTES

1. For example, see George Wead and George Lellis, *Film Form and Function* (Boston: Houghton Mifflin, 1981), 452; Gerald Mast, *A Short History of the Movies*, 4th ed. (New York: Macmillan, 1986), 448; Thomas Sobchack and Vivian C. Sobchack, *An Introduction to Film*, 2d ed. (Boston: Little, Brown, 1987), 384–85.

2. David Bordwell and Janet Staiger, "Alternative Modes of Film Practice," in *The Classical Hollywood Cinema: Film Style and Mode of Production to 1960*, ed. David Bordwell, Janet Staiger, and Kristin Thompson (New York: Columbia University Press, 1985), 381.

3. Ibid.

4. Ibid., 382.

5. For elaborations of the avant-garde as a cultural opposition, see Renato Poggioli, *The Theory of the Avant-garde*, trans. Gerald Fitzgerald (Cambridge, Mass.: Belknap Press, 1968); Peter Bürger's *Theory of the Avant-garde*, trans. Michael Shaw (Minneapolis: University of Minnesota Press, 1984) argues that avant-garde art must attack not only prevailing styles of aesthetics but the institutions of art as well.

6. T. J. Clark, "On the Social History of Art," in *Modern Art and Modernism: A Critical Anthology*, ed. Francis Frascina and Charles Harrison, with Deirdre Paul (New York: Harper and Row, 1982), 253. Clark's position on the subject is also established in his book *Image of the People: Gustave Courbet and the Second French Republic 1848–1851* (Greenwich, Conn.: New York Graphic Society, 1973).

7. Clark, "On the Social History of Art," 253.

8. Two excellent art books that exemplify this approach are Serge Guilbaut, *How New York Stole the Idea of Modern Art: Abstract Expressionism, Freedom, and the Cold War*, trans. Arthur Goldhammer (Chicago: University of Chicago Press, 1983); Francis Frascina, ed., *Pollock and After: The Critical Debate* (New York: Harper and Row, 1985).

In addition, sociologists have begun to examine the postwar avant-garde in New York City as a cohesive group of artists who participated in a social and economic network of specialized art organizations. Howard S. Becker's *Art Worlds* (Berkeley: University of California Press, 1982) emphasizes the New York avant-garde as a support structure of organizations in which individual artists competed for goals and rewards. Diana Crane's *The Transformation of the Avant-garde: The New York Art World, 1940–1985* (Chicago: University of Chicago Press, 1987) addresses the continuity and shifts by which dominant contemporary art styles are associated with art communities and the reward systems of those communities.

9. Gregory Battcock, ed., *The New American Cinema: A Critical Anthology* (New York: E. P. Dutton, 1967); Sheldon Renan, *An Introduction to the American Underground Film* (New York: E. P. Dutton, 1967); Parker Tyler, *Underground Film: A Critical History* (New York: Grove Press, 1969); David Curtis, *Experimental Cinema* (New York: Universe Books, 1971); Jonas Mekas, *Movie Journal: The Rise of the New American Cinema, 1959–1971* (New York: Collier Books, 1972).

10. P. Adams Sitney, *Visionary Film: The American Avant-garde, 1943–1978* (New York: Oxford University Press, 1974). Sitney's volume was revised for a second edition in 1979.

11. For an excellent critique of Sitney, see Dana B. Polan, *The Political Language of Film and the Avant-garde* (Ann Arbor, Mich.: UMI Research Press, 1985), 64–66.

12. Amos Vogel, *Film as a Subversive Art* (New York: Random House, 1974); John G. Hanhardt, ed., *A History of the American Avant-garde Cinema* (New York: The American Federation of the Arts, 1976); Robert Russett and Cecile Starr, *Experimental Animation: An Illustrated Anthology* (New York: Van Nostrand Reinhold, 1976); Annette Michelson, ed., *New Forms in Film* (Montreux, Switzerland,

1974); Dennis Wheeler, ed., *Form and Structure in Recent Film* (Vancouver: Vancouver Art Gallery/Talon Books, 1972); Peter Gidal, ed., *Structural Film Anthology* (London: British Film Institute, 1978); Regina Cornwell, *Snow Seen: The Films and Photographs of Michael Snow* (Toronto: Peter Martin Associates, 1979).

13. Peter Wollen, "The Two Avant-Gardes," *Studio International* 190, no. 978 (Nov.–Dec. 1975): 172; reprinted in Peter Wollen, *Readings and Writings: Semiotic Counter-strategies* (London: New Left Books, 1982), 93.

14. Wollen, *Readings and Writings*, 93.

15. Ibid.

16. Ibid., 97.

17. Peter Wollen, " 'Ontology' and 'Materialism' in Film," *Screen* 17, no. 1 (Spring 1976): 7–23; reprinted in Wollen, *Readings and Writings*, 193.

18. See, for example, J. Hoberman, "After the Avant-garde," in *Art after Modernism: Rethinking Representation*, ed. Brian Wallis (New York: New Museum of Contemporary Art, 1984), 59–74; Patricia Mellencamp, "Receivable Texts: U.S. Avant-garde Cinema, 1960–1980," *Wide Angle* 7, nos. 1–2 (1985): 74–91; Patrice Petro, "Reception Theory and the Avant-garde," *Wide Angle* 8, no. 1 (1986): 11–17.

For a discussion of the reception and effects of Wollen's essay, see Pam Cook, "Teaching Avant-garde Film: Notes toward Practice," *Screen Education*, nos. 32–33 (Autumn-Winter 1979–80): 83–97. For a full elaboration of Wollen's essay and its underlying assumptions, see David Rodowick, "Modernism, Epistemology, and Politics," *Millennium Film Journal*, nos. 16–18 (Fall-Winter 1986–87): 126–41. For Wollen's own update on his initial ideas, see Peter Wollen, "The Avant-gardes: Europe and America," *Framework*, no. 14 (1981): 9–10.

19. See, for example, Polan, *The Political Language of Film and the Avant-garde*, for an overview of Eisenstein's writings and how Eisenstein has frequently been misappropriated by semiologists.

20. David E. James's *Allegories of Cinema: American Film in the Sixties* (Princeton, N.J.: Princeton University Press, 1989) provides a significant antidote to Wollen's historiographic approach by studying formal properties of the independent cinema in relation to their political contextualization.

21. See the bibliography for a list of Maya Deren's critical and theoretical writings; for bibliographies of the others, see *The International Dictionary of Films and Filmmakers: Volume II, Directors/Filmmakers*, ed. Christopher Lyon (Chicago: St. James Press, 1984), 61, 196–97, 354, 416, 508, and 545.

22. Constance Penley and Janet Bergstrom, "The Avant-garde: Histories and Theories," *Screen* 19, no. 3 (Autumn 1978): 118.

23. Mellencamp, "Receivable Texts," 78.

24. Michel Foucault, "What Is an Author?" in *Language, Counter-Memory, Practice*, ed. Donald F. Bouchard, trans. Donald F. Bouchard and Sherry Simon (Ithaca, N.Y.: Cornell University Press, 1977), 129.

25. Walter Benjamin, "The Author as Producer," in *Reflections: Essays, Aphorisms, Autobiographical Writings*, ed. Peter Demetz, trans. Edmund Jephcott (New York: Harcourt Brace Jovanovich, 1978), 220–38.

26. Polan, *The Political Language of Film and the Avant-garde*, 53–77.

27. J. Hoberman and Jonathan Rosenbaum, *Midnight Movies* (New York: Harper and Row, 1983).

28. Foucault, "What Is an Author?" 137.

29. Ibid.

30. Ibid.

31. Kaja Silverman, *The Acoustic Mirror: The Female Voice in Psychoanalysis and Cinema* (Bloomington: Indiana University Press, 1988), 209.

32. Nancy K. Miller, "The Text's Heroine: A Feminist Critic and Her Fictions," *Diacritics* 12 (Summer 1982): 53.

33. For an additionally elegant feminist critique of Foucault's position on authorship, see Peggy Kamuf, "Dialogue: Replacing Feminist Criticism," *Diacritics* 12 (Summer 1982): 42–47.

34. Russell Campbell, "Eight Notes on the Underground," *The Velvet Light Trap*, no. 13 (Fall 1974): 45–46.

35. Ellen Freyer, "Formalist Cinema: Artistic Suicide in the Avant-garde," *The Velvet Light Trap*, no. 13 (Fall 1974): 49.

36. Penley and Bergstrom, "The Avant-garde: Histories and Theories," 113–27.

37. P. Adams Sitney, ed. *The Essential Cinema: Essays on the Films in the Collection of Anthology Film Archives* (New York: New York University Press and Anthology Film Archives, 1975).

38. Penley and Bergstrom, "The Avant-garde: Histories and Theories," 115.

39. Ibid., 123.

40. Ibid.

41. The Camera Obscura Collective, "Excerpts from an Interview with *The Legend of Maya Deren* Project," *Camera Obscura*, nos. 3–4 (Summer 1979): 177.

42. The Camera Obscura Collective, "Interview with *The Legend of Maya Deren* Project," 179.

43. VèVè A. Clark, Millicent Hodson, and Catrina Neiman, *The Legend of Maya Deren: A Documentary Biography and Collected Works. Volume I, Part One: Signatures (1917–1942)* (New York: Anthology Film Archives/Film Culture, 1984).

For a more complete analysis of the Project's methodologies and relationships to feminist critical practice, see Lauren Rabinovitz, "*The Legend of Maya Deren: A Documentary Biography and Collected Works*," *Wide Angle* 8, no. 4 (1986): 131–33.

44. VèVè A. Clark, Millicent Hodson, and Catrina Neiman, *The Legend of Maya Deren: A Documentary Biography and Collected Works. Volume I, Part Two: Chambers (1942–1947)* (New York: Anthology Film Archives/Film Culture, 1988).

45. Wendy Dozoretz, "Dulac versus Artaud," *Wide Angle* 3, no. 1 (1979): 46–53; Sandy Flitterman, "Montage/Discourse: Germaine Dulac's *The Smiling Madame Beudet*," *Wide Angle* 4, no. 3 (1980): 54–59; Anne Friedberg, "And I Myself Have Learned to Use the Small Projector: On H. D., Woman, History, Recognition," *Wide Angle* 5, no. 2 (1982): 26–31.

46. E. Ann Kaplan, *Women and Film: Both Sides of the Camera* (New York:

Methuen, 1983), and Annette Kuhn, *Women's Pictures: Feminism and Cinema* (Boston: Routledge and Kegan Paul, 1982).

47. Kuhn, *Women's Pictures*, 179–96 *passim*.

48. Ibid., 196.

49. Kaplan, *Women and Film*, 196–97.

50. Lucy Fischer, *Shot/Countershot: Film Tradition and Women's Cinema* (Princeton, N.J.: Princeton University Press, 1989).

51. Ibid., 9.

52. Ibid., 162–71.

53. Ibid., 5–7.

54. Claire Johnston, "Women's Cinema as Counter-cinema," in *Notes on Women's Cinema*, ed. Claire Johnston (London: SEFT, 1974), 24–31; Laura Mulvey, "Visual Pleasure and Narrative Cinema," *Screen* 16, no. 3 (Autumn 1975): 6–18. Mulvey's article has been reprinted in numerous anthologies on cinema, feminist theory, and contemporary art. It also appears in Laura Mulvey, *Visual and Other Pleasures* (Bloomington: Indiana University Press, 1989), 14–26.

55. An excellent introduction to psychoanalysis within a feminist framework is Chris Weedon's *Feminist Practice and Poststructuralist Theory* (New York: Methuen, 1987), 43–73. For an overview of the issues surrounding psychoanalysis and feminist film theory, see Judith Mayne's review essay "Feminist Film Theory and Criticism," *Signs: Journal of Women in Culture and Society* 11, no. 1 (1985): 81–100.

56. I am thinking here not only of Mary Ann Doane's "Woman's Stake: Filming the Female Body," *October*, no. 17 (Summer 1981): 23–36; Kuhn's *Women's Pictures;* Kaplan's *Women and Film;* Mary Ann Doane's, Patricia Mellencamp's, and Linda Williams's *Re-vision: Essays in Feminist Film Criticism* (Frederick, Md.: University Publications of America and American Film Institute, 1984); and Teresa de Lauretis's *Alice Doesn't: Feminism, Semiotics, Cinema* (Bloomington: Indiana University Press, 1984), but also of such recent work as Charlotte Brunsdon's *Films for Women* (London: British Film Institute, 1986) and Kaja Silverman's *The Acoustic Mirror*.

57. Most notable are Michel Foucault, *The Birth of the Clinic: An Archaeology of Medical Perception*, trans. A. M. Sheridan-Smith (New York: Vintage Books, 1975); Michel Foucault, *Discipline and Punish: The Birth of the Prison*, trans. Alan Sheridan (New York: Vintage Books, 1979); Michel Foucault, *The History of Sexuality, Volume I: An Introduction*, trans. Robert Hurley (New York: Vintage Books, 1980); Michel Foucault, *The Archaeology of Knowledge*, trans. A. M. Sheridan-Smith (New York: Pantheon Books, 1972).

58. Weedon, *Feminist Practice and Poststructuralist Theory*, 124–25.

3
Avant-garde Cinemas
before World War II

In early 1946, Maya Deren rented a small Manhattan theater to show three short films she had made over the last three years. She mailed announcements to friends and acquaintances, and she posted small notices at Greenwich Village bookstores. On February 18, 1946, so many people showed up for her screening that the two-hundred-seat Provincetown Playhouse could not accommodate the crowd. When Deren saw so many people clustered around the theater doors, she thought the building was on fire and rushed inside to save her film prints.[1] Shortly after that night, she wrote to film critic Manny Farber, "I feel that the crowd was some kind of a landmark. . . . It was proof of a hunger for some new developments in film. Moreover, this response should give experimental film a new lease on life, proving that one can, as I have, produce and exhibit 'outside the law.' "[2] Deren became a filmmaker as well as her own exhibitor when new excitement in independent film sparked Deren's confidence in her undertaking as well as public curiosity about alternative kinds of cinema.

In all the writings on Deren, few have said anything about her entrance into the film culture of postwar New York City. Discussions of her socioeconomic models for an American avant-garde cinema have been less prominent than arguments regarding Deren's legacy of European avant-garde aesthetics. Parker Tyler's *Underground Film: A Critical History* was, perhaps, the first book to connect Jean Cocteau's and Luis Buñuel's films from the 1920s and Deren's work in the 1940s.[3] P. Adams Sitney's thesis of a continuous cinematic avant-garde from the 1920s through the 1940s is based on the ways that Deren transformed the European Surrealist cinema for the American avant-garde.[4] Annette Michelson refines Sitney's argument, elaborating the formal relationships between Soviet and European film aesthetics of the 1920s and Deren's films and writings in the 1940s. Without discussing *how* Deren absorbed European aesthetics, these authors claim that she provided "the crucial, climactic elaboration of a totalizing, transcultural project."[5] By ignoring the practical structures of the very cinemas their essays celebrate, they create a gap between the conceptualization of a new avant-garde cinema and how it was historically instituted. Deren's and other filmmakers' efforts to join theory and practice followed specific well-established practices of the film cultures in Europe and the United States during the 1920s and 1930s.

French Avant-garde Cinema in the 1920s

European artists in the 1920s had already established a widespread artisanal tradition that explored film's formal elements, frequently applying contemporary aesthetics from other visual art forms. In France, absurdist Dada films that were poetically edited for visual puns, graphic continuity, and rhythmic textures surfaced at avant-garde soirees, and Marcel Duchamp's *Anemic Cinema* (1926), Man Ray's *Le retour á la raison* (1923), and René Clair's *Entr'acte* (1924) achieved scandalous acclaim as well as critical brickbats. In the latter half of the decade, French avant-garde filmmakers frequently concentrated on narratives that expressed the deliberately irrational, nightmarish images of Surrealism. Germaine Dulac's *La coquille et le clergyman* (1927), Man Ray's *L'etoile de mer* (1928), and Luis Buñuel's and Salvador Dali's *Un chien andalou* (1929) played an important role in this movement. These individual films were not one unified model of film as art, but they were unified by their reception in the United States as products of and referents to the Parisian avant-garde's intellectual excitement for cinematic experimentation within the antibourgeois politics and aesthetics of Modernist art.

The Parisian avant-garde films, otherwise, offered only a limited example for how to implement a system of alternative practices. The artists-turned-filmmakers who made these films may have occasionally shared their ideas, worked together on productions, and frequently appeared in each other's films. But they developed neither a philosophy nor a design for cinema as an artistic activity—including its production, distribution, and exhibition. The production of their films depended on their personal economic resources or the patronage of wealthy individuals. In fact, several of the most memorable films of the period were funded solely by the famous patron of early twentieth-century modern art, the Vicomte de Noialle. He produced Man Ray's *Les mystères du chateau du dé* (1929), Luis Buñuel's *L'age d'or* (1930), and Jean Cocteau's *Le sang d'un poéte* (1930). They brought their 35mm films to avant-garde events that were multimedia affairs (i.e., ballets, theater pieces, poetry readings) or, more infrequently, to commercial theaters as short subjects before feature films. It was only because the notoriety of the films spread beyond Paris that commercial distributors marketed the films to other countries.

What is important for understanding how these films became models is that their application of visual art aesthetics became well known throughout Europe primarily due to the cinema club movement. Cinema, or ciné, clubs were film screening and discussion groups comprised of students and artists who often lived together on the fringes of universities that hosted lively intellectual atmospheres. Ciné club participants watched European and Soviet avant-garde films, made their own experimental movies, and often wrote about the aesthetic experimentation of artisanal filmmaking in small journals and newsletters. Particularly influential were the theories of Soviet filmmakers Lev Kuleshov, Sergei Eisenstein, and V. I. Pudovkin, emphasizing the importance of rhythmic and graphic editing over narrative continuity.[6]

Critical to the development of a European avant-garde cinema in the 1920s, the ciné club movement provided an institutional basis for production, exhibition, and consumption. Richard Abel and David Bordwell have argued that the aesthetics of the French Impressionist film movement can only be understand within its context of new cinema journals and ciné clubs.[7] Anne Friedberg's study of *Close Up* magazine demonstrates the importance of both unified film exhibition and film discourse in the ciné clubs and journals for a new international film culture asserting cinema's role as an art form.[8] Such studies point to a definition of avant-garde cinema linking contextual factors to aesthetic matters as a well-publicized model of cinematic practices.

Independent Filmmaking and the Ciné Club Movement in the U.S.

The ciné club movement did not initially catch on in the United States the way that it did in Europe, and North Americans made only isolated, sporadic attempts at artisanal filmmaking as an alternative to Hollywood movies. Occasionally, artists from other media experimented with film. For example, painter Charles Sheeler and photographer Paul Strand teamed for *Manhatta* (1921), an abstract film of the city that was shown at a commercial Manhattan theater. After photographer Ralph Steiner met Strand, he experimented with texture photography in H_2O (1929), a short film about the beauty of water patterns. Other films made by individuals, such as Robert Florey's and Slavko Vorkapich's *The Life and Death of a Hollywood Extra* (1928) and

James Sibley Watson's and Melville Webber's *Fall of the House of Usher* (1928), used expensive, cumbersome 35mm equipment and film stock. Florey and Vorkapich were a writer and a painter trying to get work in Hollywood, and Watson was a wealthy man of leisure living in upstate New York. In both cases, the short narrative films featuring a distinctively Expressionist style were made primarily for the enjoyment of the filmmakers and their friends, and they received no systematic distribution or exhibition.[9]

Within a few years, however, a handful of new film societies and journals did espouse European cinema aesthetics, experimentation, and a vanguard modernism. Perhaps one of the first was the New York Film Society, a 1932 screening club. *Experimental Cinema* provided an American counterpart to the European cinema journals from 1930 to 1934. It published English translations of the film theories of Eisenstein, Pudovkin, Dziga Vertov, and Alexander Dovzhenko.[10] It also celebrated formalist cinema aesthetics, raised concerns about aesthetic and labor conditions in Hollywood, and reported on the reception of Soviet films in the United States.[11]

But most significant was the Museum of Modern Art's (MOMA) circulating film program begun in 1935. MOMA exhibited European and Soviet avant-garde films and distributed them all over the United States. Film historian and *Experimental Cinema* editor Lewis Jacobs notes that selections from the museum's collection went to hundreds of colleges, universities, museums, film appreciation clubs, and study groups.[12] Coupled with the museum's frequent New York City showings, such national screenings were a major stimulus for broader appreciation and production of experimental films.[13]

The ciné club legacy had its greatest effect in the United States not on societies and journals espousing modern aesthetics, but on Leftist political and cultural clubs. In Europe, ciné clubs were often politically allied with the Left and advocated cinema as an important medium for political action. Such clubs looked to the postrevolutionary model of Soviet cinema and, indeed, the clubs were often started in order to see Soviet and other films that were banned from public viewing.[14] For the American Left of the 1930s, the successes of European practices provided a model of unified production, exhibition, and consumption independent of the Hollywood cinema.

Radical Politics and Film Culture in Depression America

The Workers Film and Photo League (WFPL) began in 1930 as an independent branch of the Workers' International Relief, a Communist party organization with cultural goals. Photographers, artists, writers, and other intellectuals were drawn throughout the 1920s and early 1930s to the Communist party because they felt it was the only organization with a solution to American economic and social problems. Among its well-known members were Harry Potamkin and Lewis Jacobs, as well as filmmakers Leo Hurwitz, Irving Lerner, and Ralph Steiner. The WFPL proclaimed that its specific goal was to arouse the working class through cinema. Armed with Soviet filmmaking theory and examples, members began film production with WFPL equipment. The WFPL also hosted film screenings of member newsreels and shorts, as well as classic Soviet films, such as *The Battleship Potemkin, Arsenal, Ten Days That Shook the World, Man with a Movie Camera,* and *Storm over Asia.*[15] Often, the WFPL sponsored public educational lectures to accompany screenings. It ran a film and photography school and distributed members' and Soviet films throughout the United States. It was the first American organization that understood the efficacy of coordinating production, distribution, exhibition, and education efforts to insure an alternative cinema system.

But in 1935, increasing factionalism in the WFPL led to its demise. Some members questioned which was more important, art or politics. Several key members, including Steiner and Irving Lerner, argued that the league held to a narrow concept of film form, requiring them to sacrifice their desire for cinematic poetry in favor of a rigid political analysis.[16] Representative of their dissident position is the film they made in 1933 with members of the Group Theater—*Pie in the Sky.*

Improvising at a Long Island dump, Steiner and Lerner codirected with Elia Kazan, Elman Koolish, and Molly Day Thatcher a short ironic attack on religious relief measures. *Pie in the Sky* shows two young men at a Christian prayer mission. Unmoved by the minister's haughtiness and preaching, they grow even more disgusted when the church's thin slices of pie run out before they can receive their share. They leave for the local dump, where they use the junk around themselves to act out episodic parodies of religious charity and contemporary bourgeois life. Based on agitprop techniques in which members of the Group Theater were experienced, the film artistically conveys a smoothly paced, graphically uncluttered, and streamlined narrative. Documentary film historian William Alexander applauds the film: "What is most impressive is the film's spirit, which is realized cinematically in the pace and in some of the cutting and which is derived principally from the imagination, wit, and humor with which the two men again and again aid themselves and one another in resisting their hunger and despair. This spirit endows the film with its essential and bitter-sweet vitality."[17] *Pie in the Sky* is significant here because it marks an American turn toward socially conscious films that steeped political content in a discourse of film art.

Soon after the completion of *Pie in the Sky,* Lerner and Steiner, with
other League filmmakers, left the WFPL and cooperatively reformed
as Nykino. *Pie in the Sky* became the first film they exhibited and
distributed, a bellwether of the cinematic approach and style they
advocated. Among the other films that members made were *The Wave*
and *The World Today.* The organization folded when members reorga-
nized in 1937 as Frontier Films, uniting with a large number of other
Popular Front groups to fight fascism. Throughout the latter half
of the 1930s and early 1940s, Frontier Films advocated a "serious
theoretical goal of combining a profound personal sense of the human
condition with political art."[18] The WFPL, its spin-off descendants,
and satellite organizations in New York City during the 1930s provided
a continuous self-contained system of production, distribution, exhibition, and education independent of the dominant Hollywood movie
industry.

World War II and Film Culture in the U.S.

If the rise of fascism in Europe created new dedication among artists
and intellectuals to political coalitions, it also completely reshaped the
American arts, their institutional affiliations, their discourses, and aesthetics. Because of World War II, the international art capital generally
shifted from Paris to New York City, and a similar transcontinental shift
occurred in independent filmmaking activities. European painters immigrated to America to escape Nazi concentration camps, and they subsequently influenced a generation of American painters and sculptors.
Filmmakers were among the European artists who immigrated to the
United States, and they acted as mentors to a new generation of young
filmmakers. In particular, Hans Richter began the City College Institute
of Film Techniques at the City College of New York in 1943. Richter
directed the institute and oversaw the production of instructional films,
courses in film production, history, editing, cinematography, animation, and film distribution. Among the institute's students in the early
1950s were Shirley Clarke and Jonas Mekas.

Other famous European filmmakers relocated in New York City.
Luis Buñuel spent the war years in Manhattan and worked at the Museum of Modern Art Circulating Film Library. For a short time during
and after the war, Man Ray lived in Los Angeles. Marcel Duchamp became a permanent resident of New York City, and, although he was no
longer an actively producing artist or filmmaker, he was well known to
American artists. Maya Deren met with him periodically in the mid-

1940s, and Joyce Wieland and Michael Snow visited him when they lived in New York City in the 1960s.

Other developments that were part of the American war effort indirectly enabled the expansion of an independent film culture. Newly available 16mm film stock and equipment offered an economic alternative to the 35mm commercial gauge stock and equipment employed in Hollywood studios. Film stock and printing cost less than did 35mm, and the equipment was lighter in weight, portable, and more easily manipulated by one or two individuals. Although not widely available before the 1940s, 16mm stock and equipment had existed since 1923. When the government adopted 16mm during World War II for military training films and for war documentaries, the advantages of 16mm received new publicity. More important, the surplus of used equipment after the war and Eastman Kodak's need to find new markets to replace dwindling military consumption resulted in economical, readily available materials and processing. The commercial marketing of such affordable materials designed for the individual consumer revolutionized the possibilities for independent filmmaking.

A new generation of filmmakers learned the advantages of 16mm format while watching government films during World War II or while reading about the way the government made its films. Still others became familiar with 16mm while making films in the armed services or in the employ of the government. Deren's husband Hammid, Willard Van Dyke, and camera operator Peter Glushanok (Clarke's film teacher at City College) were among those who worked in film services for the Office of War Information.

In addition, new educational programs that grew out of the armed services' benefits packages and postwar economy helped expose students to the materials, models, and techniques of 16mm filmmaking. The G.I. Bill subsidized college bound veterans. The resulting increase in college enrollments and tuition revenues allowed schools to expand curricula and to introduce such new subjects as filmmaking and film appreciation. In 1947 the California School of Fine Arts became the first art school in the United States to teach 16mm filmmaking as a regular part of its curriculum. The school's move to integrate filmmaking into its curriculum helped to legitimate independent cinema's status as an artistic medium among the vanguard arts.

In the postwar arts economy, cinema emerged as the object of a film culture similar to the prewar European ciné club movement. Measured in sheer numbers alone, the growth of film culture is impres-

sive. By 1949, there were more than two hundred film societies in
the United States with an estimated audience of approximately one
hundred thousand.[19] The museum art schools and university art departments that taught filmmaking also sponsored film appreciation
courses, film societies, and screenings of classic European films and
independent cinema. For example, New York University offered a
course on the previous twenty-five years of experimental film and
frequently invited filmmakers as guest lecturers. In 1947, the University of Rochester established the George Eastman House as an
archive for films that have contributed to cinema's history as an art
form. Two students at the San Francisco Museum of Art launched a
series of screenings on independent cinema in 1947.[20] Their program
was so successful that the "Art in Cinema" series ran at the museum
until the early 1950s as a film society with approximately six hundred
members.[21] When Frank Stauffacher, one of the organizers, published
a catalogue based on the programs, he publicized independent exhibitions and provided a national model for successive programs in other
cities.

Whereas the San Francisco "Art in Cinema" series served as a West
Coast center for independent cinema screenings, Cinema 16 was the
East Coast showcase for independent film. Cinema 16 soon became
the largest film society in the United States and, by 1949, it boasted a
membership of 2,500.[22] In addition, Cinema 16 began distributing
independent films in 1948.

From their first screenings, Cinema 16's directors Amos and Marcia
Vogel emphasized a discourse of film appreciation in the selection,
arrangement, and presentation of film programs. Films were packaged
in programs not so much for their similar themes or styles but for the
contrasting ways they commented upon or approached the nature of
cinema in general. Film critic Scott MacDonald characterizes such
programming policy as "dialectical" in nature, "One form of film
collides with another so as to create a maximum intellectual engagement on the part of the audience, not simply in the individual discrete
films, but with film itself and the implications of its more conventional
uses. This similarity to Eisensteinian dialectic is more than acciden-
tal."[23] Programs regularly included scientific films, government-spon-
sored documentaries, independently made documentaries, experimental films, animation, foreign features, and classics of cinema art.

The Vogels supplemented the films with written program notes
and even with appearances by the filmmakers themselves. Among
those who authored program notes were film critics Arthur Knight,
Parker Tyler, and Siegfried Kracauer.[24] The program notes estab-

lished cinematic aesthetics within a context of modern psychological and literary thought. They implicitly defined artistic cinema through the use of symbols and spatiotemporal experimentation.

At the same time, postwar expansion of art house cinemas and a small independent system of film distribution nurtured new audience interest in significant alternatives to Hollywood movies. The number of theaters devoted to foreign films, documentaries, and reissued classics greatly increased throughout the country. In his study of emergent art film exhibition in postwar Chicago, Richard deCordova notes that by 1947 every major city except Cincinnati had an art house.[25] He cites *Variety*'s national estimates for 1947, which range from twenty full-time art houses to four hundred playing foreign films on a part-time basis.[26] DeCordova further explains that such statistics and any generalizations they might yield are skewed by the overwhelming flood of art houses in New York City alone, "The success of foreign films [in New York City] was often attributed to the presence of an extremely heterogeneous ethnic population and a large, sophisticated cultural elite. Whatever the reasons though, it is clear that New York City provides the most dramatic example of the rise of the art film after the war."[27] Whatever the lure of art house cinema, non-Hollywood films became a more visible part of the American urban movie culture, and more people experienced new types of cinema.

Newly converted art houses attempted to compete in the commercial marketplace by booking foreign films thought to be more sexually explicit than Hollywood fare. Even a 1947 *Variety* article acknowledged that a foreign or art film policy was one way to "cure" a sick house.[28] Newspaper ads for Italian and French films frequently featured tags saying "Adults Only." The 1945 Italian Neorealist film *Rome: Open City* was the subject of an ad campaign that promised "sexiness Hollywood rarely approaches."[29] In 1946, ads similarly promised that an Italian Neorealist film about the life of two young boys on the streets of Nazi-occupied Rome (*Shoeshine*) would "shock the world," and even a French version of *Carmen* promised to "make Jane Russell look like Lena the Hyena."[30]

However humorous these campaigns retrospectively appear, such marketing made these films big American hits. *Rome: Open City* grossed over a million dollars and was booked into thirty-five hundred theaters in a two-year period.[31] The Italian Neorealist films *Paisan* and *The Bicycle Thief* enjoyed such successful extended runs in downtown art houses that they were picked up by large, first-run theater chains.[32] DeCordova concludes from this evidence that an important feature distinguishing the art film from typical Hollywood fare was its promise

of a certain depiction of sexuality.[33] While not a direct model for
avant-garde cinema campaigns, the foreign and independent films
differentiated through art house marketing and exhibition provided
a highly visible discourse for the future of aesthetics and sexuality in
the avant-garde cinema of the 1950s and 1960s.

Literary journals and arts magazines also supported foreign, experimental, and independent films in articles that promoted cinema as an
art form. Such periodicals as *Saturday Review, New Directions, Kenyon
Review* and *Theater Arts* featured stories on a new independent cinema,
and magazines such as the *New Republic* and the *Nation* regularly
reviewed non-Hollywood films.[34] By their very act of including cinema
among discussions of the arts, these popular magazines promoted
cinema's status as a contemporary art form.

Neither the first nor the only advocate for a system of alternative
cinema, Maya Deren soon became the individual most closely identified
with the emergent postwar film culture in New York City. She assumed
for her generation the legacies of the ciné club movement, the WFPL,
and European aesthetics in a new, unified avant-garde cinema. Her position and what she symbolized may best be illustrated in another story
about the Provincetown Playhouse screening. Writing about Deren in
her diary, Anaïs Nin said that as she waited to get into the theater, "The
crowd was dense, and some policeman thought he should investigate.
He asked: 'Is this a demonstration?' Someone answered: 'It is not a demonstration, it is a revolution in film-making.' "[35] To others, Deren personally combined the theatrical outrageousness associated with the European avant-garde, the WFPL's commitment to Leftist political ideals,
and the administrative acumen necessary to deploy a new film network.
She represented the continuity of a film discourse begun in the 1920s in
Europe and reconstituted in a series of alternative practices in Europe
and the United States throughout the 1930s and 1940s.

NOTES

1. Arthur Knight, "The Far-out Films," *Playboy,* Apr. 1960, 42.

2. Maya Deren, Letter to Manny Farber, 24 Feb. 1946, in *The Legend of
Maya Deren: A Documentary Biography and Collected Works. Volume I, Part Two:
Chambers (1942–1947),* ed. VéVé A. Clark, Millicent Hodson, and Catrina
Neiman (New York: Anthology Film Archives/Film Culture, 1988), 370.

3. Parker Tyler, *Underground Film: A Critical History* (New York: Grove
Press, 1969), 7.

4. P. Adams Sitney, *Visionary Film: The American Avant-garde, 1943–1978,*
2d ed. (New York: Oxford University Press, 1979).

5. Annette Michelson, "On Reading Deren's Notebook," *October*, no. 14 (Fall 1980): 48.

6. Numerous filmmakers have attested to the vital role that ciné clubs played in their filmmaking careers. Deren's husband, filmmaker Alexander Hammid, received his first exposure to experimental film at a Prague ciné club. As a result, he wrote about cinema for local art journals and then, in 1930, made a short movie about a man taking a walk who observes himself (*Aimless Walk*). For further discussion of Hammid's career, see Thomas E. Valasek, "Alexander Hammid: A Survey of His Filmmaking Career," *Film Culture*, nos. 67–69 (1979): 250–322.

7. Richard Abel, *French Cinema: The First Wave, 1915–1929* (Princeton, N.J.: Princeton University Press, 1984); David Bordwell, "French Impressionist Cinema: Film Culture, Film Theory and Film Style" (Ph.D. diss., University of Iowa, 1974).

8. Anne Friedberg, "Writing about Cinema: Close Up, 1927–1933" (Ph.D. diss., New York University, 1983).

9. For a discussion of *Fall of the House of Usher*, see Lucy Fischer, "The Films of James Sibley Watson Jr. and Melville Webber: A Reconsideration," *Millennium Film Journal*, no. 19 (Fall 1987-Winter 1988): 40–49.

For a detailed discussion of Vorkapich, Florey, and the making of *A Hollywood Extra*, see Bozidar Zecevic's article, "The First of the Independents or How a Hollywood Extra Was Made," *Framework*, no. 21 (Summer 1983): 10–12; and Richard Allen's "The Life and Death of 9413, a Hollywood Extra," *Framework*, no. 21 (Summer 1983): 12–14.

10. For example, V. I. Pudovkin, "Film Direction and Film Manuscript," *Experimental Cinema* 1, no. 1 (Feb. 1930): 5–6, and no. 2 (June 1930): 7–11, trans. Christel Gang; S. M. Eisenstein, "The Cinematographic Principle and Japanese Culture: With a Digression on Montage and the Shot," *Experimental Cinema* 1, no. 3 (Feb. 1931), 5–11, trans. Ivor Montagu and S. S. Nalbanov; V. I. Pudovkin, "Scenario and Direction," *Experimental Cinema* 1, no. 3 (Feb. 1931), 16–18; S. M. Eisenstein, "The Principles of Film Form," *Experimental Cinema* 1, no. 4 (Feb. 1932): 7–12, trans. Ivor Montagu; A. Dovzhenko, "My Method," *Experimental Cinema* 1, no. 5 (1934): 23–24, trans. K. Santor; Simon Koster, "Dziga Vertov," *Experimental Cinema* 2, no. 5 (1934): 27–28.

11. For example, Alexander Bakshy, "Dynamic Composition," *Experimental Cinema* 1, no. 1 (Feb. 1930): 2–3; René Clair, "The Kingdom of Cinema," *Experimental Cinema* 1, no. 5 (1934): 43; Kirk Bond, "Formal Cinema," *Experimental Cinema* 1, no. 5 (1934): 49–51; Seymour Stern, "Hollywood and Montage: The Basic Fallacies of American Film Technique," *Experimental Cinema* 1, no. 4 (1932): 47–52.

12. Lewis Jacobs, "Experimental Cinema in America: Part Two—The Postwar Revival," *Hollywood Quarterly* 3, no. 3 (Spring 1948): 278.

13. Ibid.

14. See Friedberg's "Writing about Cinema: Close Up" for a complete discussion of the British situation.

15. William Alexander, *Film on the Left: American Documentary Film from 1931 to 1942* (Princeton, N.J.: Princeton University Press, 1981), 8–9.

16. Ibid., 56–64.

17. Ibid., 63.

18. Ibid., 241.

19. M. Pryor, *New York Times,* 18 Sept. 1949, as quoted in Stephen J. Dobi, "Cinema 16: America's Largest Film Society" (Ph.D. diss., New York University, 1984), 116.

20. Frank Stauffacher, ed. *Art in Cinema* (San Francisco: Art in Cinema Society, San Francisco Museum of Art, 1947).

21. Ibid.; Archer Winsten, as quoted in Dobi, "Cinema 16," 118.

22. Dobi, "Cinema 16," 117.

23. Scott MacDonald, "Amos Vogel and Cinema 16," *Wide Angle* 9, no. 3 (1987): 43.

24. Ibid., 42.

25. Richard deCordova, "The Rise of the Art Film in Post-war Chicago," paper delivered at the College Art Association, Boston, Massachusetts, 13 Feb. 1987, 2.

26. Ibid.

27. Ibid., 2–3. Quoted with the permission of the author.

28. *Variety,* 8 Jan. 1947, 74, as quoted in deCordova, "The Rise of the Art Film in Post-war Chicago," 13.

29. Ibid., 10.

30. Ibid.

31. Ibid., 9.

32. Ibid.

33. Ibid., 11.

34. Manny Farber was the regular reviewer for *New Republic* throughout this period. James Agee wrote a movie column discussing various types of experimental, documentary, and foreign films as art for the *Nation* from 1942 to 1948; these reviews are collected in James Agee's *Agee on Film: Reviews and Comments* (New York: McDowell, Obolensky, 1958), 21–319.

Other articles of special interest are Sara Kathryn Arledge, "The Experimental Film: A New Art in Transition," *Arizona Quarterly* 3, no. 2 (Summer 1947): 101–12; Maya Deren, "Cinema as an Art Form," *New Directions,* no. 9 (Fall 1946): 111–20; Arthur Knight, "Ideas on Film," *Saturday Review,* 27 May 1950, 38–40; Arthur Rosenheimer, Jr., "The Small Screen," *Theater Arts* 31, no. 5 (May 1947): 1, 9–10; Parker Tyler, "Movie Letter—Experimental Film: A New Growth," *Kenyon Review* 11, no. 1 (Winter 1949): 141–44.

35. Anaïs Nin, *The Diary of Anaïs Nin, Volume Four: 1944–1947,* ed. Gunther Stuhlmann (New York: Harcourt Brace Jovanovich, 1971), 137.

4

Maya Deren and an American Avant-garde Cinema

When Maya Deren bragged, "I make my pictures for what Hollywood spends on lipstick," her metaphor was well chosen.[1] She contrasts Hollywood's material construction of women's lips as both icon and sexual fetish with the possibility of her films as a confrontation to an entire system of economic practices. Long before Claire Johnston called for a women's countercinema that would rewrite patriarchal film language, Deren asserted an oppositional voice to Hollywood cinema and confronted Hollywood's formal aesthetics as a set of political practices. Yet her ongoing roles as lecturer, writer, organizer, and filmmaker have been largely received and understood within the concerns of postwar arts discourses rather than through feminist analysis.

Deren continuously attacked the Hollywood film industry's artistic, political, and economic monopoly over American cinema throughout the 1940s and 1950s in her articles, books, and public lectures. She frequently complained that though Hollywood movies were big on expenses they were small in artistry, "[Hollywood] has been a major obstacle to the definition and development of motion pictures as a creative fine-art form."[2] Deren advocated a cinema that would stylistically explore and expand specifically cinematic language. Always setting herself and her films in opposition to Hollywood standards and practices, Deren led a new postwar movement that combined radical formal aesthetics with efforts to tie the movies themselves to prevailing arts discourse and institutions.

Deren became the best-known representative of the postwar independent cinema discourse, perhaps, because she herself was the object of attention as often as the films and ideas. Her bodily appearance is important not because she was a woman but because it was the site for Deren's "star" construction as a filmmaker marked by contradictory desires for power and the pursuit of a feminine image within discourse.

Deren has always been represented as a strikingly beautiful woman
with a strong will and a forceful, self-centered personality. Her biogra-
pher Catrina Neiman said, "She was extremely conscious of herself as
a central figure, whether she was at a party or being featured in a film
program. Even . . . [to her closest friends] she was 'larger than life.' "[3]

Friends imaginatively captured Deren's spirit in their descriptions
of her. Anaïs Nin said, "Under the wealth of curly, wild hair, which
she allowed to frame her face in a halo, she had pale-blue eyes, and a
primitive face. The mouth was wide and fleshy, the nose with a touch
of South-Sea-islander fullness."[4] The poet Harry Roskolenko described her as "an overwhelming woman . . . [who was] short, stocky,
had a dancer's body. She looked like a Russian peasant."[5] Filmmaker
Willard Maas completed the picture, "She would always wear some
wild costume, a Haitian-line dirndl dress, perhaps, a skin-tight striped
jersey, and costume jewelry enough to stock an Eighth Street silver
shop."[6]

As often as not, she made a theatrical entrance in her colorful
costumes and jangling jewelry. The dancer-choreographer Katherine
Dunham said, "She would do almost anything for attention. She would
work like a bee to get noticed, shaking around, carrying on."[7] When
she had an audience, she often broke into impromptu Caribbean or
Russian folk dances. She even changed her name from Eleanora to
Maya to create a more exotic persona. Deren herself once said to a
friend, "Get different, and once you get here, stay different, individual, that's the secret."[8] Literally meaning "illusion" in Hindu philosophy, Maya lived up to her name among the arts and literary crowd of
Greenwich Village in the 1940s and 1950s.

However much her friends articulated her exotic image, Deren
herself participated in the formation of how she was recognized and
perceived. Maas explained, "Maya was always the center of it all. . . .
There was nothing that was not ordered with her, all planned to come
off as she would have it."[9] Deren's assistant, Miriam Arsham, agreed
that Deren created the self-image that she wanted: "Her day was spent
. . . according to her concept of how an artist lives. . . . She worked
very hard at this—the way she dressed, the way she spoke, the way she
wrote—everything to cultivate the idea of what the artist was."[10] Nin
describes the degree to which Deren's self-willed control over her
image construction was effective: "The power of her personality, the
unblinking of her blue eyes . . . her determined voice, the assertiveness
and sensuality of her peasant body, her dancing, drumming: all
haunted us. . . . We were influenced, dominated by her, and did not
know how to free ourselves."[11] Another story told by former *Village*

Voice editor Jerry Tallmer recalls Deren's sense of how one invents a
public persona, "[I]f she did not like your name or you, she might
blithely go ahead and give you another one; not perhaps her most
endearing habit. I saw her do this with Frances Stillman. . . . She
thought Frances looked a lot more like a Chekhov heroine than a
Frances . . . so she switched it without a moment's hesitation to a Sonia
or Varya or one of those."[12]

The very act of naming represents the way that one masters language as a symbolic system structuring one's individual relationship
to the world as well as the way one controls social relationships. Deren's
stepmother generalized her situation: "It really was difficult for her
with people, because she wanted, but she wanted it the way she wanted.
It wasn't as though she could accept other people from where they
were, and could have something back and forth."[13] Arsham concurred,
"She was a very, very difficult woman. She was a people-swallower. It
was very hard to be your own person with her, even with that generosity. It wasn't malicious. . . . She was just difficult and demanding."[14]
The women close to her depict Deren mapping her order, her organization, onto her personal and social realms, thereby empowering herself in the process. The result, as the Legend of Maya Deren Project
noted, is a tension between the woman as her friends knew her and
the image that Deren created and projected for the world.[15]

Such a portrayal of Deren's intense desire for control, achievement,
and fame became intricately bound to her sexual identity and to her
sense of pleasure. In her diary, Anaïs Nin recalls that Deren's artistic
crises and momentary setbacks became intertwined with aggressive
sexual seductions, "We all live on pins and needles as she has a need
to seduce everyone. . . .We may have to draw lots. Now you, Number
Nine, go to Maya, and make love to her and make her happy."[16] Deren
likewise used the private, personalized form of a diary to understand
her sexuality, "It is when I feel badly or intellectually unsuccessful that
I want men's arms about me because, failing on one plain [sic], on the
higher plane of asexuality, I descend to dominate on the plane of
feminity [sic] and sex. Sexual domination is in this sense a part of . . .
domination of the environment by the ego. Most women are feminine
in their activities because they cannot dominate their environment on
any other plane."[17] Deren represents her own sexual desire as a political weapon for some small measure of power within patriarchy.

Her private statement, her public persona, and her political activities resist the ways that women's social identities were cast as sexual
inside patriarchal institutions. They represent a position of refusal
while still being defined by the very sexual terms against which they

rebel. There is ultimately a corollary between Deren's difficult position as a woman filmmaker-activist in postwar America and the ways in which her films rework existing film language to inscribe a place for female subjectivity.

A Short Biography

Deren was exceptionally verbal and literate from an early age and was encouraged to be a prolific writer. She recorded her experiences and thoughts in letters and diaries; she reported on college activities as a journalism major and reporter; and she created poetry, short stories, and expository pieces as an adult.

Writing was a habit that she maintained for her entire life. "Maya wrote up a storm," admitted her husband.[18] She kept endless lists; scrap sheets of paper became diaries of private thoughts; and she spent hours rewriting three and four drafts of letters that she never mailed to friends and movie critics. In an unfinished biography on Deren, Robert Steele said, "Had her life gone smoother, she would not have been driven to write some of the letters she wrote out of frustration. . . . She shows herself as a woman who could express terrific anger, deep hurt, and great passion."[19]

Deren's voluminous writings may have been the important means by which she could claim a position of authority inside patriarchy. But they were also the way she rebelled against a society that systematically denied women a voice of power. In Deren's hands, language and language systems became a weapon.

Deren's childhood and development as a young woman may be portrayed as the process by which she learned domination through the art of language. Born Eleanora Derenowsky in a bourgeois Jewish family in Kiev, Russia, on April 29, 1917, Deren and her parents immigrated to the United States in 1922. Deren's father Solomon shortened his family's surname to Deren shortly after their arrival. Solomon Deren became a staff psychiatrist and later the director of the State Institute for the Feeble-minded in Syracuse, New York. He and his only child Eleanora developed a close, stormy relationship. Years later, she recalled their constant arguments about mathematics and how they would chase each other around the dinner table.[20] Training her at an early age in contemporary scientific theories and mathematics, he impressed upon her the importance of complex intellectual systems as a way of understanding and mastering the world.

Deren's mother, hoping to escape an unhappy marriage, found an excuse to live separately from her husband when she placed Eleanora in a private European school and moved to Paris to be near her daughter. From 1930 to 1933, Eleanora Deren attended the League of Nations School in Geneva, Switzerland.[21] Her education there so exceeded the average American girl's that the Syracuse daily newspaper ran a story on her when she returned home in 1933 to enter college at sixteen.[22]

Deren attended Syracuse University for two years. During her freshman year, she became active in the Youth Party of the Socialists League (YPSL) and subsequently married Gregory Bardacke, a student she met in YPSL.[23] After his graduation in 1935, Bardacke became a union organizer in New York City. Deren went to Manhattan with her husband and completed her studies at New York University.[24]

Separated from Bardacke by the fall of 1937, Deren began work on a master's degree in English literature. She started her degree at the New School for Social Research in New York City but finished at Smith College in Massachusetts in 1939 after her divorce was final. As an English student, she studied not only literature but perception and the creation of artistic form as theorized in gestalt psychology.[25] Her master's thesis analyzing French Symbolist poetry's influence on the Imagist poets sought historical continuity for objectifying emotions through verbal and visual associations.[26]

Between 1939 and 1941, Deren pursued a free-spirited existence in Greenwich Village. She earned her livelihood as a free-lance secretary at different times to writers Max Eastman, Edna Lou Walton, and William Seabrook.[27] She occasionally sold portrait photographs to magazines. She had several short-term love affairs. She wrote poetry and short stories.

In 1941, Deren took decisive steps to further her professional success. She asked modern dance choreographer Katherine Dunham to hire her as a personal secretary. Dunham occupied a public, central position during a resurgence of cultural interest in Latin entertainment. Dunham, a dancer and University of Chicago–trained anthropologist, was famous for her explorations into the origins of black dance. She had recreated and popularized African-Caribbean dances in a series of Broadway revues that mixed ballet vocabulary with Latin flavor. According to one dance critic, Dunham's choreography joined the "hip-shaking, pounding feet and undulating spine of African and Caribbean dances with the extensions and turns of Western forms."[28] When Deren met her, Dunham had just finished collaborating with George Balanchine on the Broadway musical *Cabin in the Sky*.

Dunham hired Deren and sometimes worked her secretary as many as seventeen hours a day. Since her own daily schedule went from noon to 5:00 a.m., she expected her secretary's to follow suit.[29] Dunham, who performed nightly in the show, kept her energy high by taking vitamin supplements prescribed by a New York physician, and she referred Deren to her doctor.[30] From this time, Deren became a life-long patient of Dr. Max Jacobson, a man whose practice consisted largely of pep pill prescriptions and vitamin injections given to celebrities and politicians.[31] Deren took amphetamines to stay alert without any sleep.[32] Deren learned much from Dunham that profoundly affected the course of her career, but nothing may have been as subtly significant as her introduction to Jacobson.

Jacobson was Deren's doctor, counselor, and friend throughout the 1940s and 1950s. By the time she died on October 13, 1961, Deren was seeing Jacobson several times a week and taking daily amphetamines and sleeping pills prescribed by him.[33] Like her father, she may also have had high blood pressure, putting her at greater risk for a stroke. The combination of high blood pressure and high use of amphetamines is particularly deadly, and her sudden death from a series of cerebral hemorrhages at forty-four was most likely a result.

Although Deren's death has never been publicly linked to amphetamines or even to drug addiction, Jacobson's medical practice was based solely on developing drug dependencies among his patients. Jacobson's practice was so notorious that in 1972 the *New York Times* began an investigative report on his medical practices, ethics, and patients.[34] A medical licensing board hearing, a New York state attorney general's investigation, and private lawsuits followed; all linked Jacobson's injection treatments and prescriptions to patients' deaths, drug addictions, and breakdowns.[35] In 1975, the New York medical licensing board took away Jacobson's license to practice medicine.[36]

Throughout the varied investigations, no one raised questions regarding Deren's death, although the circumstantial evidence suggests that Jacobson may have contributed greatly to it. Like most of her contemporaries in the 1940s and 1950s, Deren did not know about the medical risks, and the doctor that she trusted indiscriminately passed out the drugs. What appeared safe to one person was compounded by the fact that everyone else she knew was taking drugs prescribed by "Dr. Feelgood," and no one seemed any the worse for it.

Dunham's influence also touched every other aspect of Deren's life when Deren became Dunham's private secretary and traveled with her dance troupe on its cross-country tour of *Cabin in the Sky*. Deren drove Dunham's car, handled hotel arrangements on occasion, ran errands, took dictation, and typed correspondence.[37] Dunham, who had written a master's degree thesis on Haitian dances based on firsthand experiences in Haiti in 1936, passed her enthusiasm onto Deren. Deren assisted Dunham on a proposed book about Haitian dance and religion and learned about Haitian culture and rituals, jazz, and anthropology from her sessions with Dunham. While in Dunham's employ, she published the first article of many that she wrote on the subject of religious possession and dance.[38] Deren became passionately interested in the religions and dances of the Caribbean.

Once the *Cabin in the Sky* tour concluded, the Dunham dance company stopped in Los Angeles to work for several months in Hollywood films. In Los Angeles, Deren met an immigrant cinematographer named Alexander Hackenschmied who was staying with Dunham's friend, documentary filmmaker Herbert Kline. Hackenschmied (who changed his name to Hammid in 1947) was from Prague, Czechoslovakia, where he had worked for the Czech movie director Gustav Machaty and had made short experimental films.[39] He met Kline in 1938 and collaborated with him on a series of documentary films. Hammid and Kline together fled war-torn Europe in 1941 for Los Angeles. According to Dunham Company design director John Pratt, Deren "went after" Hammid, and the two were married in Los Angeles in 1942.[40]

Meshes of the Afternoon (1943)
as Woman's Discourse

The impulse and direction for Hammid's and Deren's filmmaking efforts as a team appear to have originated in Deren's enthusiasm for mastering a new language system. As soon as Hammid started to teach filmmaking to his new wife, she developed ideas for how to express her sense of self-awareness,

> I started out by thinking in terms of a subjective camera, one that would show only that which I could see by myself without the aid of mirrors and which would move through the house as if it were a pair of eyes, pausing with interest here and there, opening doors, and so on. This beginning developed into a film about a girl who fell asleep and saw herself in her dream, and it soon became obvious that I could not both photograph and act myself, so I waited until my husband was free to develop further the concept of the film and to execute it with me.[41]

With his lighting, photographic, and editing expertise and her desire to extend her previous experiences as a poet to film, the two collaborated on an eighteen-minute, black-and-white, silent film that cost

$260—*Meshes of the Afternoon.*[42] Hammid has described the collaboration as "so involved between the two of us that it's hard to separate what was one person's idea and what was the other's."[43] Although the film owes some stylistic and conceptual debts to Hammid's first experimental film, *Aimless Walk* (1930), *Meshes of the Afternoon* expresses more intense emotions and an overall mood unlike anything that Hammid had previously done.[44] The film is significant, then, as a woman's discourse that rewrites Hollywood's objectification of women by addressing a female subject who must contend with her own objectification.

In a typical Hollywood narrative film from the time period, a woman's body is appropriated as the site of pleasure for the presumed male spectator. Through the story's presentation, a woman occupies visual space only insofar as she is physically fragmented within an extensive system of shots organized by a male gaze—both the spectator's and an on-screen male subject's.[45] The purpose of such an arrangement is to eroticize and fetishize Woman as Other.[46] Nowhere is this more apparent than in the *film noir* emerging in the early 1940s. The *femme fatale* as a character type, who is visually seductive yet progressively more dangerous as the storyline unfolds, is represented only in these visual terms of sexual seduction and sexual threat. In such films as *Double Indemnity, Cat People, Laura,* and *Farewell, My Lovely,* stylized narratives emphasize both women's sexual threat as part of a sinister, alienating world and the need to contain that threat to restore order.[47] *Meshes of the Afternoon* adopts the dominant visual vocabulary associated with the emerging *film noir*—high contrast lighting, extreme camera angles, character point-of-view shots—but displaces it onto a narrative of a woman subject contending with her own fragmentation and disequilibrium. It was not until 1978, however, that film critic J. Hoberman suggested such a cinematic context for the film, "*Meshes* seems less related to European surrealism than to the Freudian flashbacks and sinister living-rooms that typify Hollywood's wartime 'noir' films. Located in some hilly L.A. suburb, the house where Deren's erotic, violent fantasy was filmed might be around the corner from Barbara Stanwyck's place in *Double Indemnity.*"[48] Hoberman is the only writer who has noted the film's ideological and aesthetic debt to Hollywood *film noir.* Writing at precisely the same moment that major critical work on the relationships among *noir,* representations of female sexuality, and psychoanalysis was being published, he has provided a pivotal point from which to reassess the meaning of the film as a woman's discourse.[49]

There is a second Hollywood genre to which this film implicitly

Meshes of the Afternoon (1943), directed by Maya Deren and Alexander Hammid. The opening shot.

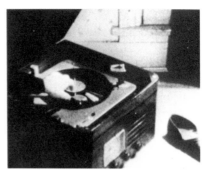

Meshes of the Afternoon. The "hypersignification" of domestic elements.

Meshes of the Afternoon. Her subjective point of view of the bedroom she is about to enter.

Meshes of the Afternoon. His point of view of the woman's entrance into the bedroom.

Meshes of the Afternoon. His point of view—the woman's body as a sexual object of desire in relation to the male gaze.

At Land (1944), directed by Maya Deren. The ongoing physical centering of a female protagonist. Photo courtesy of Boston University, Mugar Memorial Library, Maya Deren papers.

At Land. The protagonist (Maya Deren) in the house interior. Photo courtesy of Boston University, Mugar Memorial Library, Maya Deren papers.

At Land. The closing shot. Photo courtesy of Boston University, Mugar Memorial Library, Maya Deren papers.

A Study in Choreography for the Camera (1945), directed by Maya Deren. Dancer Talley Beatty in a solo freed from its geographic backdrops and real-time constraints. Photo courtesy of Boston University, Mugar Memorial Library, Maya Deren papers.

Ritual in Transfigured Time (1946), directed by Maya Deren. In the beginning, a woman (Maya Deren) winds a ball of yarn while being watched by a woman. Photo courtesy of Boston University, Mugar Memorial Library, Maya Deren papers.

Ritual in Transfigured Time. The courtship *pas de deux* between dancers Rita Christiani and Frank Westbrook. Photo courtesy of Boston University, Mugar Memorial Library, Maya Deren papers.

Ritual in Transfigured Time. It is the first woman who begins the action of running into the water until she is submerged up to her waist. Photo courtesy of Boston University, Mugar Memorial Library, Maya Deren papers.

Photo of Maya Deren. Photo courtesy of Boston University, Mugar Memorial Library, Maya Deren papers.

speaks. That is the woman's melodrama, a type itself coded through specifically cinematic structures of female subjectivity—relying upon such devices as point-of-view shots and dream sequences in relation to a female character. Mary Ann Doane's *The Desire to Desire: The Woman's Film of the 1940s* traces and analyzes the trajectory of the female as subject and object in the woman's film, and she identifies as recurrent the following spatial and temporal structures: "a marked preference for mistiming which facilitates the production of pathos . . . and an expansion of time which simulates the type of time most fully associated with women—the time of waiting and duration"; space constriction, usually the space of the home; oppositions between outside and inside the home, where difficulties often arise when a figure invades the home from the outside; uncanniness or claustrophobia associated with the space of the home; a hypersignification of domestic elements—doors, windows, kitchen, bedrooms—resulting in a "signifying glut" or overabundance of signs referring to the traditionally trivial; and the staircase as a privileged and multiple site of the woman's specularization, her pathway from curiosity to terror, and her symbolic prison.[50] Doane concludes, "In watching a woman's film, one actively senses the contraction of the world attributed to the woman, the reduction of meaning and the subordination to affect."[51] Anyone familiar with *Meshes of the Afternoon* could rapidly identify the ways that the film literalizes all these coordinates within its narrative. But, more important, it makes such processes of signification the central substance of the film's genre rewriting—they become the on-screen signified.

Meshes of the Afternoon begins by introducing a woman—played by Deren—who becomes mysterious because only her arms, legs, and shadowed profile are seen. She picks up a paper flower from a sidewalk, follows the sidewalk up a flight of stairs to a house's front door. She takes a key out of her purse, drops the key, retrieves it, and unlocks the door. She enters the house. P. Adams Sitney notes, "There is no establishing shot, no view of the whole figure in her environment."[52] The sequence of events is comprised entirely of close-up shots—her hand reaches for the flower, the hand lifts the flower, sandaled feet alternate with a shadowy profile moving up the flight of stairs to the house. The body parts substitute for an unseen but implied "whole" woman. The arm, the shadow, the flower—as objects of equal size and depth—reinforce one's sense that the parts are autonomous objects. By following and tightly framing the limbs and body shadow, Deren and Hammid inhibit any sense of manipulation or movement extended from a female subject.

The end of the opening sequence reenforces the point. When the hand takes a key from a purse and drops the key, the key falls in slow motion to the ground, bounces, and heads off-screen. A hand enters following the same trajectory of movement as the key. Across several similarly composed alternating shots of hand, key, and feet, one continuous trajectory of movement creates metamorphosis from object to body part to object to body. The relation of subject to object is reversed: the woman becomes passive while the object acts aggressively. *Meshes* visually suggests a strong sense of subject fragmentation, psychological disturbance, and dislocation underlying the simple narrative progression of a woman doing an everyday activity in an ordinary environment.

When the woman enters the house, she examines such mechanical devices as a phonograph and a telephone. She stops to rest in a chair, and she falls asleep. An iris or telescopic shot symbolically expresses travel to the internal world of her dream imagination, where she arises, chases a hooded figure with a mirrored face into the house, and encounters ordinary domestic objects. The sequence of events occurs three times, each constructed around a search through the domestic space whereby the staircase provides a pathway to dramatic spatial and temporal disruptions of the environment. The searches end with the three "dream Mayas" facing off around the dining room table in order to determine which one will kill the fourth "Maya" asleep in the chair.

The transition into the subjective or dream experience expresses cinematic ambivalence between the "alienated" world of female objectification and the "imaginary" one of female subjectivity. It is a transition from cinematic construction of shots around an objective point of view to a subjective point of view. The woman approaches the living room chair as seen in medium shot from her point of view. The next shot is an objective eye-level close-up of her feet approaching the chair, and the camera tilts up to follow the bottom half of her body lowering into the chair. An arm drops a flower into her lap, and the hand continues the line of established movements by caressing her stomach and breast. The gesture follows the line of the body, which is the line of diagonal compositional movement within the frame. The sequence ends with an extreme close-up of her eye. One moves from what the woman sees and her controlling gaze to her physical entrance into the space already defined by her sight. Her body's active control over the space continues through the motion and rhythm of the swing of her body lowering into the chair through the sweep of the hand across her body. Both actions are self-originating. Yet the woman still appears as a series of fragments, as autonomous parts linked together only by the continuity of movement. They imply "a whole person" only by the visual "gaps." The sequence ends by returning to the subject's eye, now represented objectively as the gateway to the woman's imagination.

Only after the woman subject's point of view becomes the dominant means of ordering vis-à-vis the dream sequence is her face finally made visible. Close-ups and medium shots from objective points of view occur frequently within her dream. Full shots of her body within the environment are also introduced.

The woman, represented as a whole figure and the source of her bodily movement, is now unable to master her environment because abruptly changing camera angles and jump cuts present the space itself as constantly changing around her, according to the categories of temporal and spatial disturbance outlined by Doane. Film critic Parker Tyler describes the process: "Physical laws are transcended and implemented by filmic devices. Slow motion, weird angles, magical mutation and transitions. Time is not literal . . . but a means of poetic expression. *Meshes* is an afternoon revery of erotic suspense."[53] It is worth noting that Tyler enjoins both the narrational motivating terms associated with female desire in the woman's film—*erotic*—and in *film noir*—*suspense*. It is a domestic world of dream logic where objects turn into other objects, where the speed of motion does not correspond to physical laws, and where geography is neither constant nor consistent. Time and space are so fractured that such everyday occurrences as walking up the stairs, entering a bedroom or a dining room, or answering the telephone become traumatizing experiences. Even Deren herself wrote that the film presents a malevolent vitality to inanimate objects.[54] There is little sense of illusionistic depth, and spatial orientation occurs primarily through the continuous movement within the frame and across shots. In the terms set up by Doane, the dream narrative then is largely preoccupied with the woman's physical placement and inability to find containment in a traditionally female world of domesticity that has suddenly become *noiresque*.

At the moment when the woman's self-destruction in this world seems imminent—a "dream Maya" lowers a knife toward the "sleeping Maya"—the dream ends. The dreamer's view of the sleeping woman retrospectively becomes a male point of view when she opens her eyes and her view of a man's face bending over her replaces the consummation of the dream. Although he has interrupted and "saved" her from the dream, her view of him entirely from below codifies him in a domineering position of intrusion. His view looking down at her makes her still appear vulnerable.

The man—played by Hammid—leads her to the bedroom, where

his viewpoint and actions control the flow of images. He "returns her to normalcy," that is to say, to representation within a narrative where her body is portrayed as a sexual object of desire in relation to the male gaze: in an establishing shot of a third-person or objective viewpoint, she lies on the bed with the man seated next to her; from his point of view, a high angle close-up reveals her outstretched body, and he runs his hand along its contours; after his hand has followed a path of movement along the diagonal of the frame, an extreme close-up of her lips frames her mouth on the same axis as the preceding movement.

In contrast to the earlier sequence where she caressed her body before falling asleep, one moves here from a fixed sense of space to a male gaze governing female placement within the shot. In the former instance, it was a female character who originated and controlled movement across a sequence spatially defined by her gaze. Again to quote Doane on the woman's film as a genre, "The attempted eroticization of the gaze is turned back on itself to produce the narcissism traditionally associated with the woman, the mirror constituting its most exemplary figure. The narcissistic relation of [a specifically female] spectator to screen is transformed into a divided identification with the male character loving the woman and with the woman in the process of being loved."[55] The female character has lost not only the authority of the gaze but also her position as the subjective voice and is instead repositioned as narcissistic within traditional terms of female representation.

Given this kind of recuperation, any effort to wrest back a female subjective voice must necessarily be violent. What follows then is a rapid montage organized around the figures of mirror reflections and their rewriting into destructive signification: the flower suddenly changes to a knife; she moves her head and her eye is both framed by and reflected against the knife. From her point of view, his face tilts forward and she pitches the knife at him. His face is both a broken mirror and an open space revealing waves crashing on the shore. The pieces of mirror fall onto the beach. The sequence that began as a static presentation of her body as a sensual object within the frame ends with images of her eye and hand intercut together as the dynamic agents for the flow of motion and succession of images. She destroys the objects governing a woman's sexual reflection, the man who is both male sexuality and a mirror for narcissistic female sexuality. She has literally reached out to control the definition of her self.

The woman's bold attempt to overthrow external representations of herself and to create her own self-image leads her literally to the sea, a metaphor for rebirth frequently used in women's writing. But when she reaches her destination, a place Joyce Wieland thirty years later would call "the far shore," the film acknowledges her passage with yet another narrative that returns the spectator outside the home and to another difficult entry into the domestic milieu. The melodramatic epilogue pivots dramatically on its shifts from an objective point of view to his point of view after the man approaches and enters the house. It is a syntactical repetition of camera position and point-of-view shifts from the first dream Maya's entrance into the house. Now, though, he sees the woman with her throat slit, mirror fragments strewn around her, and seaweed dripping down her clothing. His final close-up images, then, of her dead eyes and bloody mouth are a conclusion whose significance is dependent on how one contextualizes the woman's "death." Is it, as Doane would observe about women characters who appropriate the gaze in woman's films, that her desire is so excessive the only closure possible is her death? Or is it the result of her revolt against the cinematic structures of containment? Or is her death dramatically signifying her end as a construction of Woman within *his* dream world? *Her* dream world?

At Land (1944)

By the time Deren and Hammid had finished *Meshes*, they had moved to New York City because Hammid got a job there working for the Office of War Information. Once again, Deren conceived of a film idea and depended upon Hammid to help her execute it. But, this time, she unified and controlled all aspects of the film *At Land*. She directed a larger ensemble of actors as well as a second cinematographer (Hella Heyman), shot on Long Island on weekends, and then later worked with Hammid in the film's editing.

At Land significantly departs from *Meshes*'s oppositional stance to Hollywood genres and from its division of imaginary and waking terrains. But it does maintain narrative causality as well as space and time continuities across disparate times and physical locations that are organized by the ongoing physical centering of a female protagonist. The protagonist has a series of picaresque adventures in which the constantly changing objects, people, and environments around her contrast and ultimately test the strength and stability of her identity.

The woman, again played by Deren, washes out of rolling waves onto the seashore. She rises, crawls over rocks and driftwood into the middle of a banquet table. Unnoticed by those seated at the table, she pulls herself down the length of the table and, at the table's end, she steals a chess piece from a board on which the pieces move by themselves. The middle of the film records her travels through other landscapes—down a country road where she encounters a chameleon-like male companion and into a house interior of fluid space and a "planted" occupant.

Finding another chess game in progress back on the beach, she again steals a chess piece. Clutching the piece and looking around her, she is watched by other selves from places where she previously was in the film—the rocks, the banquet, the trees. The film closes with a long take of the heroine running down the beach until she almost disappears from view.

Much of the thematic work of *Meshes* is reapplied here. Shots are constructed around her acts of looking. But what she *sees* follows no conventional rules of physical stability since the objects, people, and environments frequently become transformed into something else. What is constant are both her ongoing presence and controlling gaze—even if it cannot control the stability of the world around her. In relation to the protagonist's construction as the film's subject, the spectator also watches her framed as a central object for being looked at. There are numerous male figures who become on-screen markers for gazing at the woman. In this way, the protagonist's journey, governed by her active sight, is also made the object of pleasure for frequently inscribed male viewers who offer the spectators a shared identification with the pleasure of their gaze at the woman. Once again, the terms of subjectivity Deren engages are ambivalently inscribed in relation to patriarchal representation of women.

More interesting, perhaps, *At Land* expands *Meshes*'s confrontation among multiple selves. *At Land*'s multiple selves occupy contiguous spaces rather than a single space, and they provide the continuity for a series of eye-line matches that direct the narrative's activity. When each self gazes off-screen followed by her subjective point of view of herself in another location, the woman now becomes both the originator and the object of her own gaze. In its outcome, *At Land* is finally able to write woman in relation to herself, albeit still constructed around the act of seeing.

Deren's recurring use of multiple selves suggests that an examination of plural identities is not so much a schizophrenic disorder or psychoanalytic interpretation than a radically original means toward self-discovery. This approach, in fact, abounds in women's writing. In addition, both *Meshes* and *At Land* tie such self-discovery to the sea—*At Land* allowing the character whose physical identity flows unperturbed throughout the film to originate from and return to the sea in the end.

Even the title playfully reverses the expression *at sea* while visually applying all the connotations of being at sea to the world of the terra firma—objects and people disappear and change identity, time and space are dislocated and constantly changing. Literally being at sea is the opposite of the confusion "at land." The opening and closing image of rolling waves suggests that their rhythmic flow provides a symbolic order as well as an index to the literal flow of movement that formally orders the film.

Woman's Discourse and Critical Reception within Surrealist Cinema

Neither *Meshes* nor *At Land* were necessarily understood as a woman's discourse when they were first seen by Deren's friends at private screenings and at New York film societies in 1943, 1944, and 1945. Anaïs Nin, famous for her sensitivity to the language of feminine celebration, responded in a fairly typical way when she saw the films at Deren's and Hammid's apartment, *At Land* "had many strange effects which reminded me of Cocteau. . . . [But Deren] did not acknowledge any link with the Surrealists or with Cocteau. We did not insist."[56] At that time, the Surrealist films of the 1920s were the audiences' primary cinematic comparison for the dream imagery, logic disturbances, and concern for the subconscious expressed in her films.

The critics also contributed to the films' reputation as Surrealist cinema. They constantly likened both *Meshes* and *At Land* to *Le sang d'un poète*, *Un chien andalou*, and other European Surrealist films of the 1920s. For example, dance reviewer Richard Lippold said, "*Seashell and the Clergyman* might have sprung from the heart of an identical twin of Maya Deren. Jean Cocteau's *Blood of a Poet*, too, is not far from *Meshes of the Afternoon*."[57] Parker Tyler compared her work to "the visions of Cocteau and Dali."[58] *Nation* film critic and well-known novelist James Agee did not particularly like the films but still made the inevitable comparison, "I cannot feel . . . that they do anything . . . which was not done, and done to an ill-deserved death, by some of the European avant-gardists, and especially by the surrealists, of the 1920's."[59] Even when they were writing from divergent backgrounds and contexts—dance, literature, cinema—the critics agreed that the films were stylistically linked to the European avant-garde of the 1920s.

Deren, though, claimed that *Meshes* and *At Land* were mistakenly called Surrealist because they were not involved in registers of the irrational. Contemporary feminist theorists have said much about the ideological role of the irrational realm within patriarchy as a feminized register of experience that cannot be known or understood through linear argumentation and language of scientific rationalism. Looking to Sigmund Freud's works as the exemplary site for this binary opposition within Western thought, French psychoanalytic feminists locate the rational as a masculine structuring of experience that can be known and explained in language as knowledge and truth. The irrational, however, is that which through its gaps and disruptions remains outside such knowledge. It is that which threatens the rational order and, like Woman, its threat of castration and destruction is displaced representationally within patriarchy as a "lack." If Woman is defined by what she "lacks"—the phallus—and is relegated to significance only as a negative site, then so is the irrational realm also made a site for relocating and containing patriarchal fears of Otherness.[60] It is, perhaps, particularly interesting that Deren rejected Freudian psychoanalysis since Freud's theories were built up around the "curative" process of making that which was irrational the object of rational explanation and analysis.

What is more significant here is that while Deren did not champion her own films as woman's discourse, she curbed the possibilities of interpretations linking her pleasures in the irrational to woman's language by surrounding the films with intellectual discourse emphasizing the rational order of the films. The program notes that she mailed with her films or handed out at film screenings baldly stated, "Under no conditions are these films to be announced or publicized as surrealist or Freaudian [sic]. This is not only a serious misrepresentation of the films, but also confuses the audience by inspiring a false interpretation of the films according to sustems [sic] to which they bear no relation. The preoccupation with conscious control of form which is involved . . . is obviously at variance with the Sur-realist esthetic of spontaneity."[61] Deren's disclaimer represents one effort among her many to deny the films the critical discourse of Surrealism being built up around them and the latent possibility that such Surrealist celebration of irrational subconscious spontaneity was feminine. Instead, Deren's program notes, lectures accompanying her film presentations, and published commentaries on her films critically locate the films within the patriarchal language of scientific rationality.

Maya Deren and New York Surrealism

Deren's efforts to counter the historical reception of a Surrealist critical context must be understood as something more than an effort to locate herself within patriarchal structures of power because Surrealism itself was a dominant aesthetic and critical context among the avant-garde arts in New York City during World War II. The importance of the wartime presence and leadership of expatriate Surrealists for American painters and for the arts in general is well documented. In particular, Surrealist painter Encharito Roberto Matta gathered a coterie of up-and-coming Manhattan painters around him, and they forged Surrealism's new role for abstract painting. Matta was a Chilean expatriate who studied art in Paris and traveled with André Breton and other Surrealists until coming to New York in 1939. By 1941 and 1942, he was meeting regularly with Robert Motherwell, Jackson Pollock, and William Baziotes. He was teaching the artists who shaped the major direction of American art after World War II how Surrealist automatism might be made compatible with more conscious control of form—how it might be "masculinized." Matta's commitment to the New York painters and his desire to focus attention on his methods may have resulted from arguments between him and Breton; his activities were a political challenge to Breton's leadership among the Surrealists.[62] It is this particular set of social relationships within Surrealist activity that constituted Deren's rhetorical claims for "conscious control" and her alignment with Matta.

Deren had met Matta a few years earlier. Together they started a film that they never finished—*The Witch's Cradle*. Filming Matta and Marcel Duchamp at the famous Surrealist "Art of This Century" Gallery, Deren never realized a formal plan for the film footage, but she developed sympathy for Matta's artistic position.

He encouraged automatism as a means to reveal universal mental symbols, a move that helped New York abstract painters break from a Freudian orientation to Carl Jung's concept of the collective unconscious. Pollock, Motherwell, and Baziotes as well as Mark Rothko and Adolph Gottlieb all followed Matta's approach and turned to primitive, ancient myths as an important subject for contemporary art. Rothko expresses their position: Myths "are the eternal symbols upon which we must fall back to express basic psychological ideas. They are the symbols of man's primitive fears and motivations, no matter in which land or what time, changing only in detail but never in substance . . . and our modern psychology finds them persisting still in our dreams, our vernacular and our art for all the changes in the outward conditions of life."[63] Deren, too, considered Matta's approach. It was a way to articulate her psychological self-awareness without defining it through a "lack" of rationality.

A Study in Choreography for the Camera (1945)

Deren initially tested her ideas in *A Study in Choreography for the Camera*. It is a four-minute film of Dunham dancer Talley Beatty performing a dance in several locations. Deren match-cut the dance in the midst of slow motion leaps and turns, moving from one location to another while continuing the fluidity of the dance movement. She literally freed the gestures and rhythms from their geographic back-drops and real-time constraints in an attempt to make dance the direct representation of universal expression.

Deren literalized through cinematic means what modern dance choreographers such as Martha Graham and Katherine Dunham could only imply within the time-bound, spatially limited medium of the live stage performance. Both choreographers followed a formalist approach to modern dance that restrained the emotional impulse and made stage dancing resemble ritual dancing. Such modern dance classics as Graham's *Primitive Mysteries* (1931) and *Dark Meadow* (1946) employ angular movements, sparsely abstract settings, and dramatic lighting effects not to tell a story but to serve the dance itself. Dance critic Marcia Siegel suggests that the works abstract personal feelings and national identity to a more cosmic level by using symbol, myth, and psychoanalytic exploration.[64] Dunham's *Shango* (1945), based on Haitian Voudoun rituals, and *Rites de passage* (1941), which adapted African tribal rites, likewise drew viewers into the universal feelings expressed through ritual dance.

Ritual in Transfigured Time (1946)

Ritual in Transfigured Time is the more fully developed outcome of Deren's artistic reorientation. The film applies the choreographic style of *Choreography* to a universal ritual that profoundly charges women's position in culture—courtship and marriage. The act of ritual itself is particularly important to Jungian followers because it formally ex-presses deep-seated, primitive emotions that one is otherwise unable to name during important life or environmental changes. It is, per-haps, not coincidental then that Deren's personal life was undergoing profound change since she and Hammid had separated, and they divorced soon after.

Deren's film weaves a ritual by combining activity among several people and cutting on motion. For example, a first woman (played by Deren) winds a ball of yarn in slow motion, and a second woman dressed in black (a widow) completes the gesture. The continuity of motion binds the two together. When the widow enters a roomful of people at a party, one person begins a gesture, a second continues it, and a third completes it. Fluid activity results neither from the identity of a single performer (as in *At Land*) nor from the narrative progression(as in *Meshes*), but from the combined movements themselves. Freeze-frame and shot repetitions further break actions in progress and reinforce the rhythm of the movements extended over time. Isolated from narrative function or performance completion, the repetitive gestures become a privileged formal device that, through their estrangement from an ordinary environment, assume the form of a primitive religious rite.

The second half of the film focuses on the courtship ritual that begins when the widow meets and touches a man at the party. Suddenly transported to a classical portico in the middle of a park, they perform a slow motion *pas de deux* while three female party guests hover nearby. During the dance (itself a rite of courtship), the man and the three other women are metamorphosized and frozen into statues, but the man suddenly revives and chases the widow. As she flees in panic, the widow is intercut and interchanged with the woman she saw winding yarn at the film's beginning. The widow reaches the edge of the sea. But it is the first woman who begins the action of running into the water until she is submerged up to her waist. As she turns, the widow completes the movement and floats downward through the water. Through negative photographic processing, her widow's black weeds are transformed into a flowing, white bridal gown. Instead of wedding the man, she becomes a bride of the sea.

Ritual is less a direct confrontation of patriarchal cinema than the intersection of dominant activity in three fine art forms. *Ritual* combines the Jungian underpinnings of postwar abstraction painting with the dramatic, symbolic structure of contemporary dance and the unique vocabulary of cinema. *Ritual* did not so much rewrite a woman's cinema but rather situated an alternative base *within* the vanguard arts from which one could sound a woman's voice. *Ritual* is, after all, a woman's exploration for personal fulfillment through her sociosexual role, and the film expresses the incompatibility of fulfilling that role and oneself as a woman.

Maya Deren and Reception Practices

It is interesting to note, however, that it is not *Ritual* but *Meshes* that is Deren's most highly regarded film. One 1974 film textbook stated that while *Meshes* has been widely imitated, none "could equal or surpass its intricately woven structure and the depth of its mood."[65] *Meshes* is the film that has been the most frequently shown; it is the single American independent film most likely to be in every school, film club, and museum collection. It is, according to film critic J. Hoberman, "probably the most widely seen avant-garde film ever made."[66] Whereas *Ritual* has been called the most artistically accomplished of Deren's films, *Meshes* may be the most popular because of its intervention and confrontation with the dominant Hollywood cinema, a language widely understood and shared.

Ritual's reception has been, perhaps, less problematic and more consistent than that of Deren's previous three films. Critics have continuously discussed the film as both preoccupied with form and an outward manifestation of Jungian concepts regarding women, courtship, and marital status.[67] By the time *Ritual* was completed, Deren had assumed greater personal mastery over the exhibition tactics and participated more fully in the critical reception of her films. She rented the Provincetown Playhouse not just once for a film screening but four more times in 1946 and four times again between 1947 and 1949.[68] She personally wrote film critics for the New York literary magazines inviting them to these screenings and, more significant, she suggested to them her intentions and the best way to interpret her films if they should review them.[69] She likewise produced program notes for audiences watching her films and distribution notes for other exhibitors. In all cases, she tried to encourage people to interpret the films with the same contextual guidelines that she used.

Deren was concerned about how people viewed her films and whether or not they saw them the same way she did. It may have been partially attributable to her obsession that her relations with others, including her public relations, be on her terms. But she was also politically astute enough to know that her potential audience consisted of the film society members, museumgoers, and university students who were already encountering art house movies, foreign films, experimental films, and classic reissues identifiable and marketed by their "otherness" to the current Hollywood output. She made sure that she situated her work in opposition to Hollywood forms and language.

An Anagram of Ideas on Art, Form and Film and Deren's Theory of Cinema

Deren's concern for audience reception was so great that at the same time she was finishing *Ritual* she was also writing a book on film art. Deren published *An Anagram of Ideas on Art, Form and Film* through

a small, vanguard arts press in 1946.[70] Using an anagram as a trope
for interlocking ideas, the monograph articulates her beliefs about art,
the historical significance of naturalism and surrealism, and Hollywood's failure to develop a cinematic vocabulary as part of a continuum
of artistic practice reflecting personal consciousness. Deren's book
extended to American cinema the foregone tradition among other
modern art forms—dance, theater, literature, and painting—that it is
the artist who provides the theoretical discourse in which to situate his
or her work.

An Anagram provides only an introduction to Deren's written cinematic discourse. Through lectures and in numerous articles written
for literary magazines, amateur photography periodicals, vanguard
arts magazines, dance publications, and mass-circulation women's
magazines, Deren elaborated her film theory.[71] She wrote and spoke
for whatever venue she could since the fees from her speaking engage-
ments, articles, and photographs were the major part of her income.[72]
At the very moment that film societies were increasing in size and
number, Deren defined cinema as an art, provided an intellectual
context for film viewing, and filled a theoretical gap for the kinds of
independent films the societies were featuring. In a new field where
there were few other film theory books currently available in English,
Deren's ideas were privileged theoretical discourse.[73]

Deren argued against the assumption that cinema is a realistic art
form. It was this belief, she asserted, that informed Hollywood's practices of making cinematography, sound, and editing as invisible as
possible to preserve the illusion of an objective world, "The photographic medium is, as a matter of fact, so amorphous that it is not
merely unobtrusive but virtually transparent, and so becomes, more
than any other medium, susceptible of servitude to any and all the
others. . . . [Its] own character is as a latent image which can become
manifest only if no other image is imposed upon it to obscure it."[74] She
said that Hollywood is able to provide a convincing artifice primarily
because the photographic image itself represents an optically realistic
illusion of the world. A photograph acts as a substitute for nature and,
as such, the spectator ascribes to it an identity with an object from a
preexistent reality, "The photograph not only testifies to the existence
of that [prior] reality (just as drawing testifies to the existence of an
artist) but is, to all intent and purposes, its equivalent."[75] Her belief
that the photograph carries a discourse of the referent is shared by
André Bazin, who was writing at the same time as Deren, and they
both anticipate lengthier, more elaborate analyses of the photograph
by contemporary semiologists (most particularly, Roland Barthes).[76]

In this regard, the photograph may be placed in the system of cultural signs that signify or establish an indexical relationship to reality and always refer back to a historical moment of consciousness.

The moving photograph or, more correctly, the cinema adds a property of "motion" that in and of itself need not sever or alter the relationship between the sign (or image) and its referent (or object in reality). As Soviet semiologist Yuri Lotman explains, "The 'moving photograph' is a natural continuation of this essential property of the basic material, which results in the illusion of reality becoming a major element in the language of the feature cinema."[77] However suspect the word *natural* may appear in this context, Lotman's statement reasserts Deren's argument almost twenty years later. The illusion of motion, when attributed to a photographic image, refers to properties already associated with the referent, and the image's capacity to admit more aspects of the referent may even strengthen the indexical bond between the sign and the referent. Out of this relationship, however, she decried documentary realism because the filmmaker relinquished his or her artistic intervention or relationship to the basic material. Documentary film could not be art because the filmmaker refused to acknowledge a position relative to shaping or altering a photographic reality.

As opposed to photography's attributes, the painting always signifies a constructed image rather than testifying to the actual existence of an object in nature. For Lotman, an ontology of painting is steeped in its semiotic status as a sign of signs, an image of mental images.[78] Again, Deren also articulated this difference by arguing that painting is always understood as an abstraction of the real. "A painting is not, fundamentally, a likeness or image of a horse; it is a likeness of a mental concept which may resemble a horse or which may, as in abstract painting, bear no visible relation to any real object."[79] Within this system of differentiation, Deren considered animation an extension of painting and not akin to photographically based cinema. For that reason, she rejected the work of such animators as Hans Richter and Oskar Fischinger as steeped in the "plastic" image and not inherently cinematic because the cinema must be photographically based.

Deren theorized a cinema defined as much by editing as by the cinematographic image and the authority of reality as its basic material. Borrowing freely from the work of both Sergei Eisenstein and Dziga Vertov, Deren advocated spatiotemporal leaps as a privileged means of cinematic organization, "The editing of a film creates the sequential relationship which gives particular or new meaning to the images *according to their function;* it establishes a context, a form which transfigures them without distorting their aspect, diminishing their reality and authority, or impoverishing that variety of potential functions which is the characteristic dimension of reality."[80] Deren's words imply the Soviet filmmaker-theorists' concern for a cinema form that would reflect a new, modern world. Indeed, she concluded that cinema's unique capability to create synthetic constructions across time and space make movies the best art form to reflect not only the modern sense of speed and alienation but the ways in which the airplane and radio have led to a "relativistic reality of time and space" so that "the absolutistic differentiation between *here* and *there* loses meaning as *here* and *there* [and] . . . the chronology of the past, present, and future has also increasingly lost its meaning."[81] Deren, however, selectively ignored that Soviet film theorists understood film language as the didactic means to social awareness and political practice.[82] Deren fully understood Vertov's and Eisenstein's theories, which she had studied in college, but she was rethinking formalist cinema as the basis for expressing psychological introspection. Deren displaced the rationale of Soviet film theory onto contemporary psychological thought prevailing in the postwar arts economy.

Deren understood the importance of contemporary semiology's basic assumption that cinema is fundamentally a language system, and her arguments regarding cinema's ontology as a formalist medium were both theoretically sophisticated and prescient. She further anticipated the concern within contemporary semiotics for studying basic linguistic units of a language system when she identified a dual structure in cinema that is consistent with modern categories of the syntagmatic and the paradigmatic: the "horizontal" (syntagmatic) mode whereby images are decoded through their connectiveness, generally according to principles of spatial and/or temporal continuity, and the "vertical" (paradigmatic) mode wherein images' graphic or symbolic connections to larger abstract orders are privileged. She likened her categories to those in literature: the story or novel is analogous to the "horizontal" film, and imagistic poetry is analogous to the "vertical" film. Her classification of vertical and horizontal modes is a truncated version of Eisenstein's more elaborate editing theories put forward in *Film Form: Essays in Film Theory* and *The Film Sense*. But, even though she admired Eisenstein's montage sequences and poetic concepts, she still found the overall form of such films as *Potemkin* too steeped in literary narrative.[83] Her argument, original in its thinking, shifts the dominant emphasis from the horizontal to the vertical axis as the way to reorganize cinematic material more subjectively and to break from Hollywood mimesis.

Maya Deren and Postwar Film Culture

Deren presented her views at every opportunity, but especially
when she appeared with her films across the United States, Canada,
and South America. She alone brought film theory and independent
cinema to the Ivy League schools as well as to state teacher colleges
and film societies in the Midwest and far West.[84] In many regions of
the United States, her audiences were unfamiliar with the art discourse
Deren represented. Art historian Dore Ashton has described Deren's
terrain, "[These were] vast geographical areas in the United States
where no living painter or sculptor could be found, much less a museum. Although culture, as conceived by Americans, had penetrated
the hinterland in the form of public libraries, literary societies, and
even music circles, the plastic arts had, for various reasons, lagged far
behind."[85] However much Ashton poses the state of art culture in the
rest of the country as inferior to that of New York City, there is
something worthwhile in maintaining Ashton's division. The postwar
expansion of art activities and a support structure in New York City
is already well documented.[86] The number of galleries, the types of
museum exhibitions and collections, artists' social networks, and critical discourse all increased and were the sites for an interwoven web of
cultural authority on art. Although there existed outside New York
City some 143 museums and art centers and 67 more that began
during the years when Deren traveled around the country, the institutions were more often spatially isolated, inadequately funded, and not
so closely integrated with a full support structure.[87] Deren was an
emissary representing arts culture from New York City at a time when
there were few local authorities to compete with her.

On these travels, she insisted on talking about her films *first*. Nin
reported that this arrangement caused resentment among some college students who felt that Deren did this to "make sure they would
look at [the films] in *her* way."[88] But this was precisely her goal; the
verbal discourse always provided the context for the visual discourse.
Deren told audiences that if her films initially produced confusion or
surprise it was because her audiences' "habits of vision" had made
them blind.[89] Her very words denied her audiences the authority of
their power of sight because they did not possess the language for
critical interpretation that she did.

Deren's manner as well as her claims to power through language
could be abrasive to audiences especially unaccustomed to taking their
intellectual training from a woman. At a poetry and film symposium
organized by Cinema 16 in 1953, Deren's male copanelists refused to

take seriously her clearly defined ideas regarding the vertical and horizontal modes of film form, and they responded by making fun of her.[90] Hoberman characterizes Deren's resolute rebuttals to "Dylan Thomas's shameless hot-dogging and Arthur Miller's windy pontifications" as indicative of the cultural climate she was up against.[91]

But Deren's forceful personality and intimidating presence could also be her greatest assets. Her striking good looks and her offbeat appearance drew journalists to interviews and people to her talks. Her love at being the center of attention and her self-conscious awareness of how to hold a crowd when she was center stage helped Deren become a charismatic speaker. Younger male filmmakers like Kenneth Anger, Curtis Harrington, and Stan Brakhage became devoted to her.[92] Joyce Wieland remembers Deren's reputation in Toronto in the 1950s as a "Pied Piper" who would lead a workshop and then be followed to New York City by mesmerized filmmakers.[93]

The end of Deren's filmmaking partnership with Hammid in 1946 seems to have fanned her need for verbal as well as sexual domination. She spent more time traveling, writing, and lecturing than making films. She did embark on a fifth film project, drawing up elaborately detailed plans of the abstract intellectual concepts the film would illustrate.[94] But without Hammid's assistance, *Meditation on Violence* (1947) was simply "a kungfu remake" of *Choreography* in which a young man performs the dancelike movements of Chinese boxing.[95] The only other film that she finished more than ten years later—*The Very Eye of Night* (1959)—is another dry exercise in filming dance. Ballet dancers perform superimposed over a starry sky, and critics generally responded in a lukewarm fashion. Deren slowly made the transition from making art to organizing the critical and theoretical discourses surrounding the films.

Divine Horsemen and the "Divine" Artist

Simultaneous to shifting the emphasis of her film activities, Deren applied for a John Simon Guggenheim Foundation fellowship to finance her future film work. Although she never realized the proposed film, she received the first Guggenheim ever awarded to a filmmaker in 1946. Her ambition had outgrown the small scale of her first films and, despite increasing monies from film rentals, lecture fees, and free-lance articles, she needed the income to support both herself and her film production. With the money, Deren went to Haiti to observe Voudoun rituals for a proposed film on the ritualistic, dancelike continuity of children's games in different cultures. It was the first of three trips that she would eventually make to Haiti, and she recast her personal experiences not in a film but in an anthropological book.

Deren's book compares the priests in Haiti to Western artists because she identifies with their social status as individuals whose special talents are exploited or mocked. Both provide rituals for the perpetuation of cultural myth in their respective societies. She sets the stage for her ability as an outsider to understand Haitian Voudoun, "My background as an artist resulted in a discretion which . . . provided an alternative mode of communication and perception: the subjective level."[96] Granting herself the special perceptual and communicative powers that she saw in the Haitian priests, Deren functions as both translator and subject of a journey into spiritual awareness.

Divine Horsemen: The Voodoo Gods of Haiti (1953) is not an anthropological study of a foreign culture. It is, rather, an ethnography of psychological introspection in a nonindustrialized culture. In the Haitian Voudoun priests and their role among societal relationships, Deren saw displayed transcultural human patterns, "This adventure is composed . . . from the specific physical conditions which time composes for each individual race. The differences between the tales of the venerable ancients of the various nations are differences, then, between the matter of them. But in all this cosmic variety, the constant is the mind of man."[97] Progressing from a discussion of such Jungian assumptions to specific experiences, the book can be divided into five parts: how Haitian religion is an outward manifestation of universal conflicts; the religion's structure and how it has evolved; the order of supernatural and human roles within the structure; the rites themselves as the formal manifestations; drums and dances, the materials that are utilized in ritual. Deren moves from the general conception of Haitian religious activity tapping the collective subconscious to a more culturally specific examination of its details.

The structure provides a conceptual order leading to the book's climax—Deren's possession by a Haitian *loa*, or god. As part of this order, Deren switches from her expository writing style to create the culmination of her subjective investigation. Deren describes her possession in terms reminiscent of her film imagery, "As sometimes in dreams, so here I can observe myself. . . . My sense of self doubles again, as in a mirror, separates to both sides of an invisible threshold. . . . I see the dancing one here, and next in a different place, facing a different direction, and whatever lay between these moments is lost, utterly lost. . . . The white darkness starts to shoot up."[98] Deren's words suggest that her possession provides an experience similar to her visual expression of female subjectivity and representation of "multiple selves" in *Meshes of the Afternoon* and *At Land*. But unlike anything expressed in *Meshes* or *At Land*, the momentary confrontation of "multiple selves" becomes a means of transcending spatiotemporal confinement and thus a bridge between mortality and divinity, "The bright darkness floods up through my body, reaches my hand, engulfs me. I am sucked down and exploded upward at once. That is all. . . . How clear the world looks in this first total light. How purely form it is, without, for the moment, the shadow of meaning. I see everything all at once, without the delays of succession."[99] The moment becomes sheer ecstasy, and the possession experience dramatizes the spiritual fulfillment of her psychological self-definition without advancing it as rational knowledge.

One of the consequences of Deren's Haitian trips was that she forged a literal role for herself as high priestess to her community of artists in New York City. Both Stan Brakhage and Willard Maas remarked upon occasions where Deren practiced Voudoun before her friends. She took the formal rituals out of their original context and made dramatic reenactments to insure that all would go smoothly on Maas's film shoot, to link her anger with divine powers of retribution, or to place curses upon friends whom she believed had injured her.[100] By making such exotic, self-centered performances part of her social gatherings, Deren imposed a "ritual" on her friends that contributed more to her status and popularity than to the group's unity.

However self-serving Deren's methods may appear, her actions did not overlook the significance of Voudoun's meaning in its native culture. British sociologist Dick Hebdige has commented on the social role and expressive function of African subculture in the West Indies, "The preservation of African traditions, like drumming, has in the past been construed by the authorities (the Church, the colonial and even some 'post-colonial' governments) as being intrinsically subversive, posing a symbolic threat to law and order. These outlawed traditions were . . . positively, triumphantly pagan. They suggested unspeakable alien rites, they made possible illicit and rancorous allegiances which smacked of future discord."[101] While Deren's book expresses the symbolic importance of ritualistic structures for community, she extended her Haitian model to the New York art community. She made her understanding of Haiti an intellectual model for her leadership in New York, and she used her knowledge of Voudoun's social function as a way to establish her own "Otherness," her exoticism, her subversive position as a woman operating outside the Law. At a time when other artists primarily achieved social stature and prestige for making art, Deren justified as artistically superior her

claims of rebellion, her priestlike work and her devotion to establish
film organizations and artistic community.

Maya Deren and Avant-garde Cinema Practices

When she was not on a trip to Haiti or traveling around the country
showing her films and promoting experimental film, Deren was working on organizations that would communally unite independent
filmmakers. Beginning in 1953, she led a small group calling together
filmmakers from all over the city.[102] The group's written statement of
purpose reflects Deren's concern for an artists' community, "To bring
together, for mutual action and protection, the hitherto isolated film
artists, [and] to act as a liaison center between the film artist and his
public."[103] Deren's words echo those used by others as a means of
characterizing the New York artists' conception of their place in society. For example, one art historian commented, "Whether factually or
not, the Abstract Expressionists thought of the artist as a solitary
individual, forced into isolation not so much by desire, as by the
insensitivity of an ill-informed public."[104] Deren's consistent calls to
other artists through opposing "community" and "isolation" were part
of a unified discourse of elite separation and privileged identity among
New York City artists in general in the 1950s.

Deren identified more than a rhetoric for unity among independent
filmmakers. She formulated in language the specific concrete actions
the group should implement so that it would have a support structure
for artistic practice.[105] To this end, she first prepared a detailed outline
that articulated her full vision of a communal artists' system, breaking
the system's function into the categories of production, distribution,
and promotion.[106] Deren's definition of an artist support system en-
compassed the following activities:

(1) provide members with price and service information on equipment
sales and rentals, labs, film stock, and studios;
(2) provide a clearinghouse for equipment swaps, transportation, and
available crew personnel;
(3) act as a collective to obtain for members bulk purchase rates and
discounts, group rental and insurance rates, and special scaled rates
from various technical unions;
(4) distribute to members information on fellowships, film festivals, legal
matters and lawyers, types of exhibition venues, the names of film critics
and journals interested in experimental film;
(5) produce a members' film catalogue for general distribution;
(6) act as a lobby group to pressure film critics and their publications, museums, and art foundations to provide more support for experimental film.[107]

Her plan enunciates all the components that contemporary sociologists see as the marks of an avant-garde social structure.[108] From the outset, Deren envisioned an elaborate system that would define and support the artist's role as a member of a special community, as an activist of social protest, and as a filmmaker.

Approximately forty people answered the filmmakers' invitation on November 25, 1953. They planned to consolidate informational services on grants, film festivals, technical data, film labs, distribution, and organizations bidding for independent films. They discussed long-range goals of making an artists' center of screening rooms and post-production facilities.[109] The newly created Film Artists Society met monthly thereafter, trying to implement their goals through exchanges of information at monthly meetings and in mimeographed newsletters. Among the active members were jazz and dance filmmakers Richard Brummer, Allen DeForest, and Roger Tilton; experimental filmmakers Shirley Clarke, Ian Hugo, Maria Korwin, Francis Lee, Walter Lewissohn, Willard Maas, John Schiff, Joe Slevin, and Francis Thompson; filmmaker-writers Lewis Jacobs and Edouard Laurot; and film score composer Louis Barron.

The meetings continued from 1954 to 1956. But by early 1955, the group had renamed itself the Independent Film Makers Association, Inc. (IFA), and its active core now consisted of thirty-three filmmakers. Those who had been in the Film Artists Society were joined by others— film composer Bebe Barron, animators Rudy Burckhardt and Douglas Crockwell, poet-turned-filmmaker Ben Moore, and filmmakers David Anderson, Stan Brakhage, Robert Campbell, Kit Davidson, Wheaten Galentine, Hilary Harris, Robert Harrison, Peter Hollander, Sam Kaner, Helena Sands, Ruth Schonthal, Noel Sokoloff, John Strang, Val Telberg, and Robert Vickery.[110] The group had expanded its activities to include participation in local film festivals by cosponsoring programs and discussions and selecting films.[111]

Monthly meetings now included film screenings of members' films, guest speakers, and postscreening discussions. During 1955, members saw not only each others' work but also films and lectures by Len Lye, James Broughton, and Kenneth Anger. Cecile Starr from the Film Council of America and Amos Vogel of Cinema 16 were among the guests invited to chat with members at a Halloween party.[112] IFA had become a monthly forum for a full-fledged social, intellectual, and professional community.

Shirley Clarke remembers the meetings as large family arguments that often ended in yelling matches. In discussions frequently dominated by Deren and documentary filmmakers Willard Van Dyke and Irving Jacoby, everyone took sides regarding the business activities

and the individual films being screened.[113] Clarke particularly recalls
the details surrounding the proposed publication of a filmmakers'
directory, "I remember screaming because Maya thought because she
had made more films than I did, she would have more pages. It was
certainly fair. But, at that time, nobody thought anything was fair.
Then the meetings would end with us looking at each other's films
and screaming about those."[114] Although the necessary funds had
been secured, the unresolved discussions regarding each filmmaker's
number of pages forever postponed the directory's production.

At the same time that Deren was but one voice among several
in the IFA, she exercised complete administrative control over the
organization that she individually founded and ran—the Creative Film
Foundation (CFF). She started the CFF in 1955 to fill a gap left out
of the IFA's diverse activities or those of other independent film
organizations that were consolidating exhibition activities. The CFF
was a nonprofit foundation that awarded filmmaking grants to independent filmmakers. Naming herself the executive secretary, Deren
ran a one-woman operation, seeking funds to underwrite the grants,
organizing film screenings and symposia, and publicizing film as a
creative art form.

The CFF was the first American organization to award money
grants and merit citations to independent filmmakers on a regular
basis. Among its fellowship recipients from 1955 to 1961 were Stan
Brakhage, Stan Vanderbeek, Robert Breer, Shirley Clarke, and Carmen D'Avino. Besides promoting these filmmakers through CFF press
releases announcing the awards, Deren and the CFF cosponsored
annual winners' films at a Cinema 16 showing. She also promoted the
organization itself at a series of five CFF symposia on the relationships
between cinema and dance, music, poetry, painting, and myth.

Other than these occasional public activities, Deren's foundation
was little more than a letterhead. She ran the entire organization
out of the Greenwich Village apartment she shared with her third
husband, composer and musician Teiji Ito. The grants were comprised
from modest amounts of monies solicited from friends and other
filmmakers. For example, Deren convinced Shirley Clarke that if
Clarke's wealthy father contributed $1,000 he was going to give Clarke
anyway, Deren would see that Clarke got a fellowship for $800.[115]
Deren netted a $200 cash contribution and the publicity attached to
a substantial anonymous donation, while Clarke benefited from the
attendant publicity as well as the status of receiving an artistic honor.
Deren eventually repaid Clarke's generosity when she awarded her
another $1,200.[116]

But perhaps more important than its awards and events was the way that Deren used the name of the organization to legitimize independent film's connections to the other fine art forms. When Deren began the CFF, she wrote to a number of celebrities and excerpted their responses in all subsequent CFF publicity as an indication of widespread artist support.[117] Trading on the name recognition of such famous artists as playwright Arthur Miller, architect Mies van der Rohe, aesthetician Sir Herbert Read, dancer-choreographer Martha Graham, and poet-filmmaker Jean Cocteau, Deren asserted that their personal endorsements of the CFF authorized independent cinema's rightful place among the postwar vanguard arts.

In addition, Deren lent credibility and respectability to the CFF by maintaining a full board of directors and officers who were nominally the fellowship committee. Although their positions on the board demanded little from them, the individual board members provided the prestige associated from their institutional affiliations within the New York arts community. Deren's board included film historian and scholar Lewis Jacobs, Cinema 16 director Amos Vogel, and film critics Parker Tyler and Arthur Knight.[118] She also included anthropologist Joseph Campbell, the two art critics Clement Greenberg and James Johnson Sweeney who championed Abstract Expressionism, art historian Meyer Schapiro, artist Kurt Seligmann, poet James Merrill, and leading gestalt psychologist Rudolf Arnheim.[119] The CFF may have been in practice a nominal apparatus of the independent cinema, but its discursive value obscured its limited economic function.

Deren's organization-building activities did not occur in isolation any more than did her educational and filmmaking activities. At the same time she was concentrating on artist-support networks in the independent cinema, film societies were developing a national support system. The Film Council of America began in 1954 and was expanded into the American Federation of Film Societies by 1956. Established to be an informational clearinghouse and facilitator for independent film exhibition, the nationally consolidated organization offered centralized support and greater power to individual, isolated film societies in the same manner that Deren attempted to unite individual filmmakers.

Even in this area Deren sought a discursive role. Writing to her friend Cecile Starr who represented the American Federation of Film Societies, Deren considered herself an authority on the film society because she had spent more than a decade traveling and lecturing to such societies, "The Film Society should continue to move forward, and to remain *in advance* [of the commercial and local art theaters],

otherwise it has no justifiable function or role to fill in the community."[120] Deren wanted to express her position in the federation's new
journal, and she asked Starr if she could outline the relationship
between the film society and the avant-garde.[121]

Deren similarly responded to Jonas Mekas soon after he began *Film
Culture* as a new film review magazine in 1955. When Mekas wrote a
blistering attack on the current experimental cinema as "a conspiracy
of homosexuality," Deren called all her friends to meet collectively
with Mekas.[122] Soon thereafter, *Film Culture* began to respond less
prejudicially and more seriously toward experimental cinema, and it
regularly publicized experimental cinema activities and filmmakers.
By 1960, it had become something of an official organ for the New
York independent cinema.

Mekas himself became one of the foremost champions for the independent cinema. His regular movie column "Movie Journal" in the
Village Voice was a frequent site for polemics, publicity, and defense of
the independent cinema. When Mekas took time off from the column
in 1960, he made Deren his guest replacement. For a few weeks
Deren took over Mekas's platform as she expressed her long-held views
regarding Hollywood's abuses and obstacles for creating a true cinema
art.[123] Deren may not have personally put together the organizational
network that was growing for independent cinema, but her efforts
reached into every aspect of it as she attempted to impress her definition of an avant-garde cinema onto the emerging apparatus.

By the time Deren died in the fall of 1961, the independent cinema
had transformed from the few isolated filmmakers, societies, and programs of a decade earlier to a self-sustaining organizational network.
Many of the organizations, including those in which Deren had a hand,
were short-lived, momentary efforts to bring together a community.
Creative Film Foundation, Independent Film Makers Association, the
Golden Reel Film Festival, the Film Council of America, and even
Cinema 16 were just a few of the New York–based organizations that
came and went during this period. But no sooner had one disappeared
than another rose to take its place. However precarious the status of
the individual organization, the overall structure that supported an
independent cinema was firmly in place by 1961.

The independent cinema depended upon a variety of filmmaker-
sponsored organizations and independent film societies. Such groups
frequently existed along the margins of arts and educational institutions, demonstrating their connection to larger cultural arts practices
by promoting a discourse of film art. Deren offered these groups both
the rhetoric and the economic model for a self-continuous system of

experimental cinema. However varied were the films brought together in these groups and however widespread or transitory were the groups themselves, Deren outlined to them a radical cinema. As J. Hoberman has astutely pointed out, "A film practice that opposes the dominant culture, resists commodity status, invents its own means of production, and sets out to challenge habitual modes of perception *is* political—no matter what it seems to be about (and sometimes because it's not 'about' anything)."[124] Deren's occupation was an important act of political opposition. Her work was no less than consolidating the first cohesive system of cinema as collective artistic activity and practices, thus defining an American avant-garde cinema.

NOTES

1. "The Film That Dreams Are Made On," *Esquire*, Dec. 1946, 187.

2. Maya Deren, "Cinematography: The Creative Use of Reality," *Daedalus* 89, no. 1 (Winter 1960), 150; reprinted in *The Avant-garde Film: A Reader of Theory and Criticism*, ed. P. Adams Sitney (New York: New York University Press, 1978), 60.

3. Catrina Neiman, as quoted in "Excerpts from an Interview with *The Legend of Maya Deren* Project," The Camera Obscura Collective, *Camera Obscura*, nos. 3–4 (Summer 1979), 183.

4. Anaïs Nin, *The Diary of Anaïs Nin, Volume Four: 1944–1947*, ed. Gunther Stuhlmann (New York: Harcourt Brace Jovanovich, 1971), 137.

5. Harry Roskolenko, as quoted in *The Legend of Maya Deren: A Documentary Biography and Collected Works. Volume I, Part One: Signatures (1917–1942)*, VèVè A. Clark, Millicent Hodson, and Catrina Neiman (New York: Anthology Film Archives/Film Culture, 1984), 333.

6. Willard Maas, "Memories of My Maya," *Filmwise*, no. 2 (1962), 27–28.

7. "Interview with Katherine Dunham," in *The Legend of Maya Deren, Volume I, Part One*, 469.

8. Maya Deren, "Letter to Shirley Lyons," in *The Legend of Maya Deren, Volume I, Part One*, 116.

9. Maas, "Memories of My Maya," 27–28.

10. "Interviews with Miriam Arsham," in *The Legend of Maya Deren: A Documentary Biography and Collected Works. Volume I, Part Two: Chambers (1942–1947)*, VèVè A. Clark, Millicent Hodson, and Catrina Neiman (New York: Anthology Film Archives/Film Culture, 1988), 439.

11. Nin, *The Diary of Anaïs Nin: Volume Four*, 147.

12. Jerry Tallmer, "For Maya Deren—In the Midst of Life," *Filmwise*, no. 2 (1962), 8.

13. "Interview with Amalie Deren Phelan," in *The Legend of Maya Deren, Volume I, Part One*, 174–75.

14. "Interviews with Miriam Arsham," in *The Legend of Maya Deren, Volume I, Part Two*, 442.

15. Clark, Hodson, and Neiman, *The Legend of Maya Deren, Volume I, Part Two*, 437.

16. Nin, *The Diary of Anaïs Nin: Volume Four*, 111.

17. Maya Deren, "On Women," n.d., MS, Maya Deren papers, Mugar Memorial Library, Boston University, Boston. Quoted with permission.

18. Robert Steele, Typescript of interview with Teiji Ito, n.d., Robert Steele Collection, Maya Deren papers, Boston University, Boston, 6. Quoted with permission.

19. Robert Steele, "Insert A," TS, n.d., Robert Steele Collection, Maya Deren papers. Quoted with permission.

20. Steele, Typescript of interview with Teiji Ito, 6.

21. "Interview with Marie Deren," in *The Legend of Maya Deren, Volume I, Part One*, 39.

22. Bobby Zimmer, "Hill Gal Makes Good," *Syracuse Daily Orange*, 3 Nov. 1950, 2, Maya Deren papers; "Girl Prepares for College in 3 Years Study at Geneva," *Syracuse Post Standard*, 21 Sept. 1933, 8; reprinted in *The Legend of Maya Deren, Volume I, Part One*, 119–21.

23. Clark, Hodson, and Neiman, *The Legend of Maya Deren, Volume I, Part One*, 195–213 passim.

24. Although there is no evidence to indicate that she knew members of Nykino or other left-wing film and photo clubs during this time, Deren was involved in the Young Socialist League and committed to studying the Soviet Union so that she should certainly have been aware of Nykino's work in New York Soviet film screenings, lectures, and publications. Nykino's position on the relationship of film art to poetic form and revolutionary content was consistent with the definition of art that Deren advocated throughout her life. In a town where the relationship between poetic form and revolutionary content was a widespread matter of concern among left-wing organizations, she would certainly have been familiar with the ideas put forward by Nykino and found them sympathetic to her own.

The authors and editors of *The Legend of Maya Deren, Volume One, Part Two* come to a similar conclusion, saying that they "presumed there might have been some transfusion of energies and ideas, however indirect," between the Worker's Film and Photo League and Deren. Their interview with Tom Brandon, a member of the WFPL who later went into commercial distribution, covers his acquaintance with Deren begun in the 1940s when she asked him to distribute *Meshes of the Afternoon*. Clark, Hodson, and Neiman, *The Legend of Maya Deren, Volume One, Part Two*, 257.

25. Eleanora Deren, "Reason of the Dyadic Relativity of the 17th c. and Its Development towards Modern Triadic Relativity in Science, Philosophy and Ethics," TS, n.d., Maya Deren papers; Eleanora Deren, "Notes on Gestalt Psychology," Smith College, 1938, Maya Deren papers.

26. Eleanora Deren, "The Influence of the French Symbolist School on Anglo-American Poetry" (Master's thesis, Smith College, 1939), Maya Deren

papers; "Table of Contents" and "Preface" reprinted in *The Legend of Maya Deren, Volume I, Part One*, 391–92.

27. For more details on this period of Deren's life, see *The Legend of Maya Deren, Volume I, Part One*, 295–417 passim.

28. Robert Coe, *Dance in America* (New York: E. P. Dutton, 1985), 155.

29. Maya Deren, Letters to "Indian," 30 Mar. 1941 and 1 Apr. 1941, *The Legend of Maya Deren, Volume I, Part One*, 434–37.

30. Clark, Hodson, and Neiman, *The Legend of Maya Deren, Volume I, Part One*, 419.

31. Known among New Yorkers as "Dr. Feelgood," Jacobson included among his patients such well-known figures as Tennessee Williams, Truman Capote, Cecil B. DeMille, Eddie Fisher, Otto Preminger, Anthony Quinn, Jacqueline Kennedy, and President John F. Kennedy; Boyce Rensberger, "Amphetamines Used by a Physician to Lift Moods of Famous Persons," *New York Times*, 4 Dec. 1972, 1.

32. In a letter to "Indian," 30 Mar. 1941, Deren wrote, "Detroit, to me will always be remembered through a sort of Benzedrine haze. . . . Friday night on the train, I didn't sleep at all and took Benzedrine." Letter to "Indian," *The Legend of Maya Deren, Volume I, Part One*, 435.

33. Maya Deren's appointment book, 1961, Maya Deren papers.

34. Rensberger, "Amphetamines Used by a Physician"; Jane E. Brody, "Patient and His Doctor: Quandry for Medicine," *New York Times*, 16 Jan. 1973, 1.

35. Jacobson was linked to the death of Mark Shaw, the photographer to the Kennedy family; Rensberger, "Amphetamines Used by a Physician." He was charged with responsibility for entertainment publicist Milton Blackstone's current condition as a drug addict; Brody, "Patient and His Doctor." He was later found guilty of forty-eight counts of unprofessional conduct in eleven specifications and one count of fraud and deceit; Lawrence K. Altman, "State Official Scored," *New York Times*, 26 Apr. 1975, 1.

Other articles covering the Jacobson hearings include Jane E. Brody, "Dr. Max Jacobson Faces State Charges on Conduct," *New York Times*, 24 Mar. 1973, 1; Jane E. Brody, "State Accuses Dr. Jacobson of Giving Himself Amphetamines for Nonmedical Purposes," *New York Times*, 19 Apr. 1973, 35; Jane E. Brody, "State Medicine Board Finishes Hearings in Dr. Jacobson Case," *New York Times*, 6 June 1974, 24.

36. "Jacobson Loses License; Doctors Ask Self-policing," *New York Times*, 26 Apr. 1975, 1.

37. Clark, Hodson, and Neiman, "Secretary to Katherine Dunham," in *The Legend of Maya Deren, Volume I, Part One*, 417–24.

38. Eleanora Deren, "Religious Possession in Dancing," *Educational Dance*, Mar.–Apr. 1942, 4–6, 9–11; reprinted in *The Legend of Maya Deren, Volume I, Part One*, 480–97.

39. For an overview of Hammid's career, see Thomas E. Valasek, "Alexander Hammid: A Survey of His Filmmaking Career," *Film Culture*, nos. 67–69 (1979): 250–322.

40. John Pratt, as quoted in *The Legend of Maya Deren, Volume I, Part One*, 467.

41. Maya Deren, "Magic Is New," *Mademoiselle* 22, no. 3 (Jan. 1946), 180; reprinted in *The Legend of Maya Deren, Volume I, Part Two*, 309.

42. The musical soundtrack that now accompanies most extant prints of the film was made in the middle 1950s by Deren's third husband, Teiji Ito.

43. Alexander Hammid, as quoted in Valasek, "Alexander Hammid," 282.

44. For a more detailed discussion of Hammid's role and influence on the film, see Valasek, "Alexander Hammid," 282–85.

45. For the basic outline of this well-known argument in film theory, see Laura Mulvey, "Visual Pleasure and Narrative Cinema," *Screen* 16, no. 3 (Autumn 1975): 6–18.

46. Ibid.

47. See E. Ann Kaplan, ed., *Women in Film Noir* (London: British Film Institute, 1978).

48. J. Hoberman, "The Maya Mystique," *The Village Voice* 23, no. 20 (15 May 1978): 54.

49. Kaplan, *Women in Film Noir*, was published in 1978.

50. Mary Ann Doane, *The Desire to Desire: The Woman's Film of the 1940s* (Bloomington: Indiana University Press, 1987), 34–35.

51. Ibid., 179.

52. P. Adams Sitney, *Visionary Film: The American Avant-garde, 1943–1978*, 2d ed. (New York: Oxford University Press, 1979), 10–11.

53. Parker Tyler, "Maya Deren as Filmmaker," *Filmwise*, no. 2 (1962): 3.

54. Maya Deren, "Program Notes on Three Early Films," n.d., Maya Deren papers; reprinted in *Film Culture*, no. 39 (Winter 1965): 1; reprinted in *The Legend of Maya Deren, Volume I, Part Two*, 78.

55. Doane, *The Desire to Desire*, 178.

56. Nin, *The Diary of Anaïs Nin: Volume Four*, 76.

57. Richard Lippold, "Dance and Film—A Review in the Form of a Reflection," *Dance Observer* 13, no. 5 (May 1946): 59; reprinted in *The Legend of Maya Deren, Volume I, Part Two*, 393.

58. Parker Tyler, "Experimental Film: A New Growth," *Kenyon Review* 11, no. 1 (1949): 143.

59. James Agee, *Agee on Film: Review and Comments* (New York: McDowell, Obolensky, 1958), 190–91; reprinted in *The Legend of Maya Deren, Volume I, Part Two*, 382.

60. For a more complete discussion of these ideas, see *In Dora's Case: Freud-Hysteria-Feminism*, ed. Charles Bernheimer and Claire Kahane (New York: Columbia University Press, 1984). I would especially recommend Toril Moi's "Representation of Patriarchy: Sexuality and Epistemology in Freud's Dora" in this volume.

61. Program Notes, 1945, Maya Deren papers.

62. Irving Sandler, *The Triumph of American Painting: A History of Abstract Expressionism* (New York: Harper and Row, 1977), 38.

63. Mark Rothko, as quoted in Sandler, *The Triumph of American Painting*, 63.

64. Marcia Siegel, *The Shapes of Change: Images of American Dance* (Boston: Houghton, Mifflin, 1979), 175–76.

65. Lincoln F. Johnson, *Film, Space, Time, Light, and Sound* (New York: Holt, Rinehart, and Winston, 1974), 136; as quoted in Louise Heck-Rabi, *Women Filmmakers: A Critical Reception* (Metuchen, N.J.: Scarecrow Press, 1984), 200.

66. Hoberman, "The Maya Mystique," 54.

67. For example, see Sitney's discussion of *Ritual in Transfigured Time* in *Visionary Film*, 30–33; Ken Kelman, "Widow into Bride," *Filmwise*, no. 2 (1962): 20–23.

68. Publicity Releases, Maya Deren papers; Maya Deren, "Screenings of the Films (1945–46)," in *The Legend of Maya Deren, Volume I, Part Two*, 630–31.

69. Publicity releases, Maya Deren papers.

70. Maya Deren, *An Anagram of Ideas on Art, Form and Film* (Yonkers, N.Y.: Alicat Book Shop Press, 1946); reprinted in *The Legend of Maya Deren, Volume I, Part Two*, 550–602.

71. For example, see the following articles by Maya Deren: "Cinema as an Art Form," *New Directions*, no. 9 (Fall 1946): 111–20; "Cinematography: The Creative Use of Reality," 150–67; "Creative Cutting," *Movie Makers Magazine*, May–June 1947; "Creative Movies with a New Dimension—Time," *Popular Photography* 19, no. 6 (Dec. 1946): 130–32; "Magic Is New," *Mademoiselle* 22, no. 3 (Jan. 1946): 180; "Ritual in Transfigured Time," *Dance Magazine* 20, no. 12 (Dec. 1946): 9–13; "Some Metaphors for the Creative Process," *Village Voice* 5, no. 39 (21 July 1960): 6, 8.

72. Financial records, Maya Deren papers.

73. A sampling of English language film theory books around 1950 would be largely limited to the following: Rudolf Arnheim, *Film* (London: Faber and Faber, 1933); Sergei Eisenstein, *Film Form: Essays in Film Theory*, ed. and trans. Jay Leyda (New York: Harcourt, Brace and World, 1949); Sergei Eisenstein, *The Film Sense*, ed. and trans. Jay Leyda (New York: Harcourt, Brace and World, 1942); V. I. Pudovkin, *Film Technique and Acting: The Cinematic Writings of V. I. Pudovkin*, trans. Ivor Montagu (New York: Lear, 1949).

74. Maya Deren, "Cinematography: The Creative Use of Reality," 150.

75. Ibid., 154.

76. André Bazin, *What Is Cinema? Volume I*, trans. Hugh Gray (Berkeley: University of California Press, 1967); Roland Barthes, *Camera Lucida: Reflections on Photography*, trans. Richard Howard (New York: Hill and Wang, 1981).

77. Yuri M. Lotman, "On the Language of Animated Cartoons," trans. Ruth Sobel, *Russian Poetics in Translation* 8 (1981): 36–37.

78. Ibid.

79. Deren, "Cinematography: The Creative Use of Reality," 153.

80. Ibid., 159.

81. Deren, "Cinema as an Art Form," reprinted in *The Legend of Maya Deren, Volume I, Part Two*, 319.

82. For a good overview on the function of film language for Eisenstein's overall film theories, see Dana B. Polan, *The Political Language of Film and the Avant-Garde* (Ann Arbor, Mich.: UMI Research Press, 1985).

83. Deren, *An Anagram*, 45.

84. During the late 1940s and through the 1950s, Deren lectured at New York University, Yale University, Smith College, Vassar College, the University of Wisconsin, the University of Chicago, Rhode Island School of Design, Syracuse University, Pittsburgh State University, Antioch College, Colorado State University, Ball State Teachers' College, the University of Oregon, Stephens College, and the University of Havana. In addition, she appeared at small art museums and clubs across the country and she conducted extended workshops.

85. Dore Ashton, *The New York School: A Cultural Reckoning* (New York: Viking Press, 1973), 6.

86. Diana Crane, *The Transformation of the Avant-garde: The New York Art World, 1940–1985* (Chicago: University of Chicago Press, 1987), 1–11.

87. Ibid., 6.

88. Anaïs Nin, *The Diary of Anaïs Nin, Volume 6: 1955–1966*, ed. Gunther Stuhlmann (New York: Harcourt Brace Jovanovich, 1976), 170.

89. Maya Deren, Lecture, Yale University, New Haven, Connecticut, n.d., tape recording, School of the Art Institute of Chicago, Chicago, Illinois.

90. For a transcript of the panel, see "Poetry and the Film: A Symposium," *Film Culture*, no. 29 (Summer 1963): 55–63; reprinted in *Film Culture Reader*, ed. P. Adams Sitney (New York: Praeger, 1970), 171–86.

91. Hoberman, "The Maya Mystique," 54.

92. Nin, *The Diary of Anaïs Nin: Volume 6*, 352; Stan Brakhage, "An Open Letter to Maya Deren," *Filmwise*, no. 2 (1962): 13–15.

93. Joyce Wieland, interview with author, Toronto, Canada, 11 Mar. 1980.

94. The plans are reprinted as *"Meditation on Violence," Film Culture*, no. 39 (Winter 1965): 18–21.

95. Hoberman, "The Maya Mystique," 54.

96. Maya Deren, *Divine Horsemen: The Voodoo Gods of Haiti* (New York: Dell Publishing, 1970), 8.

97. Ibid., 21–22.

98. Ibid., 258–59.

99. Ibid., 260.

100. Maas, "Memories of My Maya," 23–29; Brakhage, as quoted in "Excerpts from an Interview with *The Legend of Maya Deren* Project," Camera Obscura Collective, *Camera Obscura*, nos. 3–4 (Summer 1979): 177–91.

101. Dick Hebdige, *Subculture: The Meaning of Style* (New York: Methuen, 1979), 31.

102. The other filmmakers were Preston K. Munson, Roger Tilton, Allen DeForest, Walter Lewissohn, Francis Thompson, Joe Slevin, Lewis Jacobs, George Capsis, Richard Brummer, and Ian Hugo.

103. "Film Group Newsletter," Nov. 1953, Maya Deren papers. Quoted with permission.

104. Crane, *The Transformation of the Avant-garde*, 47.

105. "Film Group Newsletter."

106. Maya Deren, untitled MS, n.d., Maya Deren papers.

107. Maya Deren, untitled TS, 30 Nov. 1953, Maya Deren papers.

108. Crane, *The Transformation of the Avant-garde*, 110.

109. "The Film Group," mimeographed TS, n.d., Maya Deren papers.

110. Joan McQuary, Letter to Members, 1 Mar. 1955, Maya Deren papers; "Films by I.F.A. Members," mimeographed TS, n.d., Maya Deren papers; for more biographical information on these IFA members, see individual entries in Sheldon Renan, *An Introduction to the American Underground Film* (New York: E. P. Dutton, 1967).

111. "Memo June 1955 Independent Film Makers Association, Inc.," June 1955, Maya Deren papers.

112. "Memo November 1955 Independent Filmmakers Association Inc.," Nov. 1955, Maya Deren papers.

113. Shirley Clarke, interview with author, Chicago, Illinois, 23 Sept. 1981.

114. Ibid. Quoted with the permission of Shirley Clarke.

115. Ibid.

116. Maya Deren, Letter to Shirley Clarke, 1 Aug. 1955, Shirley Clarke papers, Wisconsin Center for Film and Theater Research, University of Wisconsin-Madison.

117. Creative Film Foundation Press Release, 1955, Maya Deren papers.

118. Creative Film Foundation Announcement, *Film Culture*, no. 1 (Jan. 1955): 61; "Creative Film Awards," *Film Culture*, no. 14 (Nov. 1957): 11.

119. Ibid.

120. Maya Deren, Letter to Cecile Starr, 15 Jan. 1956, Maya Deren papers. Quoted with permission.

121. Ibid.

122. Jonas Mekas, "The Experimental Film in America," *Film Culture*, no. 3 (May–June 1955): 15–20; reprinted in *Film Culture Reader*, 21–26; Mitch Tuchman, "The Mekas Bros.: Brakhage and Baillie Traveling Circus," *Film Comment* 14, no. 2 (Mar.–Apr. 1978): 12.

123. Maya Deren, "Of Critics and Creators," *Village Voice* 5, no. 38 (14 July 1960): 10; Maya Deren, "Some Metaphors for the Creative Process," 6, 8; Maya Deren, "Movie Journal," *Village Voice* 5, no. 44 (25 Aug. 1960): 6, 8; reprinted in *Film Culture*, no. 39 (Winter 1965): 49–55.

124. J. Hoberman, "Three Myths of Avant-garde Film," *Film Comment* 17, no. 3 (May–June 1981): 34–35.

5

Shirley Clarke and the Expansion of American Independent Cinema

In 1950, Shirley Clarke was a young dance student in New York City. As an organizer of modern dance fund-raisers and publicity she was an efficient administrator—giving orders, attending to details, enthusiastically promoting the contemporary dance scene. One day while she was coordinating a package of American dance films going to Europe, she received a telephone call from an irrepressible woman who identified herself as Maya Deren. The caller insisted that she "was the American dance film."[1] Clarke, one of the few women around town who could match the caller's outspokenness, simply told Deren that she had never heard of her; that was the end of their first conversation.[2]

Three years later, the two finally met each other face-to-face. Clarke had just finished directing her first dance film. With several friends, she went to watch Deren's dance films at Deren's apartment. "First I learned that you paid to see her films and hear her speak, even in her own home . . . and in the midst of dozens of musical instruments and double dozens of cats."[3]

Deren, who was in her mid-thirties, probably sized up the woman only a few years her junior with one withering glance. Deren, whose own plumpness belied her claim to be an expert dancer, would have noticed Clarke's disciplined dancer's body and well-trained movement. Since she was fond of her own curly mane that softened her features and contributed to her beauty, she would have looked scornfully at Clarke's trim cap of short, dark hair. Whereas Deren took in an entire room with her striking good looks and force of personality, Clarke had not yet acquired such self-confidence and self-esteem, "[Maya] spoke with [such] intense emotion and passion that at times [it] seemed like anger and practically had me curled up in my chair."[4]

Deren and Clarke had much in common. They shared a passion for dance and film. They were both headstrong and determined to get their own ways. They were both loquacious talkers eager to express their ideas and opinions—so opinionated and headstrong, in fact, that they often clashed. (They even once argued about the proper length for a woman's hair.)[5]

As female artists, however, they recognized and discussed the ways that their position marginalized them both within dominant institutions of women's lives and within the male-dominated arts world. They agreed that as women filmmakers they should always present a "united front."[6] Like Deren, Clarke resisted women's traditional roles in arts activities and in the films that she made.

Clarke learned Deren's aesthetic model of film form and, more important, watched her as a personal example of a successful woman artist. Clarke believed that Deren's aesthetics formed the basis for her development as a filmmaker, "She gave me proof that dance in film is not only created by filming abstract dance movement but that the natural actions of a human being walking, sitting, crawling, sleeping, etc. are also the stuff of cine-dance poetry and become ultimate film choreography."[7] Clarke extended Deren's formal model to narrative fiction and documentary, modes beyond those Deren imagined for an experimental cinema.

Within these modes, however, she explores neither female subjectivity as such nor her sexual desire. She, instead, displaces her sense of marginalization and Otherness onto a cinema of expressionistic urban alienation and the physical bodies of social outcasts and misfits—personified by African-Americans, homosexuals, and drug addicts. The cinema of social protest that she activates is another kind of refusal to be constructed and known within white, patriarchal terms of sight and power relations. Out of traditional modes and antagonistic relationships between documentary and fictional narrative, Clarke inscribes new positions for social subjectivity. The result is less a language of the feminized Other than a prefeminist investigation of social subjectivities.

Clarke also adapted Deren's economic model for her own position as an activist-organizer. Watching Deren's success, she believed that the increased number of experimental film organizations and screenings, as well as new international recognition, were signs that American experimental cinema was ready to challenge Hollywood more directly through commercially viable forms and outlets, "The present distribution system to some degree *has* to be subverted. Very few people are making experimental films or documentary films, and yet over the

years both have had an enormous influence on the industry."[8] She
extended Deren's artisanal-based system to a more broadly defined
independent cinema network. Clarke's work in the 1960s encompasses
the history of what came to be called the New American Cinema, and
she played a key role in its attempts to express cultural protest, expose
deep-seated political unrest, and challenge the Hollywood model of
cinema. Clarke's career exemplifies both the adaptability and limitations of Deren's model, transforming Deren's position into a model of
representation and alternative practice as an explicitly sociopolitical
activity.

A Short Biography

Though she was only two years younger than Deren, Clarke came
of age artistically much later and did not assume a position of leadership until well into her thirties. Clarke struggled with many of the
same kinds of personal and social conflicts that characterized Deren's
youth and adolescence during the same time period, but Clarke expressed greater indecisiveness in responding to society's expectations
for a young, bourgeois woman, and intense psychological turbulence
surfaced repeatedly throughout her life.

Shirley Brimberg Clarke is the eldest daughter of a Polish-Jewish
immigrant who had amassed a fortune in manufacturing before
Clarke was born. Her mother was the daughter of a New York City
multimillionaire manufacturer and inventor. Shirley and her two
younger sisters were raised by nannies and governesses in the nursery
of a large, elegant Manhattan apartment on Park Avenue. Although
the three girls were not often physically far from their parents, Samuel
and Florence Brimberg spent little time with their children and were
emotionally remote.[9] They were such extensions of Victorian ego
ideals of masculinity and femininity that Shirley grew up believing her
mother represented ladylike femininity whereas her father's swagger-
ing authoritativeness made him "a vulgar, screaming maniac."[10]

Increasingly, her feelings toward her father colored her familial
relationships and the direction of her personal life. Shirley's sister
Elaine recalled that Shirley frequently confronted their father and, in
return, got slapped.[11] As a poor academic student at one of New York's
most expensive progressive schools during the Depression, Shirley
attracted even greater ire when she began concentrating on dance
classes instead of scholarly pursuits, "As far as my father was concerned, a whore and a dancer were the identical appellation."[12] She
circumvented his prohibition against dance and his unwillingness to

pay for her lessons by attending out-of-state colleges that had modern dance classes and companies. Feigning an interest in a liberal arts education, Shirley briefly attended Stephens College, Bennington College, the University of North Carolina, and Johns Hopkins University. At each school, she would complete the few dance courses offered and then leave. During the course of a few years, she received training in the three main variations of modern dance technique: the Martha Graham method, the Doris Humphrey–Charles Weidman technique, and the Hanya Holm method, all of which stressed originality, personal expression, and the rhythm and movement inherent in human actions.

When Clarke decided in 1943 that she needed to continue advanced dance studies with the choreographers themselves in New York City, she could use neither geographic distance nor college as a subterfuge. So, she found another way to escape—she got married. She self-admittedly wed the lithographer Bert Clarke in August 1944 to run away from her father, "[Bert] was going to take care of me, and that was just fine with me."[13] Once she was legally independent from her father, Shirley used newly available stock dividends and trust funds as a means for economic independence. Bert Clarke, fifteen years her senior, displaced her own father and became the "good" paternal figure who protected and approved of her while encouraging her artistic goals. Since she was free to follow her own interests, she studied dance with Holm, Graham, Humphrey, and ex-Graham dancer Anna Sokolow.

Throughout the rest of her twenties, Shirley Clarke combined dance activities with those of an affluent wife and mother. She and her husband initially lived in a comfortable Manhattan apartment overlooking Central Park and then moved to suburban Westchester County after their daughter Wendy was born in 1946. Freed from many domestic responsibilities by the presence of a housekeeper and nanny, Clarke regularly commuted to Manhattan for her dance lessons. She performed frequently in experimental pieces organized by the students and their teachers at demonstrations, recitals, and choreographers' workshops. As a regular student at the Dance Theater of the Young Men's and Young Women's Hebrew Association (YM-YWHA), one of New York's leading experimental dance centers, she had the opportunity to work with a wide variety of choreographers and dancers. But Clarke's own dance and choreographic career was quite undistinguished. The one time in 1948 that she performed her work in a YM-YWHA Choreographers Workshop, dance critics said her portrayal of a woman's reaction to a loved one's death was "deriva-

tive-imitative," "disjointed," and left "much to be desired."[14] Clarke
herself said that she realized she was not good enough to become really
famous.[15]

After becoming increasingly frustrated because she did not think
she could achieve her professional goals and troubled because she
could not cope with the demands of both her needs and her family's,
Clarke entered into transactional analysis. In postwar America, psychi-
atric therapy was a socially acceptable—even celebrated—solution for
dissatisfied women. Feminist psychologist Nancy Chodorow describes
the social formation of women's dependency on psychoanalytic therapy: "The barrage of oughts about having babies and being a good
mother from television, toys, storybooks, textbooks, magazines,
schools, religions, laws . . . reinforce the less intended and unconscious
development of orientations and relational capacities that the psycho-
analytical account of feminine development describes."[16] Affluent
women like Clarke who had the financial access to the growing number
of private practice psychiatrists were encouraged to seek such individual solutions for their personal unhappiness so that they would be
socially fulfilled as well as "good" nurturing wives and mothers. Chodorow explains that "post-Freudian psychology and sociology have
provided new rationales for the idealization and enforcement of wom-
en's maternal role."[17] Clarke, who had "reached the limit of what she
could stand," sought relief through a psychiatrist's efforts, and he
(rather typically for the time) tried to get her to expiate her ambivalent
feelings about her father.[18]

Although psychoanalysis did little to change her hostility toward
her father, it did convince Clarke to change careers. Her psychiatrist
suggested that since she was frustrated as an unaccomplished dancer,
she should simply try something else.[19] His easy dismissal of her ten-
year investment in modern dance and desire to achieve professional
stature suggests how ideologically formed his reply may have been.
To her doctor, Clarke's professional frustrations probably appeared
as the sincere good intentions of a dilettante housewife with too much
leisure time. It is ironic, perhaps, that the man who apparently took
her no more seriously than did her father also offered her the encouragement that helped her to achieve professional stature and fame as
a filmmaker.

Clarke owned a movie camera that she had received as a wedding
gift. Amidst the boom in consumer movie camera sales, she and her
husband principally used their camera the same way as most other
amateur moviemakers: they made home movies of family gatherings,
their daughter's birthday parties, their daughter at play. Now Clarke

and her husband took out the Bolex movie camera to make a dance film.

Shirley Clarke and Ciné-dance in the 1950s

Dance in the Sun (1953) is a remarkable ciné-dance of Daniel Nagrin's fluid movements intercut between an interior and exterior location. Although Clarke had not yet seen any of Deren's films, *Dance in the Sun* resembles *A Study in Choreography for the Camera*. It adheres to Deren's formal treatment of editing on motion and creating the flow of movement across a uniquely cinematic space. Clarke began with the knowledge that most dance films that tried to preserve the stage illusion of dance composed for the entire body ultimately broke the original lines of expression by cutting from long shots to close-ups, "Dance as it existed on the stage had to be destroyed in order to have a good film and not just a rather poor document."[20]

Soon after Clarke finished *A Dance in the Sun,* she had her first meeting with Deren. More than ever, Clarke became convinced that she was onto something new and important. She even describes her conviction in terms that are reminiscent of Deren's way of talking: "All the kinds of things I discovered about the choreography of editing and . . . space/time came from making that very first film. The idea of leaping from the stage and landing on the beach . . . just strikes me as a wonderful leap of not only magic but of concept, as a way of encompassing the universe."[21] Clarke closely followed Deren's poetics of movement as a metaphor for individual consciousness no longer anchored in conventional spatiotemporal logic.

Soon after her meeting with Deren, Clarke found herself in Paris spending a lot of time with her daughter at the city's parks. She decided to make a film based on Deren's "interest in using people as well as dancers to create films where you get, not merely dance movement that has been created for the camera, but the actual Dance of Life."[22] *In Paris Parks* (1954) poetically depicts a variety of activities in a city park and uses editing rhythms, movement, and color as the organizational continuity. The film begins with a child rolling her hoop into the park in the early morning and ends with the park emptying at sunset. In between are the events of a single day: children feed the animals in the petting zoo, the elderly nap on park benches, children watch a puppet show, people visit the amusement park rides and food concessions.

But when Deren applied choreographic principles to human activity as in *Ritual in Transfigured Time,* she did so by exaggerating movement

fluidity. For example, she used freeze-frames and slow-motion cinematography, simple foreground to background relationships, editing on
motion, and match cuts to emphasize on-screen motion as the principal
means of formal unity. Clarke, however, allows continuous movement
no privileged place among a range of formally expressive pictorial and
cinematic properties, and her montage of material is without the kind
of rigid formal structure that Deren valued so highly.

In Paris Parks is most interesting though for the way that it expresses
motion through the editing tempo itself. Clarke employs a quicker,
more musically upbeat tempo than anything that Deren ever did. Her
choice of a jazz accompaniment by LaNoue Davenport further reflects
Clarke's development of a rhythmic signature that more closely corre-
sponds to the "abstract poetry of city motion."[23] Clarke, always the
New Yorker physically in tune with an urban sense of speed and
urgency, may have discovered rapid pacing as the means to reflect
her own staccato, energetic movements and gestures. Shortly after
completing the film, Clarke asserted, "[Movies are] predominantly
visual, rhythmic experiences."[24]

Shirley Clarke and New York City Experimental
Cinema in the 1950s

When Clarke returned to New York City a few months later, she
set out to become a full-time filmmaker-artist. She enrolled in New
York's only film school, the City College of New York's film program
run by Hans Richter. She took film classes and met other filmmakers.
She made another ciné-dance film, *Bullfight* (1955), featuring her former teacher Anna Sokolow dancing *Homage to a Bullfighter* intercut
with actual bullfighting footage shot by Clarke's friend Peter Buckley.[25]
She and her City College classmate Jonas Mekas joined the Independent Film Makers Association (IFA) and participated in the monthly
meetings, screenings, and shouting matches. She learned film history
by attending screenings at Cinema 16. She saw masterpieces of European filmmaking—German Expressionism, Soviet cinema of the
1920s, French avant-garde, British documentary tradition, and Italian
Neorealism.[26] She went on an IFA field trip to the George Eastman
House film archives in Rochester, New York, where she, Deren, Mekas,
and other New York filmmakers steeped themselves in classics of world
cinema.[27]

Encouraged by her new friends, Clarke began to submit her three
films to international film festivals. She won awards for *Bullfight* at the
1955 Edinburgh Film Festival and the 1955 Venice Film Festival. *A*

Dance in the Sun played at the 1954 Zurich International Film Festival and was selected as the best dance film of 1954 by the New York Dance Film Society. Such recognition, as well as the Manhattan film community's congenial, familial atmosphere, bolstered Clarke's ego and her commitment to film, and she made the transition to a life devoted to cinema.

Clarke's 1957 film *A Moment in Love* is exemplary not only of her rapid ascension to the vanguard of experimental filmmaking but of a general direction in New York City experimental filmmaking. Although Deren's obsession with formal control and the photographic realism of the cinematographic image set important precedents for experimental filmmaking in the 1950s, filmmakers were now breaking her rules. Many incorporated improvisation and freer thematic organization while disrupting the optical realism of the cinematographic image through photographic distortions, tints and color saturations, superimpositions, and various types of photographic processing. Willard Maas and Marie Menken had foreseen such possibilities as early as 1943 in *Geography of the Body,* and Sidney Peterson used anamorphic lenses to create distortions that undercut Deren's concept of realism in *Mr. Frenhofer and the Minotaur* (1948) and *The Lead Shoes* (1949). But Ian Hugo's *Bells of Atlantis* (1952) more fully explored a range of cinematic and printing techniques that eliminated the illusion of a diegetic or solidly three-dimensional narrative space.[28] The effect was to bring experimental cinema more fully within painterly discussions of Abstract Expressionism and that movement's emphasis on new image formations that explored physiological and psychological perceptions. Other contemporary films that employed such a range of expressive technique included Kenneth Anger's *Eaux d'artifice* (1953), Stan Brakhage's and Joseph Cornell's *The Wonder Ring* (1955), Francis Thompson's *N.Y., N.Y.* (1958), and Stan Brakhage's *Anticipation of the Night* (1958).

Clarke's adoption of such formal expressiveness in *A Moment in Love* represents her first attempt to adapt Deren's model of ciné-dance for new stylistic purpose. The film is a *pas de deux* composed of bits and pieces from several Sokolow works danced by Carmela Gutierrez and Paul Sanasardo. Movement within the frame as well as camera movement and match cuts on motion allow for an uninterrupted, shot-to-shot flow of motion. But the film departs from Deren's initial concept of ciné-dance by using superimpositions of the dancers over moving clouds and over each other, by employing graphic distortions, and by bathing the image in a variety of colors that flattens and absorbs background detail.[29] Completely dissolving Clarke's dependency on stage choreography or optical realism as the raw material for a dance film, *A Moment in Love* celebrates a high degree of line and color abstraction and movement as the formal beauty of pure dance.

A Moment in Love brought Clarke to the attention of Willard Van Dyke, the well-known documentary filmmaker who had worked with Paul Strand, Ralph Steiner, and the other leaders of Frontier Films. Van Dyke had agreed to make short film loops depicting scenes of American life for the United States Pavilion at the 1958 Brussels World's Fair. He conceptualized the project as "a new film form based on imagery which allows . . . a continual flow of ideas on one general theme," an orientation sympathetic to Clarke's developing film aesthetics.[30] He hired not only Clarke but also documentary filmmakers Donn Alan Pennebaker and Richard Leacock, as well as Clarke's friends from the IFA, experimental filmmakers Francis Thompson and Wheaten Galentine.

They made a total of twenty-three two-and-a-half-minute color loops from the State Department's list of such topics as traffic, people, food, costumes, and topography. Pennebaker and his assistant, Derek Washburn, traveled around the country and sent footage to New York, where Clarke edited their material into twelve loops. Clarke alone shot and edited three loops, and Pennebaker individually made one. Clarke assisted other filmmakers on four loops, and Thompson, Galentine, and Leacock each made one loop.

All of Clarke's loops used extensive, rapid editing. Clarke describes the point of view that she and Pennebaker adopted: "What we did was try to make jokes of everything because we had been told there would be no sound, and the one thing we couldn't do was jazz. So I made them all jazz."[31] For example, *Melting Pot* (a loop that Clarke made by herself) begins with shots ordered by subject similarity—people conversing, adults with children, children with children. But then similar camera positions in relation to the subjects provide the continuity for a rapid portrait series. The second minute of *Melting Pot* joins individuals making gestures into one continuously flowing and repetitive gestural salute. *County Fair* alternates shots of vertical movement with horizontal and diagonal movements. For example, the dominant vertical lines of a tall man swallowing a sword contrast the subsequent montage of a merry-go-round, go-cart, and harness horse race all dominated by horizontal lines of movement.

Similar to *Bullfight* and *A Moment in Love*, several loops also depend upon color-saturated images as a means for denaturalizing photographic representations into emotionally expressive abstract forms. For example, *Sundown*'s land- and urbanscapes are exaggerated through red tints. Intensifying the reddish illumination cast by the setting sun heightens the expressionistic value while also flattening out photographic details.

Unlike Pennebaker's *Gas Stop* loop that relies upon the narrative device of a car being serviced step-by-step at a highway gas station, Clarke's loops realize Deren's goal of vertical cinematic organization. They are ciné-poems rather than narrative dramas. Many of the ciné-poetic loops posit ironic stances. *Houses* undercuts the American myth of individualism as it incorporates nearly identical dwellings from all over the country, distorted views of various metropolitan skyscrapers and patterns of row houses, trailer parks, and tenements. The formal structure itself composed of rapid rhythms and graphic continuities represents repetition and conformity. *Ready to Eat* satirizes the variety and abundance of American food. Montages of prepackaged, frozen foods are formally matched for the artificial colors, textures, and forms of the packaging.

Neon Signs is, perhaps, the best loop of all. It is a ciné-poem of form, color, and movement that exhibits the visual richness and humor of America's brash, outdoor advertisements. It opens with a close-up of the blinking neon letters M-O-R-E, setting up the loop's dual strategy. On one level, the blinking letters themselves are a colorful, melodic dance. On another level, they spell out a connotation of American greediness that feeds and is fed by advertising. Quick shots follow of distorted neon lights, and then a high angle shot aimed at a wet sidewalk fills the frame with diffused and reflected neon light. Succeeding shots more closely examine light reflected off other surfaces— a car's windshield and shiny hood. Then the loop moves from its slower, more languid middle into a third and final section: a series of kitsch neon signs that are all dramatically colored and composed of elaborate, blinking forms. Some of the signs dance in edited rhythms: a champagne glass with blinking bubbles, a star, a cowboy, a Pepsi-Cola logo that dilates, a red eagle that flaps its wings.

The techniques and style of *Neon Signs* and the other loops represent the vanguard of American film aesthetics in the 1950s. Such intense cinematic expression was so successful in these short pieces that it was adapted for television commercials and was widespread industrial practice by the 1960s. Whereas the U.S. State Department was depending upon the loops to sell America, the filmmakers inscribed richer, more ambiguous and ironic possibilities. The filmmakers went so far that the U.S. government almost turned down *Houses* and, in fact, did reject what was arguably the most formally daring loop in the group.

Bridges-go-round (1958) depicts immobile objects but creates a continuous, fluid sense of motion through camera movement and over-lapped images so that each shot dissolves into another. Like other loops, the images employ a high degree of color-tint saturation, and the camera angles and the blending graphics further heighten the dramatic, surrealistic effect of suspension bridges whirling weight-lessly in air. When Clarke brought the footage home after the State Department rejected the loop, her eleven-year-old daughter re-sponded with fright to the imagery.[32] Clarke said Wendy's reaction made her realize that cinematic choreography applied to such inani-mate objects could deliver an emotional jolt that she had not achieved in her earlier efforts.[33]

Bridges-go-round, the three-and-a-half-minute film Clarke finished from the loop footage, became her most critically acclaimed experi-mental film. Critics particularly celebrated the perceptually disorient-ing effects.[34] As cinematic music and dance, *Bridges-go-round* evokes a rich, dreamlike atmosphere through a number of formal techniques: low angles and backlighting that emphasize two-dimensionality, zoom-ing in or out while moving through the structure, and sandwiching two of the same image in reversal so that four-way directional movement results.

Bridges-go-round generally circulates today in a seven-minute ver-sion, which is the film repeated with two distinct soundtracks for each identical set of images. This highly unusual situation occurred because the original composers Louis and Bebe Barron requested that their electronic score not be distributed. They thought they were legally unable to permit the music's distribution because they had used the same piece of music for MGM's *The Forbidden Planet.*[35] Clarke commis-sioned a second score from jazz composer Teo Macero who had done the soundtrack for *A Moment in Love.* Macero's piece consists of one vocal note filtered electronically through several voices mixed with a jazz accompaniment. In 1968, Clarke received legal rights to the Bar-rons' score, and she juxtaposed both scores on her film prints. The effect is startling because the same images take on different moods when accompanied by different soundtracks. The Barrons' electroni-cally produced tones contrast the choralelike quality of Macero's voices layered over contemporary jazz. Through this coincidence, *Bridges-go-round* became as well a study on the relationship between sound and image coloration.

By 1958, Clarke was showing *Bridges-go-round* at all the local places where experimental films played. It won an award from Cinema 16 and the Creative Film Foundation, and it was selected to represent the United States at the 1958 International Experimental Film Festival in

Bridges-go-round (1958), directed by Shirley Clarke. Sandwiching two of the same image in reversal. Photo courtesy of Wisconsin Center for Film and Theater Research, Shirley Clarke collection.

Bridges-go-round. Photo courtesy of Wisconsin Center for Film and Theater Research, Shirley Clarke collection.

Shirley Clarke on the set of *The Connection*. Photo by Gideon Bachmann; courtesy of the Wisconsin Center for Film and Theater Research, Shirley Clarke collection.

The Connection (1961), directed by Shirley Clarke. The addicts, who acknowledge the presence of the cameras, increasingly perform to the cameras. Photo courtesy of Wisconsin Center for Film and Theater Research, Shirley Clarke collection.

The Connection. Warren Finnerty. Photo courtesy of Wisconsin Center for Film and Theater Research, Shirley Clarke collection.

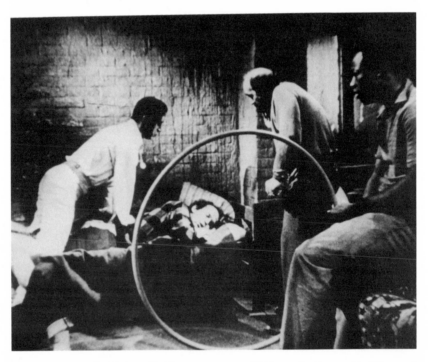

The Connection. Publicity still. Photo courtesy of Wisconsin Center for Film and Theater Research, Shirley Clarke collection.

The Cool World (1963), directed by Shirley Clarke. The street preacher in the film's opening scene. Photo courtesy of Wisconsin Center for Film and Theater Research, Shirley Clarke collection.

The Cool World. Publicity still. Photo courtesy of Wisconsin Center for Film and Theater Research, Shirley Clarke collection.

The Cool World. Publicity still. Photo courtesy of Wisconsin Center for Film and Theater Research, Shirley Clarke collection.

Carl Lee and Shirley Clarke at a press conference at the 1963 Venice Film Festival. Photo by Giacomelli; courtesy of Wisconsin Center for Film and Theater Research, Shirley Clarke collection.

Portrait of Jason (1967), directed by Shirley Clarke. Photo courtesy of Wisconsin Center for Film and Theater Research, Shirley Clarke collection.

Portrait of Jason. Photo courtesy of Wisconsin Center for Film and Theater Research, Shirley Clarke collection.

Photo of Shirley Clarke. Photo courtesy of Wisconsin Center for Film and Theater Research, Shirley Clarke collection.

Brussels. A year earlier, *A Moment in Love* had been named one of the best ten nontheatrical films of the year by the *New York Times* film critic.[36] Clarke had become among the leading avant-garde figures in New York experimental film.

Following in Deren's footsteps, Clarke also developed quickly as an advocate for the small independent film community. She accompanied film screenings and gave public lectures at Cinema 16, the Museum of the City of New York, the New York Public Library, Brooklyn Museum, Columbia University, and the City College of New York. She lectured in Rochester and spoke at a screening of her films at the Minneapolis Institute of Fine Arts.

She also attempted to get experimental films into commercial theaters. One Manhattan theater did run *In Paris Parks* as a short subject film before the scheduled feature, but Clarke was unable to get additional moviehouse bookings.[37] Clarke persisted, however, in believing that experimental film was "one of the little stilettos we can put into the commercial world, so that eventually the kind of film we're talking about can get to bigger audiences."[38] Her words express an increasing ambition to consolidate American independent cinema within the mainstream of American moviegoing rather than at its margins.

Unlike Deren, Clarke thought of an experimental cinema system as a means to an end rather than as the end itself. Clarke's attitude belongs to a larger category of criticism in the late 1950s that was increasingly disappointed by the limitations of the experimental cinema. For example, *Film Culture* editor Jonas Mekas claimed in 1959 that the New York experimental cinema had become "sterile."[39] He denigrated a style of intuitive, self-directed lyricism best represented by Stan Brakhage in such films as *Anticipation of the Night* (1958), *WindowWaterBabyMoving* (1959), and *Cat's Cradle* (1959).[40]

Such criticism developed against the backdrop of New York art institutions, where certain critics and journalists leveled new charges at the reigning avant-garde in painting—Abstract Expressionism. They said that the Abstract Expressionist content of "private myth" and its therapeutic function of artistic self-recognition was overly narcissistic, an aesthetic dead end.[41] But, as Barbara Haskell has pointed out, "At the very time that Abstract Expressionism was perceived as exhausted and bankrupt, it simultaneously exerted a hegemony so absolute that it offered young artists no room to maneuver."[42] The painting community had dissolved into a series of factions around the leaders of Abstract Expressionism and those who resisted Abstract Expressionists' success and control of the arts economy.[43] While the artistic milieu became more marked by "a set of relatively transient, interlocking subcultures," Clarke and other filmmakers simultaneously participated in a cultural repositioning against the discourse of Abstract Expressionism.

Cinéma Vérité and the Turn toward Social Relevancy in the Arts

Clarke became drawn to documentary filmmaking and a rhetoric of social relevancy. Clarke's Cinema 16 and IFA experiences had included screenings of Robert Flaherty's documentary films as well as examples of Italian Neorealism's synthesis of poetic and documentary techniques.[44] She also saw Italian and European realist styled films enjoying both popular and critical success at an increasing number of Manhattan art cinemas.

Working for Van Dyke, she became further involved in his and other filmmakers' stories of the American documentary tradition. Van Dyke had worked in documentary film since the days of Frontier Films in the 1930s and had codirected with Ralph Steiner the classic documentary film, *The City* (1939). Leacock had begun his career as Robert Flaherty's camera operator on *Louisiana Story* (1948) and worked throughout the 1950s for the U.S. Information Agency and television networks. When Clarke went to work for Van Dyke in 1958, he and Leacock were doing segments for such television magazine shows as *Omnibus* and *Twentieth Century,* making Clarke aware that television provided a new, more popular outlet for a socially committed independent cinema. In all these assignments, Van Dyke's reliance on controlled shooting situations, editing, and voice-over or musical commentaries promised a poetic style to which Clarke could easily adapt from her own experience as an experimental filmmaker. After the loops, Clarke and Van Dyke co-directed *Skyscraper* (1959), a documentary about the construction of the Tishman Building in midtown Manhattan.[45] Clarke and Van Dyke used montage editing, asynchronous sound mixes, and nondiegetic music to dramatically transform the material into a genre musical through character voices—off-screen construction workers who watch the film of their job and comment on it—and through interspersed songs about the building process, itself a series of montages.

Once she worked for Van Dyke, Clarke was among those who began to advocate new directions in American documentary and narrative cinema. Two dominant cinematic developments attracting the attention of Clarke and her peers were the French New Wave or *nouvelle vague* and the documentary movement known as *cinéma vérité.* Both

French in origin, each film movement attempted to be a topical cinema of social relevancy and contemporary realism. A theatrical cinema of low-budget, freewheeling films made by young filmmakers, the French New Wave had swept onto the international film scene since the 1959 Cannes Film Festival, where Jean-Luc Godard's *A bout de souffle* and Francois Truffaut's *Les quatre cents coups* became instant hits. *Cinéma vérité* or "cinema truth" was a documentary style associated with French filmmakers Jean Rouch and Chris Marker, who used new lightweight, synchronized-sound, portable equipment to capture spontaneous events while they interacted with their subjects. In Rouch's and Edgar Morin's classic *Chronique d'un été* (1961), the filmmakers interrogate their subjects, show the footage to the participants, record participant reaction, and then themselves reflect on their project.

Within this climate, Clarke, Van Dyke, and three other of his employees—Leacock, Albert Maysles, and Pennebaker—agreed that a better-defined community would support more ambitious documentary films. In 1958, they established Filmmakers Inc., a cooperative film company designed mainly to provide them with individual offices, equipment, and postproduction facilities. More than a business address and a place for individual work, Filmmakers Inc. was a symbolic site for communal activities among the number of independent filmmakers trying to make breakthrough documentary or narrative films. By the early 1960s, other young, hopeful filmmakers were hanging around Filmmakers Inc. Fred Wiseman, Joyce Chopra, Nell Cox, and Charlotte Zwerin all began their careers by assisting in the editing process or by working on camera or sound crews.[46] Clarke has claimed that Filmmakers Inc. coalesced the origins of the new independent cinema, "This place became a major New York headquarters. We helped John Cassavetes get started. I lent him my camera equipment to shoot *Shadows* (1958). Through him, we met Jean-Luc Godard. A lot of experimental filmmakers also came by. In other words, a lot of the American New Wave film movement and the development of cinéma vérité took place with all of us interacting with each other."[47] Like Deren, who was fond of historicizing events as illustrations of group definition, socialist purpose, and solidarity, Clarke defines her participation in an organizational structure as the origins for an American counterpart to European movements.

While Clarke made commissioned documentaries, such as *Skyscraper* and *A Scary Time* (1960), and tried to launch a feature film project, Leacock, Pennebaker, and Maysles began to assist former *Life* photojournalist Robert Drew on documentaries sponsored by Time-Life for television broadcast. Since they were initially unable to afford the purchase costs of the new portable, transistorized outfits, they adapted old cameras and sound equipment. They or other Drew Associates employees then edited the footage to recreate and simulate as faithfully as possible the original events. The filmmakers believed that by exposing social problems without explicitly offering an interpretive stance they could encourage reform efforts.

While the Drew team filmmakers called their approach cinéma vérité after the French documentary style, it is more accurately a departure from the original methods and philosophy of cinéma vérité proper. Leacock said their purpose was "to find some important aspect of our society by *watching* our society, by *watching* how things *really happen* as opposed to the social image that people hold about the way things are supposed to happen" (emphasis mine).[48] Unlike Rouch and Marker, who believed that the filmmaker's and camera's presence were catalysts that activated the profilmic event (events unfolding in front of the camera), the American cinéma vérité filmmakers believed that their presence and camera offered a minimum of interference or interpretation.

The Drew team brought to television documentary the liberal values of social reform. They presumed the moral truths that they saw would be evident to everyone, "If right-thinking people become aware of the way things 'really are,' they will take steps to correct injustices and inequities. The advocacy of a specific program of change is not the filmmaker's task; it is enough to reveal the 'truth' of a social situation to the viewer."[49] Between 1960 and 1963, Drew Associates filmmakers covered American imperialism in Latin America (*Yanki, No!* for ABC Television), desegregation in the South (*The Children Were Watching* for ABC Television), and the American political process (*Primary* for the four Time-owned television stations and *Adventures on the New Frontier* for ABC Television).

The new theme of liberal reform they espoused was part of a larger cultural shift. Art critic Max Kozloff described the shift as "A 'can-do' mentality [that] promised momentum away from the stagnation of the Republican years."[50] The optimism of the Kennedy era, fueled by a charismatic president and his programs of liberal progress, contributed to a different social frame from that of the 1950s, which produced the art world's alienated fascination for the angst-ridden personal identity crisis.

In addition, artists more freely intermingled than in the 1950s when the bars, clubs, and private parties were the chief and exclusive social organizations. In the 1960s the art scene focused around Judson Memorial Church in Washington Square and a few other downtown sites where artists from several art forms gathered for performances and happenings. As art critic Barbara Haskell observed, "The downtown scene in those days was remarkably intimate. Everyone knew everyone else . . . through encounters at performance events and gallery openings attended by dancers, painters, sculptors, musicians, poets and actors. Within this network of artists, aesthetic ideologies and loyalties were neither narrowly drawn nor mutually exclusive."[51] Art critics see in this mobility and interaction both aesthetic influence across disciplines and a broader, more encompassing arts discourse. Lawrence Alloway described it as a new, social awareness, "As an alternative to an aesthetic that isolated visual art from life and from the other arts, there emerged a new willingness to treat our whole culture as if it were art. . . . [It was] a move towards an anthropological view of our society. . . . The mass media were entering the work of art and the whole environment was being regarded, reciprocally, by the artists as art, too."[52] Alloway sees the "new attitude" as a discourse of the burgeoning Pop Art, but it also links the painterly attitude to the Camp sensibility in such films as Jack Smith's *Flaming Creatures* (1963) and Ken Jacobs's *Blonde Cobra* (1963), as well as to the New American Cinema movement and to the rhetorical claims of cinéma vérité documentaries. All these filmmakers studied life and the world rather than themselves.

Shirley Clarke and Cinéma Vérité

Clarke, however, did not always contribute to a unified position among New York cinéma vérité filmmakers. Throughout the decade in which cinéma vérité flourished as a cinematic practice, Clarke interrogated cinéma vérité's political premises and posited more self-reflexive forms of address as the means to radicalize audience experiences of social issues. Her assault on the cinéma vérité filmmaker's belief in the natural authority of his or her position is no less than a challenge to the patriarchal nature of the cinematic gaze. By challenging the inscription of the filmmaker's gaze as objective reality, Clarke began to address the politics of image construction and to show how image production itself may become conflated with the production of meaning.

In private discussions among the members of Filmmakers Inc., Clarke disagreed with Pennebaker and Leacock (the chief representatives of cinéma vérité) about their approach to cinema and reality. She argued with Pennebaker, Leacock, and others who shared the belief that their intuition for spontaneous control approximated as closely as possible an objective attempt to record the reality of the natural world.[53] Clarke denied the possibility of any such intuitive objectivity by emphasizing the inherent subjectivity in the cinematic process itself—in one's decisions regarding the subject material, in the selective nature of the editing process, and in one's choice of camera positions dependent upon a filmmaker's predisposed way of seeing.[54] Other documentary filmmakers who participated in these discussions echoed Clarke's argument. Emile de Antonio argued that "the assumption of objectivity is false."[55] Fred Wiseman agreed that "the objective-subjective argument is . . . a lot of nonsense. [My] films are my response to a certain experience."[56] Their point was that the main "truth" is the rhetorical authority of the filmmaker (as author) as well as the authority of the apparatus.

The Drew team cinéma vérité filmmakers aimed a camera at a subject to reveal some psychological insight not apparent to the cinematographic object. They believed that this revelation occurred when a subject trying to maintain her or his dignity before the camera had to struggle with a psychological defeat.[57] Robert Drew explained, "What really happens in any of these stories is that something is revealed about the people."[58] He further specified that such character revelation came about by structuring into the film specific crisis moments picked up when the camera joins an event "in progress."[59] Clarke argued with the logic of this position (both literally and in her subsequent films) by claiming that the filmmakers themselves "naturalized" such psychological revelation through the narrative (complete with crises) that they edited into their documentaries.

But outside the filmmakers' private discussions among themselves, limited debate circulated about the construction of "authority" in cinéma vérité. When it came to documentary cinema, most film critics and scholars alike espoused an aesthetics of the content. Following in the realist theoretical tradition of Siegfried Kracauer, Rudolf Arnheim, and André Bazin, documentary critics like Henry Breitrose, George Bluestone, Richard Griffith, and Paul Rotha believed simply in the ontological function of photography to reveal an undisguised and unmediated reality. For example, George Bluestone wrote about a scene inside Presidential candidate Hubert Humphrey's car in Drew's and Leacock's *Primary*, "That one sequence gives us more insight into the bone-crushing fatigue of a primary campaign than a thousand narrative assertions."[60] His words signify his proposition that the cinematographic image and narrative are set in opposition to each other, and the implication is that the image alone renders narrative logic and causality impotent. He does not admit the possibility that the image and even the entire scene may be seen as part of a narrative composition that is a structure for the whole film. Bluestone's statement is all too typical of an uncritical sentiment dominant through the 1960s regarding American cinéma vérité and the filmmakers' claims for truth revelation and psychological insight.

Not until the middle 1970s and 1980s did film historians and scholars begin to examine the theoretical assumptions of documentary film form. By that time, feminist documentary filmmakers had already begun self-reflexive examinations into the authority of image and narrative (e.g., *Daughter Rite, Thriller, Riddles of the Sphinx, Amy!*). The new critical literature that accompanied these films approached the documentary mode as an interpretive system.[61] By the early 1980s, documentary critics reached a consensus, "The tendency to see documentary films . . . as objective records of events rather than as a filmmaker's statement about events derives from a confusion of interpretive strategies: the unsophisticated assumption that filmed events can be critically interpreted as 'natural.' What such viewers fail to understand is that all mediated events are to some degree symbolic."[62] The Filmmakers Inc. discussions have become reactivated as a historical site in the 1980s and are now part of a dominant critical discourse in which documentary films are interpreted and understood. Within such shifting terms, Clarke's films in the 1960s may be seen as occupying a significant place in an ongoing debate about documentary mode, naturalist aesthetics, and the claims to truth of the documentary filmmaker. Clarke's *The Connection* (1961) is, perhaps, the first public interrogation of the objective authority of the presumed male gaze operating in American cinéma vérité.

The Connection as a Radical Critique

The Connection is about a cinéma vérité director filming a group of drug addicts who are together awaiting their "connection" (the arrival of a heroin package). Acting as a double-edged sword that self-reflexively portrays and betrays cinéma vérité, *The Connection* appears to be a cinéma vérité documentary, although it is actually a tightly scripted, acted, and edited drama. The film's controlled dramatic situation has only been made to resemble cinéma vérité to expose how cinéma vérité fails as an exposé.

The Connection's visual qualities, setting, characters, action, and temporal developments all adhere to cinéma vérité conventions. The movie was shot employing hand-held cameras and fast black-and-white stock. The resulting jiggly framing and grainy, high-contrast cinematography give it the visual style associated with the technological economy of portable equipment used for cinéma vérité. Camera angles and movements reveal a completely enclosed, naturally lighted room rather than a two- or three-sided, evenly lighted set on a sound stage. The action or, rather, the lack of conventional dramatic progression suggests a real-life situation rather than a scripted one. The on-screen subjects swear, behave badly, are silent for long stretches, stick syringes in their arms and, at one point, simply stare at cockroaches climbing the wall. Because narrative progress does not conform to Hollywood-styled "realism" and because it does adhere to the profilmic coding of cinéma vérité, *The Connection* arguably signifies that it is a cinéma vérité film.

But the film invokes more significant issues than how easily one can simulate or manipulate cinema so that it appears to be transparent reality. The conceit upon which the film hinges is that everything the spectator sees is from the subjective point of view of the white bourgeois director-character through his camera viewfinder or from that of his African-American, middle-class assistant. The second camera frequently enters the field of vision, repetitively inscribing the camera on-screen as a representation for the apparatus that mediates the production of meaning. Even though the framed image of the pro-filmic event is the subjective point of view of the director or the camera operator, *The Connection* incorporates the off-screen director as an extension of the spectacle. The identification of the image frame's subjective formation allows the director's assumptions about his relationship to the situation a privileged rhetorical position within the film. In the 1960s, Penelope Gilliatt was the only film critic who observed the centrality of this issue to *The Connection,* "In most films, the camera has no identity; it is simply a conveniently agile window through which one can stare without being seen, and one questions its superhuman perceptiveness no more than one questions the fact that a novelist has such an unlikely nose for being in the right place at the right time. In *The Connection,* on the other hand, the camera is always a palpable object."[63] Fifteen years later when critics more generally addressed these issues, Jeanne Allen elaborated on Gilliatt's initial assessment by noting that formal self-reflexivity provides a means for countering the claim of verisimilitude as a natural process.[64]

The inscription of the camera is a way to foreground the film's dominant subject position. While *The Connection*'s fictional director Dunn whines the cinéma vérité slogan, "I'm just trying to make an honest human document," he pans his camera, mobilizing the frame to bring some action to the sedentary situation. He wheedles, cajoles, and provokes the junkies into action in front of him. The addicts, who acknowledge the presence of the cameras, periodically respond and increasingly perform for the cameras. At one point, an addict tired of the director's ministrations asks him what he wants to hear and proceeds to deliver it. The irony is that there is no drama except that which Dunn invents, instigates, or shapes.

Only when the director within *The Connection* realizes that his predisposed way of seeing infiltrates and determines whatever he sees does he acknowledge his simple substitution of "objectivity" for his subjectivity. In the film's climax, he recognizes the existence of social "realities" impenetrable by his experience and his camera. His act of self-awareness, which is cinematically inscribed through the subjective camera of the African-American assistant, transforms the position of the junkies into symbols for dislocation, alienation, and a kind of turning off of the world represented by the director. The "objects" of this "documentary" ultimately become a visual representation for that which exists outside Dunn's knowledge. They are symbolic of an "Other" that cannot be known or understood within Dunn's white, bourgeois world but which may be accessible through African-American discourse as represented by the camera assistant's inscribed point of view. The very existence and identity of an "Other" finally threatens the hermeneutic not only of the director's position but also of his world. Within an argument on the representational authority and subjective positioning of direct cinema and documentary filmmaking, Clarke's film potentially stakes out a position on the brink of radical politics.

The Connection's Reception as a Beat Film

The Connection, however, received no such critical focus when it first appeared. It is not simply the case that the absence of a circulating discourse on documentary auto-critique prevented the film's radical textual position from itself becoming "known" until two decades later. But other contemporaneous discourses contextualized filmic meanings within a dialogue and practice of social liberalism, forwarding other positions within *The Connection.* Discursive formations that circulated around *The Connection's* release principally focused attention on the film in three ways: its similarities and differences to the well-known, off-Broadway play from which it was adapted, its aesthetic contextualization within the emergent New American Cinema movement, and its social position as the object of a lengthy censorship battle. In the 1960s, the burden of public discourse on *The Connection* activated unified meaning across these three overlapping formations.

Clarke's film *The Connection* drew upon the publicity attached to the Living Theatre's off-Broadway production of the play in 1959. That the two would be identified together is a function of the Beat or hipster cultural milieu from which both productions arose, as well as the specific marks of Clarke's production that referred to the earlier one. Clarke retained the play's original title, acting cast, and premise. The film and its attendant publicity always identified the "authors" as Clarke and the play's original writer Jack Gelber, and Clarke stressed the collaborative nature of the screenplay in all her interviews. She also included a jazz combo of musicians among the actors and their improvisations among the continuous on-screen activity, capitalizing on already formed associations between jazz music and hipsterdom.

In the two years between the play's midsummer premiere to bad reviews and the film's release, *The Connection* became something of a cult hit among the theatrical vanguard. Bad reviews in such established tastemakers as the *New Yorker*, the *New York Times*, and the *Village Voice* gave way to more favorable critiques in those same periodicals as well as in the liberal literary magazines, the *Saturday Review* and the *New Republic*.[65] The newer reviews emphasized the play's novelty and unconventionality, focusing on Gelber as a new speaker for the Beat Generation and identifying the play's "hipness" in opposition to the general public's "squareness."[66] Even *Esquire* magazine noted *The Connection*'s newly acquired status of being "in" among anyone wanting to be considered fashionably trendy: "Square, Beat, Hip and the Old Lady from Iowa just *had* to dig the scene."[67] The play won three off-Broadway awards (Obies) in 1960 for best production, best new play, and best actor (Warren Finnerty), and it continued as part of the Living Theatre's repertory for more than two years.

The trendiness and unconventionality surrounding the play became fused with the publicity, interviews, and reputation of the Living Theatre. In her study of the rhetoric surrounding the play and the film, Elayne Zalis points to the way that the Living Theatre's cofounders Judith Malina and Julian Beck participated in the general cultural formulation of the hipster/square opposition as an insider/outsider one.[68] In their interviews as well as in the articles about them and the Living Theatre, they establish their symbolic allegiance to marginalized and oppressed groups while they also carefully demarcate their position outside the very oppressed groups (drug addicts, African-Americans) to which they claim allegiance.[69] The Living Theatre's European tour of *The Connection* in the spring of 1961 served to extend and intensify this association to the point where an Italian critic simply referred to the theater company as "the rebels, the anti-Broadway."[70]

When Clarke entered the picture, the play and its association with the Living Theatre were already the site for a we/they opposition within which the Beat Generation's disaffection with white, bourgeois cultural norms was able to assume expression while remaining contained within white, bourgeois culture (including Broadway and off-Broadway theatrical productions). To be a hipster on these terms was to be anti–status quo and anti-square (to sympathize with the outsiders) while not actually being so marginalized as to be without political or economic power (the social outsiders).

When Clarke premiered *The Connection* at the Cannes Film Festival in the spring of 1961, she capitalized on these "connections" to the Living Theatre and the associative significance of hipsterdom. She traveled to the French festival with an entourage that included poet celebrities Allen Ginsberg, Gregory Corso, and Peter Orlovsky. Their beatnik appearances, openly expressed homosexuality, and controversially frank and unconventional poetry had made them something of an international sensation. Along with writer Jack Kerouac, Ginsberg had achieved legendary status as one of the best-known representatives of the new generation of rebels. Between 1959 and 1961, the American media were obsessed with the subject of jive-talking hipsters, bohemian pads, and subterranean espresso coffeehouses. Ginsberg, Corso, and Orlovsky were all international Beat celebrities who had already appeared in *Pull My Daisy*, a 1959 underground film hit in the United States and Europe. Their reputation as wild rebels often turned out to be just reputation. At the 1961 Cannes Film Festival, "people followed Ginsberg, Corso and Orlovsky on the streets, waiting for outrages that never occurred."[71] When another critic arranged an interview and was disappointed that they did not do anything outrageous, he still filled his article "with apocryphal quotes and invented pieces of business designed to show how wild, erratic and undependable these well-behaved young men really were."[72]

Perhaps in part because of its identification with the Beat milieu, *The Connection* became a festival hit despite being shown out of competition. One French critic said that it "made the festival."[73] The film received critical praise for its unconventionality, controversial subject matter, and frankness.[74] Critics quoted Clarke's explicit remarks linking her film to the hipster: "After all it is about this group of people who . . . are frankly escaping. But their way of escape is through a kind of revolt, they revolt against the standard. . . . The people they call beats . . . are responding against conformity. And what if it is the lunatic fringe?"[75] Even *Variety*, the American film industry's trade paper, indirectly acknowledged the film's allegiance to the nonconventional Beats and allowed that it should do well "in some enlightened spots."[76]

The Connection's Reception as New American Cinema

Clarke's enthusiastic reception at Cannes also drew out her associations with the New American Cinema. The New American Cinema Group is the name that Clarke and Mekas gave to a loose organization of American independent feature filmmakers that they had helped to found in the fall of 1960. The New American Cinema represented a cooperative effort to advocate a low-budget, personal, or auteurist commercial cinema in the United States. Mekas announced the group's aims in a manifesto that he published in the 1961 summer issue of the magazine he edited, *Film Culture*.[77] Typical of his inflammatory rhetorical style, Mekas expressed the group's aims: "We are for art, but not at the expense of life. We don't want false, polished, slick films—We prefer them rough, unpolished, but alive; we don't want rosy films—we want them the color of blood."[78] Although the New American Cinema never met regularly as a group or realized any of its ambitious plans for collective production, distribution, and marketing, the name itself became associated with an independent movement in the United States that was a counterpart of numerous new wave European cinemas. Film scholar David E. James summarizes the New American Cinema's overall cultural significance as "inventing an extra-industrial and, in fact, an anti-industrial use of the medium."[79]

For example, when Clarke and *The Connection* appeared in France and in London, critics identified her as a representative of the New American Cinema. The *London Times* critic grouped Clarke with the filmmakers of recent independent New York films like *Shadows*, *On the Bowery*, *The Savage Eye*, and *Little Fugitive*.[80] The same critic likened her style and approach to the "free cinema" movement of low-budget, independent films in Britain.[81] French cinema periodicals grouped her film stylistically with Godard's *nouvelle vague* hit, *A bout de souffle*.[82] The Italian critic writing for *Figaro* said, "It is this year's *L'Aventura*."[83] They celebrated *The Connection* because it had outdone these and other European new wave films in its ability to capture a feeling of spontaneous events and acting. One American critic reported simply that "*The Connection* flipped the French."[84] In this way, *The Connection* also became known and interpreted by its similarities to other new wave films as well as independent American films already celebrated throughout Europe for their look of spontaneity, concern with topical controversy and their apparent lack of concern for traditional aesthetics and form.

The Connection: Reception, Repression, and Shifting Discourses

With such a stunning critical debut, Clarke and her coproducer Lewis Allen arranged for an American commercial distribution. But the New York State film licensing board that reviewed films for obscenity refused its license for public exhibition. The Motion Picture Division of the State Education Department of New York voted that *The Connection*'s use of the word *shit* as slang for heroin and a suggestive magazine photograph of a woman's body that appeared briefly made the film obscene and unlawful. Under the legal counsel of well-known civil liberties lawyer Ephraim London, Clarke and Allen appealed the decision and mounted a general campaign against the constitutionality of censorship laws. London had just won a highly publicized case championing the unconstitutionality of religious censorship in the film *The Miracle*. According to Clarke, he was eager to take on a case challenging the censorship laws on obscenity.[85] The legal landmarks of *The Connection*'s case were as follows: on October 6, 1961, the appeals committee upheld the lower decision; *The Connection* company excised the "offensive" magazine photo but lost its subsequent appeal to the New York State Regents that oversaw the Education Division in January 1962; the entire case was transferred to the court system, where on July 2, 1962, the court overturned the Board of Regents decision and declared that the film was not obscene; the Regents appealed the decision, and on November 1, 1962, the New York State Supreme Court upheld the lower court's decision that the film could be shown.[86]

During the year and a half of litigation that followed the Cannes showings, *The Connection* was the subject of continuous media coverage that reconfigured the film's position for the American public. National magazines and the New York City press, in particular, developed a number of key issues and arguments around the film and its position as the object of a censorship battle. Press coverage of the court cases and *The Connection* developed a new context within which to understand the film's meanings. Critical discussions that had previously focused on the film's relationships to the play, its celebrity status at the Cannes Film Festival, its relationships to new wave cinemas, and its Beat or hipster sensibility were not necessarily dropped but reestablished within a broader discussion of rebellion and conformity. The Beat/square, we/they, outsider/insider associations already evoked be-

came further politicized in a more explicit discourse of expression/
repression.

Central to the coverage of *The Connection*'s legal battle is the continuous claim that cinema is an art form. Whereas London's appeals to the
courts challenged the legitimacy of the censorship law itself, film critics
and reporters more narrowly advocated cinema's right as art to be
outside the laws. Like the censorship laws of most states, New York's
restrictions did not apply to those products sanctioned as "literature"
or "art." In this case, *New York Times* critic Bosley Crowther argued
that "the issue is whether a screen-writer has the same right to choose
his words as does a novelist or a playwright."[87] When the Judson
Memorial Church arranged for a private screening of the film, the
church minister stated, "We believe that this film is an honest and
forthright work of art on an adult theme."[88] When the president of
the United States requested a private screening, Mekas wrote in his
Village Voice column, "Did you know that *The Connection* was clean
enough to screen at the White House but that it makes the New York
censors blush girlishly?"[89] Within the ongoing discussion, the religious
and social authorities that one would most likely expect to object to
"obscenity" became cultural voices for film's legitimacy as an art form.
Clarke's censorship struggle reactivated Deren's claims and, this time,
national as well as New York arts and literary magazines pleaded for
the legal status of that which they as cultural and aesthetic authorities
already defined as legitimate art. They repetitively positioned themselves in opposition to the courts and their valuation of cinema.

But because Clarke and Allen could not exhibit the film at a New
York public theater, they had a film whose notoriety resulted chiefly
from the many layers of extratextual discourse. In other words, few
people could actually see the film itself. Most other states had censorship laws similar to those of New York, and exhibitors throughout the
country awaited the outcome of the New York case before committing
themselves to exhibit the film. While the film played successfully in
Paris and London (where it passed the censorship boards), only a small
handful of screenings occurred in the United States. The film actually
had its United States premiere in Scottsdale, Arizona, in February
1962, almost a year after the Cannes Festival appearance. A four-
hundred-seat art cinema owned by a teacher at Phoenix College capitalized on the controversy surrounding the film. Interviews with
Clarke and ample coverage of the film's court battle filled the local
papers and the theater's advertisements, and *The Connection* enjoyed
a successful run.[90]

Although the film was not playing anywhere, the New York papers kept it alive before the public by covering the court decision.[91] The *New York Times* featured a profile on Clarke as a feisty director whose film was being championed by "New York's small but dedicated movie colony."[92] But Clarke remembered, "I kept saying, 'We've got to do something drastic. Maybe we've got to show the film somehow and maybe even get arrested or something because soon nobody but us is going to care whether they ever see it.' "[93] In the fall of 1962, the film's distributor convinced the newly renovated D. W. Griffith Theater that it could sensationalize itself as a competitive art cinema by promising that it would open with *The Connection*. The announcement stimulated an upsurge in press coverage. The New York papers now detailed the unfolding drama as the New York State Supreme Court issued an injunction against the film's exhibition, arrested the projectionist, and closed the theater after two showings.[94]

Renewed New York publicity prompted other theaters outside New York City to exhibit *The Connection* as a notorious film. The Cinema Theater in Los Angeles opened the film on October 5, 1962, and broke the house's twenty-six-year box office record for opening three performances.[95] Allen noted that the theater's advertising capitalized on the film's New York controversies but was not enough to attract audiences for more than a few days.[96] Clarke noted a similar situation in Los Angeles and other cities: "For three or four days, the reactions would be good. People had heard or read about it some place. . . . [But] people couldn't identify with the film at all. They thought: those dirty characters—they're bums."[97]

When the New York Court of Appeals finally made a unanimous decision for *The Connection* on November 2, 1962, the film resumed its New York City booking at the D. W. Griffith Theater. Now that the critics and public alike could see the film, the same thing happened in Manhattan as in other cities. The film was a product of such a storm of controversy that the experience of the film itself failed to live up to expectations aroused by the dramatic censorship struggle. One New York critic summed up the prevailing attitude: "Outside of the notoriety that 'The Connection' has because it is the center of a contention over the legality of censorship . . . there is little about it to warrant the clamorous interest of the average movie-goer or to distinguish it as a significant piece of cinematic art."[98] The reviews now reversed direction from the accolades initially heaped upon the film by both the European and American press, and the film's early contextualization as outsider, socially relevant art seemed buried beneath the sensationalized aesthetic aura acquired through obscenity charges, lawsuits, arrests, and injunctions.

The Cool World (1963): New American Cinema and Cinéma Vérité as African-American Cinema Discourse

If *The Connection* suggests a highly dramatic example of how New American Cinema became discursively positioned in the 1960s, one may more productively turn to *The Cool World* as an example of Clarke's social protest through representation and practice. In many respects, however, *The Cool World* is more of a collaboration between Clarke and African-American actor Carl Lee than a specifically auteurist movie. Lee (who was in both the play and film versions of *The Connection*) had become Clarke's lover and companion after her marriage to Bert Clarke ended in 1961. It is the film's cinematically constructed invocation of African-American discourses and activation of a black subject position that offer a radical alternative framework for defining and organizing meanings about social problems.[99]

Lee and Clarke based their film on Warren Miller's best-selling novel about Harlem teenagers. They incorporated Clarke's filmmaking style of gritty black-and-white realism, marked as such because of its location shooting, improvisation, and rambling narratives. Like *The Connection*, *The Cool World* privileges cinéma vérité techniques. Clarke used hand-held cameras, fast film stock for high contrast black-and-white images, and she and Lee shot the film in outdoor Harlem locations with nonprofessional actors who Lee coached and directed to speak "naturally," that is, to speak swiftly and in street slang.

But *The Cool World* also employs such uncharacteristic vérité devices as montage sequences, a first-person voice-over narration, and nondiegetic jazz soundtrack. In this respect, it more accurately resembles the style of an Italian Neorealist drama than a cinéma vérité documentary. From the opening scene, the young, African-American male lead provides an introspective voice that frames plot developments and comments on characters in relation to his interior identity. Blues and jazz accompaniment colors the combination of dialogue, sounds, and images and is specifically tied to an important tradition of African-American culture. The montage sequences convey a poetic sense of black street life from the inside of Harlem culture.

Unlike other contemporary theatrical narrative films that addressed issues of racism, *The Cool World* does not enunciate a unified discourse of white address through subject positioning of white characters. It might be contrasted, for example, with *To Kill a Mockingbird*, which identified race problems with the South and filtered the issues of racism through the viewpoint of a white girl and "the heroic actions of her Lincolnesque father."[100] In other contemporary films, Hollywood represented African-American cultural experience in stereotypical, "prettified" portraits (*Porgy and Bess* and *A Raisin in the Sun*) that demonstrated more of Hollywood melodramatic conventions than a discussion of current social and economic conditions among African-American communities. Not only does *The Cool World* attempt to explore racism in a contemporary Northern setting, but it enunciates a black subjectivity through identification with a principal African-American character.

The film's opening organizes three different forms of address as specifically "African-American" address. *The Cool World* begins with an extreme close-up of a street preacher's face as he speaks directly to the camera. His words, shouted out, are as expressive of rights to power as their visual and auditory assertiveness, "Do you want to know the truth about the white man? The white man is the devil. The black man is the original man. . . . Join with me in reclaiming what is rightfully ours." Although this character only appears for the first few minutes of the film, it is his address—set within the discourse of black resistance and revolution associated in the 1960s with the Nation of Islam movement—that sets the stage for the discursive framework of the film.

The preacher's speech is followed by a visually rambling introduction to Harlem streets and the lead character Duke, while Duke's voice-over situates who he is and what he wants. Duke wants to get a small-time racketeer's Colt revolver so that he can become the leader of his street gang. His recourse to "power" as a "cool killer" presents a disturbing corollary to the preacher's program for responding to racism.

The next scene follows Duke hopping onto his class's schoolbus. While the bus of bored teenagers rides along Fifth Avenue en route to the stock exchange, their white male teacher lectures the students on stocks, bonds, and investments. Attempting to appear affable and knowledgeable, the teacher breaks cadence in his speech only to yell at the students to keep their hands inside the window and not to touch the white female passengers on a passing city bus. Hand-held camera shots reveal midday Manhattan outside the window while close-ups of the bus interior cover boys discussing the acquisition of a gun and singing a cappella rhythm and blues.

The characters lack self-consciousness but display an open awareness of the jiggling camera's presence, a key component in many cinéma vérité films. Their treatment contrasts the teacher's closely scrutinized face while he is unable to maintain disciplinary control. His facial pretense (for the camera?) that he is in control and is respected signifies his deeper fear and misunderstanding of his charges, who openly display contempt for white authority and economic achievements.

This scene presents a third form of address—from direct persuasion in the opening to the subjective meditation that follows to dramatic argument—that asks the audience to identify with an African-American subject position and to assume an attitude of superiority. Thus, *The Cool World* may be heralded as a celebration of black experience from African-American viewpoints and, indeed, it has been retrospectively repositioned in this way in black film festivals of the 1980s. But, even in this context, contemporary African-American spectators have commented on the fact that the film portrays cultural victimization without allowing the victims any recourse to successful resistance or opposition.[101]

In the narrative that follows, Duke meets the other gang members at their clubhouse, a run-down apartment deserted by another boy's father. He consults with Priest (played by Carl Lee), the former gang member who is now a small-time racketeer, as well as with an upwardly mobile, college student freedom rider. He spends time with his mother, his grandmother, his prostitute-girlfriend Luanne, and Priest's girlfriend, each of whom talks about the way patriarchal institutions—family, church, marriage—have defined her life and how each has ultimately failed to provide for her. Ultimately, he and his gang engage in a street fight that ends in a knifing and Duke's brutal arrest.

Each plot development is framed both by Duke's interior monologues and the montage sequences of Harlem street life. Such expressly poetic devices bridge narrative episodes with numerous scenes of street life, portraits of neighborhood residents, and visions of nighttime Harlem, often made available to the spectator because of Duke's presence on the streets. *Newsweek*'s enthusiastic review offers a descriptive example, Clarke "invents visual rhymes, cutting from a cigar smoker to a fat man smoking a ceramic pipe, to a man with a cigarette; or from a little girl skipping, to a man doing a trick dance on a manhole cover, to a group of young women twisting outside a record shop."[102] The visuals and their accompanying jazz soundtrack are emotional, highly kinetic manifestations of the restless energy and sense of frustration expressed in Duke's monologues.

The Harlem montages edited by Clarke are reminiscent of her earlier work in *Brussels Film Loops* and *Skyscraper* as well as Dziga Vertov's theories of "kino-glaz" ("cinema eye"). Soviet filmmaker-theorist Vertov heralded a new cinema based in the organization of camera-recorded documentary material. Whereas Clarke's peers at Filmmakers Inc. interpreted the Soviet formalist's definition of the filmmaker as that of a passive recorder, Clarke emphasized Vertov's approach to editing as the best means to recreate an essence of reality. *The Cool World*'s discourse of cinéma vérité counterpoints its interpolations of a cinema-eye, Vertov-styled documentary about Harlem. The film ultimately plays one style against the other, synthesizing them in a superstructure that is an atmospheric story of social realism.

If *The Cool World* is a problem-oriented film, then the problems to which it responds are neither historically specific to the 1960s nor so easily eradicated as the liberal optimism of the time indicated. The opening scenes actively work in this way, not only to situate "the problem" outside the dominant discourse of liberalism in the early 1960s, but to inaugurate a trajectory toward the destruction of the film's characters who seek violent power as well as the teenagers who try not to take sides in the gang wars. The film portrays a cultural situation far more complex than the liberal political solutions being purveyed at the time.

It might be worth noting here that the film's only African-American characters who have achieved upward mobility are presented somewhat ambivalently. The freedom rider Douglas, who dresses in suit and tie and carries books, is a visual representative of an outside world when he engages Duke in conversation. When Douglas argues with his brother Blood, the dope addict and former gang leader, Blood accuses him of turning into a "white man." Douglas's argumentation is logical and reasoned in grammatically correct English. Blood's drug-induced response of "it's a black dirty world out there" is an emotionally charged refrain to Douglas's solutions as personal ones that will neither alter the course of his victimization nor the rest of Harlem's. His curse of "stay in your white world" suggests that Douglas's campaign of liberal activism has also meant his assimilation into white culture.

Elsewhere, the college-bound basketball player teaching neighborhood kids on the playground is unable to defend himself or the kids from the sadistic teasing of the rival gang. He depends upon Duke's intervention. His visual isolation within the mise-en-scène and pauses of speech surrounding his subsequent brief conversation with Duke literalize as well how isolated and ambiguous is his escape from the problems of the ghetto.

Lastly, it is important to note how the rhetoric of the civil rights movement offers no solutions for the oppression experienced by the film's women—oppression that results from both race and gender barriers. The issue is not one the film takes up as a significant theme but is, nevertheless, introduced dramatically through all the female characters. For example, the young Hispanic girl Luanne who becomes a prostitute to the gang and then Duke's girlfriend when he heads the gang, speaks to Duke of her individual dreams and aspirations. Her voice affects narrative direction only after her exchange value as a sexual commodity for the gang has been repetitively inscribed. Even then, Duke recognizes the obvious poverty of her fantasy to see the sea when it is only a short subway ride away. His gesture of love in a Coney Island trip becomes narratively short-circuited when she disappears from the beach, Duke's life, and the film.

The absence of available alternatives to women is more forcefully represented in Duke's mother. Her narrative importance, like Luanne's, is set in relation to Duke's character, and she functions through a set of appearances either arriving at the apartment with a man in tow or leaving to go work in a laundry.[103] But when Duke rather sarcastically asks her about one of her past "husbands," she delivers a tongue-lashing monologue in which the camera focuses on her (not on Duke's reaction) while she describes repetitive desertions and single-handed efforts to support herself and a child. Her conclusions tie her economic condition to gender as much as to racism, "Things always get too much for men. . . . One day they just doesn't come home. It's easy for you, you a man and you just like the others. . . . You only know how to give a woman sadness and cause her pain and suffering."

This moment in the film provides the movie's most obvious point of rupture, not simply because the terms of oppression have shifted within the dominant rhetorical strand of racism to incorporate sexual difference but also because the speech is itself made within the syntax of melodrama. In other words, a film whose style so self-consciously sets itself against Hollywood standards incorporates an African-American woman's declaration of her problems only in the language of Hollywood melodrama: the acting style becomes hyperbolic and overly gestured; the actress is centrally framed and expressionistically lighted for dramatic focus; the language itself is more obviously theatrical and delivered in clear, dramatic tones without any external sound interference. The scene is anomalous within the film both for its style and for its intimation that poverty and racism have different effects on women and that problems of sexual difference are beyond the range of civil rights campaigns.

Similarly, when Priest's white girlfriend tries to confess her problems to Duke, her dilemma is so outside the perspective represented by Duke that she largely causes his character embarrassment. Depressed, physically abused, boozy, and lonely because she spends most of her time waiting for Priest, she tries to reach out to Duke, who panics at her efforts of friendship. (Of course, his on-screen panic can also be linked to his acculturation, as demonstrated on the schoolbus, not to "touch" white women.) Suspended in a "woman's time" of endless waiting, she still serves as a momentary reminder that, questions of racism aside, there still remains sexual oppression.

The Cool World: White Liberalism and Reception Practices

In 1963, *The Cool World* offered a much different "preferred reading" when it initially played to largely white liberal audiences. The film's reception may be best understood for the ways that the film was situated within the rhetoric of the civil rights movement. The civil rights movement addressed the achievement of black equality through due legal processes and advocated only nonviolent means to publicize its goals. Unlike the Black Power movements of the late 1960s or the Black Muslim movement, the civil rights movement of the early 1960s as led by Martin Luther King, Jr., maintained a voice that was neither radical nor revolutionary. *The Cool World* arrived on the art cinema circuit at the moment when white Northerners had stepped up their involvement and sympathy for civil rights marches, acts of civil disobedience, and integrationist demonstrations in the South. In a retrospective twenty years later, film scholar Noël Carroll attempted to recreate the context, "The rhetoric of the movement was grounded in simple justice, claiming for blacks only that which most whites already had. . . . [*The Cool World*] bear[s] the pre-Watts and pre-Black Power stamp of this stage . . . [and is] underwritten by the hope that the documentation and explanation of injustice will move people of good will to eradicate it."[104] Carroll's statement not only presupposes the discursive mark of a unified politics among the film, the New American Cinema, and cinéma vérité but incorporates the spectator within a rhetorical field of liberal humanism. What Carroll's analysis of the film does not acknowledge, however, is the ways that *The Cool World* problematizes the liberal sensibility that he sees it celebrating.

The film initially played both the Venice Film Festival in September 1963 and commercial art cinema houses catering to white, bourgeois audiences in the United States. Unlike *The Connection, The Cool World* was not surrounded by a storm of controversy, European labels of vanguard style, and Beat subcultural associations. But Clarke and her producer Fred Wiseman privately agreed that their public statements about *The Cool World* should offer a positive point of view so as to avoid some of the negative public reactions to *The Connection*.[105] Clarke further stated that their promotion should set the film within traditions of *la politique des auteurs* and European art cinema while denying its connections to classical Hollywood cinema.[106] A significant effect occurred, however, when they attempted to book the film into the midtown Manhattan movie houses patronized by Harlem teenagers. They found that the film's already formed associations with Clarke and the New American Cinema, with European film festivals, and with the uptown art cinemas made it impossible to sell their product to a venue that did not specialize in independent or European cinema.[107]

The film was constantly kept in the public eye throughout its subsequent New York run even though the film itself received mixed critical reviews.[108] When the film was not being reviewed, newspapers as well as national magazines (*Newsweek* and *Life*) and film journals (*Film Comment, Films and Filming*) continued their coverage by interviewing Clarke and the film's teenage stars. The nonprofessional actors from Harlem, Brooklyn, and the Bronx fielded questions about how the film was changing their life expectations.[109] Amidst optimistic, upbeat dialogues on new career goals and educational aspirations, the stories made the film's production the socially therapeutic object of their own discourse of egalitarianism.

Film magazine interviews with Clarke emphasized her status as a Jewish woman filmmaker in a man's world as a measure of her sympathy and identification with racial discrimination. In this context, the displacement of white racism by anti-Semitism and sexism argues for the reader's identification with Clarke as the successful filmmaker-star while suppressing both the idea of miscegenation and an African-American man's artistic role in the film's production. The same articles always named individual African-American workers to emphasize that the production crew was racially mixed (a significant inclusion in film journals presumably aimed at a narrower professional audience when there were practically no African-Americans with either the technical training or access to film craft unions).[110] Stories and tag lines on production stills explicitly admired the crew's courageousness for shooting a film on the streets of Harlem—an admiration obviously directed from a white, bourgeois position.[111] Making known the narrative of the film's production played a central role within the film's larger discourse of white liberalism and social justice.

Following its New York City commercial run, *The Cool World* played throughout the summer and fall of 1964 at small art house cinemas in scattered North American cities. Supporting the rhetoric of the New York articles as well as those in nationally distributed periodicals, Clarke herself made personal appearances in many of these places.[112]

Her speeches to the local presses and to the audiences attending the film
explicitly invoked the rhetoric of contemporary civil rights discourse,
"If we 'whites' really know what the life of the Negro living in the ghettos
of America is like, we will join our fellow Americans, the Negroes, and
bring about true brotherhood."[113] Her presence helped to coalesce the
film's position within the personal cinema while it defined a specifically
white point of view that could place the end of racism within nonthreat-
ening, ecumenical terms. The primary significance of the film's meaning then was not in its residual claims for formal aesthetic authenticity
but in the way that it promised to achieve what Robert Drew had earlier
outlined as the goal of cinéma vérité—to unveil social injustices so that
"right-thinking" people could enact reforms.

Amidst such social activism during *The Cool World*'s 1963 and 1964
release, competing discourses were repressed and made "audible" only
several years later. While Clarke claimed that she needed a male
producer to acquire economic investors, it is equally important that
she said investors would only back an African-American film because
it had a white director.[114] Though Clarke told all her interviewers that
such a film about African-American culture could not have been made
without Lee, Lee not only received far less public mention than did
Clarke but his name was left out of the initial advertisements and he
got less significant screen credit. Clarke later said that she fought with
Wiseman over this very point because Lee was systematically being
denied authorial valorization.[115] Furthermore, the contextualization
of *The Cool World* within a rhetoric of personal cinema and Clarke's
status as an auteur privileged Clarke's participation over that of Lee's
as well as other members of the production crew.

Clarke's relationship with her producer Fred Wiseman and their
struggles for power over the film are equally important sites for considering how traces of race and gender conflicts that were smoothed over
or erased in the public discourses participated in the film's historical
meanings. Seven years after the film's completion, Clarke was angrily
saying, "Fred Wiseman screwed me on *The Cool World*."[116] Although
none of the public statements or publicity surrounding the film's initial
release speaks of any friction, Clarke's subsequent interviews and private correspondence between Clarke and Wiseman as well as between
Clarke and several friends resonate with anger about the film's labor
relations. While Clarke's publicly expressed anger may be attributed
to her indignation at Lee's treatment, it also appears to stem from the
financial relationships and division of producer-director roles on the
film. As part of their contractual agreement, Clarke gave Wiseman exclusive rights for financing, distribution, and exhibition while Wiseman
relinquished any power over the production. But when their company

ran out of money on the projected $250,000 film and put its future in jeopardy, Clarke personally loaned the company $50,000.[117] Wiseman never repaid her and refused her access to the film's financial statements, and her requests for economic information continued into the 1970s.[118]

When Wiseman, Clarke, and Lee went to the Venice Film Festival in 1963, Clarke and Wiseman spent more time arguing with each other than publicizing the film. A 1963 *New Yorker* column hints at some of the pressures underlying their relationship when it details the last-minute struggles to get the film accepted and completed for the festival.[119] It does not mention that many of Clarke's friends felt the recent death of Clarke's father was affecting her emotional stability.[120] As she worked round-the-clock to finish the film for the festival, she was plunging into a nervous breakdown. Clarke herself said later, "I looked like the end of the world."[121] By the time she arrived in Venice, Clarke fought with Wiseman over the hotel arrangements, the advertisements, Lee's marginalization, and even Wiseman's commitment to the film's success.[122] Clarke accused Wiseman of producing the film only so that he could "cop a career" for himself as a filmmaker, and she subsequently claimed that he spent the trip promoting himself instead of the film.[123] It might be worth considering that many of Clarke's statements have been made retrospectively after Wiseman's career as the cinéma vérité filmmaker of *Titicut Follies, Hospital, High School, Law and Order,* and other films had outshone hers.

But it is also important to see Clarke's relationship with Wiseman in a larger context than that of bitter memories and confrontation. When she later asserted that she needed Wiseman because people would not invest in her films unless they were produced by a man, Clarke articulated the limitations of her social power and the practical, frustrating dilemma of her professional situation. It seems not so coincidental that the terms of economic control and ego domination that marked her relationship with Wiseman were also the terms by which she characterized her relationship with her father. The ensuing mental breakdown that she linked to the conditions surrounding these two relationships was, perhaps, her only recourse for rebellion. By January of 1965, Clarke was admitted to a private Connecticut mental hospital for several months.

Clarke and Film-Makers Distribution Center:
An Apparatus for a Commercial Avant-garde

The season of 1965–66 was a transitional one for Clarke, the American independent cinema, and the arts in general. After being released from the hospital during the summer of 1965, Clarke had taken up

residence in Greenwich Village's legendary hangout for bohemians—
the Chelsea Hotel. She slipped back into the large downtown network
of filmmakers, actors, photographers, jazz musicians, dancers, painters, and poets. As another artist described their highly informal social
scene of the mid-sixties, "We had a lot of close friends, a floating group
of about 200 people."[124] The popular press considered the downtown
arts world an immoral bohemia marked by frequent parties, sexual
indulgence, and hallucinogenic drugs, whereas artists' nostalgic re-
membrances express a localized moment of imagined powerfulness,
self-contentment, and optimism, "The sixties esprit . . . [was] optimistic, experimental and feverishly intense . . . [an] anything goes philosophy."[125] The entire art market flourished, and new government and
corporate funding contributed to accelerated economic growth. The
creation of the National Endowment for the Arts (NEA) symbolized
an institutionalized recognition of the artist's important role in society.

   While Clarke began reorganizing her life around activities that
supported the independent cinema, the Village itself provided a central headquarters for an increasingly wider range of cinema support
activities. Those activities garnered a lot of publicity in the media,
"Virtually every magazine in the country—from *The Saturday Evening
Post* to *Playboy*—had run one sort of article or another on the phenomenon; the Museum of Modern Art had organized a symposium on the
New American Cinema; and in addition . . . two East Village venues
. . . were regularly screening underground films."[126] The two-year-old
Film-Makers' Cooperative established by Jonas Mekas was thriving as
a national clearinghouse for experimental films aimed at noncommercial outlets.[127] In 1965, Millennium Film Workshop provided a new
regular venue for cooperative film production, class instruction, and
exhibition. Mekas's "Movie Journal" column weekly covered the independent cinema in the *Village Voice*. The fourth annual New York Film
Festival headed by Amos Vogel included numerous events, panels,
and screenings on the independent cinema. Even CBS planned a
special program on the New York filmmakers, and its camera crew
followed Clarke, Amos Vogel, Stan Brakhage, Carmen D'Avino, Stan
Vanderbeek, Ed Emshwiller, and Bruce Conner all the way to Berlin,
Germany, for a New American Cinema symposium.[128]

   In early 1966, Clarke met with Mekas and independent filmmaker
and exhibitor Louis Brigante to set up a nonprofit cooperative for
distributing independently made films to commercial theaters. They
took over space in the Film-Makers' Cooperative office, hired a general
manager, and became the board of directors of the newly formed
Film-Makers Distribution Center (FDC). Modeled on the Coop, the

FDC perpetuated the Coop's artist-centered philosophies and democratic policy of accepting all submitted films. But, unlike the Coop's practice of allowing the filmmakers to set their own individual rates, the FDC assumed authority for determining rates and for withholding a larger percentage of the profits than did the Coop. They simultaneously incorporated the Film-Makers Lecturers Bureau as an auxiliary means of tying the FDC to a personal, auteurist cinema where the filmmaker's copresence would be an important incentive to small art houses around the country.

The FDC was initially successful both in the number of filmmakers who chose to participate and in its economic practices. The first year's catalogue included feature-length films by Clarke, Mekas, Storm De Hirsch, Lionel Rogosin, Gregory Markopoulous, Robert Downey, and Andy Warhol. Andy Warhol's participation was particularly important because his film *Chelsea Girls* (1966) was the FDC's first and only big commercial hit.[129]

Chelsea Girls represented all the extremes and outrages that were publicly associated with the Greenwich Village scene in the mid-sixties, and the film became an established hit among the New York City art subculture, hangers-on, and would-be bohemians. By December of 1966, the FDC moved the film from a small art house into a larger, first-run commercial theater and hired additional office staff to handle bookings in other cities.[130] *Chelsea Girls*, a two-screen, three-and-a-half-hour epic about the events, conversations, and boredom in a series of Chelsea Hotel rooms, also became immediately popular in Los Angeles, Dallas, and Washington, D.C., while the film played continuously in Manhattan through May of 1967.

Attempting to duplicate *Chelsea Girls*'s success, the FDC booked Robert Downey's *Chafed Elbows* (1966) into a New York City commercial theater in January of 1967. Although the film about a subcultural hero who gets welfare payments and marries his mother did moderately well, it was neither the object of public fanfare nor critical dialogues, and its bookings never extended to other cities. Additional efforts to create more hits failed.

Although *Chelsea Girls*'s commercial toehold encouraged the board of directors that other independent filmmakers would join the FDC, the cooperative's initial success was momentary. Warhol withdrew *Chelsea Girls* from the FDC in May of 1967 because commercial distributors were promising better deals. As usual, Mekas was quick to assess the political implications of the situation; he issued a manifesto in his *Village Voice* column, "All kinds of clever commercial fishermen are beginning to tempt us with promises, contracts, sweet tongues. It's time to sound a warning. . . . Our direction should remain inward, and homeward. . . . Director's cinema as against producer's cinema. Self-expression as against 'public' expression. Cooperative distribution as against private distribution. Multiple distribution as against 'exclusive' monopolistic distribution."[131] Mekas's statement offers a timely warning of the potential exploitation and Hollywood recuperation of the independent cinema's success as a commercially viable cinema. Indeed, Hoberman's and Rosenbaum's *Midnight Movies* illustrates how the regularization of the midnight-movie time slot in commercial film practice in the early 1970s was linked to the midnight showings of films like *Chelsea Girls* as a marginalized but alternative practice to Hollywood cinema. The seeds of the FDC's success could also sow its destruction.

Without another *Chelsea Girls*, the FDC continued to distribute films by the original group of filmmakers while it battled mounting losses. The sudden withdrawal of *Chelsea Girls* was particularly problematic because, based on the film's expected income, the FDC had already contracted expensive promotion and distribution campaigns for other films. Clarke and Mekas turned over their meager film profits, and Clarke appeared at film festivals and colleges promoting the FDC. She successfully convinced several Hollywood directors to lend their names as well as money to the FDC. Clarke reproduced all the strategies that she had seen Deren use.

Meanwhile, the community of independent filmmakers itself expressed divisiveness over Clarke's goal of a commercial alternative cinema. Some filmmakers, like Stan Brakhage, publicly denounced the FDC and stated disapproval of any forays into the commercial film arena.[132] When filmmakers accused Clarke of being "nothing more than a commercial filmmaker," they were leveling their worst insult at her, articulating a pronounced ideological split regarding the definition of the independent cinema itself.

The struggle over two competing definitions was due as much to shifting economic and cultural forces in the arts as to the filmmakers' internal group politics. During the late 1960s, independent cinema became an increasingly visible part of established cultural institutions like museums and universities. Such a shift occurred not only in New York City, where relations among colleges, museums, and marginal film organizations already existed, but across the country. The American Film Institute was founded in Washington, D.C., in 1967 as an archives and center for the study and support of film as an art form. But, perhaps, a more decisive factor was the National Endowment for the Arts's policies of disbursement, which made new monies available for museums outside of New York City. Following the lead of the NEA created in 1965, state arts councils were mandated, and state funding agencies likewise provided more widespread support for the arts.

Universities, too, incorporated more film activities into their museums and curricula alike. In the middle and late 1960s, cinema studies became widely recognized as a professional academic discipline, and the number of courses devoted to the study of motion pictures as an art form rose from fewer than 40 in 1953 to 428 in 1965, an increase of 1000%.[133] Academic expansion of cinema arts occurred during a time of economic growth at universities that could afford the support systems of film rentals, library purchases, filmmaking equipment purchases, and trained faculty necessary for new film degree programs and courses. Such institutions provided all the apparatus necessary for a self-contained economic base of production, exhibition, and promotion of independent cinema.

Brakhage, one of the most quickly valorized filmmakers within the new art institutional network, advocated an orientation to independent cinema that was consistent with museums and universities' redefined practices for supporting cinema activities as an artistic, noncommercial form. Universities were hiring independent filmmakers as regular faculty members to teach in their film and art departments. Many filmmakers who had argued for a personal, artist-centered cinema now found that educational institutions associated with the more traditional arts were ready to absorb them. New regional film festivals likewise accorded particular artistic prominence to artisanal filmmaking. Once again, Mekas astutely described these events and their significance, "The success of the underground film, the success measured in crowds and by crowds, is . . . in the suburbs and in the country. Every university has a film festival going. . . . The film culture is rolling across the country."[134] As a distributor to nontheatrical venues, Film-Makers' Cooperative experienced a sharp increase in revenues.[135] The museum and college market represented a steadily growing and easily identifiable set of structures whereas, in pure economic terms, Clarke and the FDC were advocating that independent cinema expand, diversify, and, to some degree, compete with both Hollywood and the greater number of nontheatrical showings.

Although the position identified with Brakhage suggests the existence of a philosophical bifurcation, many filmmakers found in practice that they could participate in both camps. Clarke, as well as the other filmmakers who were members of the FDC, still had films at the Coop that were routinely rented to nontheatrical outlets. Clarke's films, among others, received wider exposure through the college market. In fact, *The Connection* played a profitable seven-college tour in the spring of 1967.[136] Clarke herself was lecturing more frequently to university audiences. But she initially interpreted the growth in college film rentals and lecture fees as complementary to commercial expansion and not as competition.[137]

Portrait of Jason (1967): Joining the Commercial and Artisanal of the Independent Cinema

Clarke's own *Portrait of Jason* is an example of how a film typically straddled both distribution markets and diverse audiences in the late 1960s. *Portrait of Jason* is a feature-length cinéma vérité interview with a would-be nightclub entertainer and African-American gay prostitute. Made with Clarke's own funds and several cans of surplus film stock that an NBC-Television employee had given Clarke, *Portrait of Jason* was a low-budget enterprise that required only a small crew of three and no outside investors or producers. Its chief expense was the cost of blowing up the 16mm film to 35mm gauge for commercial distribution. After entering it in the 1967 New York Film Festival, Clarke turned the film over to both the Coop and the FDC for simultaneous theatrical and nontheatrical exhibition.

Portrait of Jason is a more overt auto-critique of cinéma vérité than either of Clarke's earlier films. Its raw material is a single stationary camera view from one continuous twelve-hour take edited down to ninety minutes. The film presents Jason's stories, mood swings, breakdowns, and improvisations to a series of off-screen questions fired by Clarke and Carl Lee. Jason covers such topics as his name and image change from Aaron Paine to Jason Holliday; his lifestyle as an African-American gay man who has worked as a houseboy and prostitute; his proposed nightclub act of songs, jokes, and female impersonations; his feelings about being filmed; his childhood and his parents; and his fears and personal secrets. Unlike *The Connection* where the drama hangs in the tension between the characters' ennui and the director's on-screen obnoxious provocations to reveal "something personal," *Portrait of Jason* begins as its sole character's intimate revelations but turns upon the horror of their absolute falsity.

It is the off-screen voices acting as a catalyst—they first prod Jason onward and then challenge his pose—that get Jason to reveal that he is acting: he is lying. The off-screen voices establish unseen characters whose even, well-modulated tones suggest a self-control that contrasts Jason's vocal and visual mood swings. As one of these "characters," Clarke self-consciously acknowledges her role in the process of the film's production and construction. Not unlike the movie director in *The Connection,* she becomes a provisional if invisible participant in the film's unmasking of itself as a discursive process rather than simply as an artifact.

The film's narrative drama hinges on the expectation, delays, and subsequent anticipation that one will truly find out whether or not Jason is lying and that some truth will be revealed in the outcome. Such an assumption derives from the discourses of narrative drama that promise a restored order by the film's end and of cinéma vérité that promise the sheer force of the cinematographic image will strip bare the object of the camera's scrutiny and will reveal some naked truth about the character. But the point of *Portrait of Jason* is that in a situation where a single character knowingly does an emotional striptease for public consumption, the reality of his confession is hollow.

Jason's polished performance draws upon the most intimate, along with the most mundane, details of his life in order to make himself an object of art. As the central object of the camera's unrelenting gaze, Jason never rules the frame but is ruled by it. But Jason's self-aware expertise at playing the victim and at manipulating his position puts in doubt his role as the unassuming object of the camera's gaze. What results is an ambiguity about whether it is the camera or the actor that is the site of enunciation. As one writer has suggested, the film articulates Jason's game of "exploit and be exploited" with the off-screen but cinematically inscribed director, with the camera and with the implied audience. Jason is "a homosexual who had found ersatz sexual power in skillful, repetitive games of using and being used; a Negro ex-housemaid who knew the ins and outs of making men knaves to their manservants; a sensitive and beautiful psychologizer who played on the nerves of his psychiatrists."[138] The political dimensions are important here: an African-American homosexual man's only power here comes from undercutting his victimization by the camera. Once again, Clarke addresses questions of power and resistance in relation to both sexual and social identities and offers at least a negotiated position in response to dominant cinema categories.

In *Portrait of Jason,* the cinematographic image organized by the filmmakers controls its object (Jason) while the object simultaneously and self-mockingly manipulates his objecthood. Film critic Parker Tyler recognized *Jason's* political and cinematic significance, and he labeled it "the climax for the Underground film camera['s] . . . morally sanctioned, altogether self-righteous voyeur[ism]."[139] *Portrait of Jason,* along with Jim McBride's *David Holzman's Diary* released the same year, addressed filmmaking practice and representation processes to identify and denounce the ideological underpinnings of cinéma vérité.[140]

While *Portrait of Jason* received enthusiastic reviews as a cinéma vérité exposé about its own practices of psychological investigation and claims for truth, such critical reception participated in two different kinds of marketing. The film's initial commercial release occurred when Clarke and the FDC "four-walled" the film at a Manhattan theater. The FDC rented the theater outright for three months and covered all operational and publicity expenses against recovery of all box office receipts. Four-walling is a common practice among smaller, independent commercial film distributors operating on the fringes of the Hollywood film industry and has often led to enough public prominence and economic return in a significant market to offset the costs and to generate more widespread exhibitor interest. The FDC chose this practice because it could not otherwise obtain commercial exhibition in New York City. Rather than try to attract commercial exhibitors outside New York City on the limited basis of its festival reviews and nontheatrical rentals, the FDC went this route as the only viable way to acquire a widespread commercial distribution. Despite such an approach and the publicity that supported the film's connections to cinéma vérité and the personal auteurism of the New American Cinema, the film lost $7,500 during its three-month run.[141] But on the basis of its critical momentum and limited economic possibilities, the FDC was able to arrange additional screenings at a few other American art cinemas scattered throughout the country. Clarke herself appeared and spoke at screenings. In each of these cases, however, the economic terms required to convince exhibitors to show the film were such that the FDC did not realize any profit from the film.

At the same time, *Portrait of Jason* circulated on the college campus and film festival circuit throughout North America and Europe. As distributed by Film-Makers' Cooperative, the film played regularly throughout 1967 and 1968, and Clarke was often present as a speaker with the film. In the nontheatrical market, the overhead was not only smaller, but the profits were based on a smaller margin of economic success and attendance. The film received more numerous nontheatrical bookings and consistently made a profit when the rental fees were scaled to educational and arts institutions.[142] Although the film would have had to show many more times in this market to achieve the kind of profit that one successful art cinema run could boast, it could at least depend upon readily identifiable, smaller constituencies while maintaining a consistent economic profit at each individual showing.

Why was the film successful nontheatrically and not theatrically?

One reason might be that the college and museum market provided a context where the identifiable discursive formation for a personal, self-reflexive cinéma vérité feature would have been easily contained within the overlapping intellectual and artistic valorization practices of the university and museum network. Another theory is that new Hollywood films were increasingly depicting nudity, explicit sex, and obscene language while appropriating the independent cinema's technical and conceptual conceits. In short, they supplanted the independent cinema. Calvin Tomkins argued that "the commercial cinema was increasingly innovative, while the underground seemed to have lost energy and direction," but it is hard to tell whether he is describing a cause or an effect.[143] One could also argue that the FDC's failure to achieve widespread commercial success may have even contributed to the film's popularity in universities and museums. As suggested by Brakhage, the independent cinema audience was marked by a cinema discourse of art that pitted their self-identified apparatus against those tied to films of popular commercial appeal.

The End of (Independent) Cinema as an Independent System of Practices

By early 1970, however, the FDC was in serious financial trouble. The filmmaking community's expressions of support had so eroded and the debt had grown so large that Mekas told Clarke and Brigante he wanted to close the organization. When Clarke asked for more time to turn around the FDC's finances, Mekas argued that he was afraid the FDC's creditors would attach liens to the Coop and destroy it as well.[144] In the spring of 1970, Mekas dramatically informed Clarke and Brigante that a city marshall was threatening to auction both the FDC's and the Coop's property, and they agreed to close the FDC.[145] Mekas assumed legal liability for a reduced debt claim of $40,000 against the FDC, a move he said he made to keep Coop monies from being secured.[146]

The closing of the FDC marked the end of one era and the beginning of another for Clarke. It was the summer of 1970, and it was a time of transition for the independent film community as a whole and the country in general. Throughout the spring of 1970 as the FDC's finances collapsed, Clarke was surrounded by the mounting crises and political tensions associated with President Richard Nixon's war offensive in southeast Asia and protests in the United States. When Nixon acknowledged that U.S. troops had crossed into Cambodia in May of 1970, widespread student demonstrations closed numerous

college campuses, created an atmosphere of domestic conflict and
turmoil, and resulted in the deaths of four students when the Ohio
National Guard was called in to Kent State University to quell a protest.
Clarke marched in protest parades, she participated in acts of civil
disobedience and got arrested, she attended meetings where members
of the artists' community planned ways that their art could be political
tools in the fight. She worked alone experimenting with super 8mm
film and portable video in short, personal diary compositions. Since she
was no longer part of large-scale film collaborations or an institutional
drive for an alternative cinema, Clarke said that her mood regarding
both cinema and politics was pessimistic, a mood of depressed frustration that was echoed in the public discourses of the counterculture.[147]

As the summer wore on, Clarke said she increasingly fell into a
state of despair. Only weeks after Mekas circulated a memo to Coop
members in which he complained about the financial martyrdom he
had incurred due to the FDC's closing, he publicly announced new
plans to establish a film archive and theater.[148] Calvin Tomkins commented, "Astonishingly enough, money had become available for another Mekas project—a film 'academy' dedicated to showing in repertory, the highest achievements of avant-garde film."[149] Mekas claimed
he had started a fund two years earlier to raise money for the project,
and with enough now accumulated to finance the construction of a
viewing theater and the purchase of a film library, he planned a
December 1970 opening for the new Anthology Film Archives. Clarke
said that she learned about her former partner's plans by reading
about them in the newspaper.[150] Not only had Mekas excluded her
from organizational plans, but he also appeared to be omitting her
work from the repertory. When Clarke tried to discuss the matter with
Mekas, he simply told her that she did not understand the project.[151]

Anthology Film Archives functioned as a self-institutionalization of
independent film history in a museum of cinema art. Sitney described
Anthology Film as an institution that would "formulate, acquire, and
frequently exhibit a nuclear collection of the monuments of cinematic
art."[152] Anthology Film set about canonizing a specific set of films
that would be selected by Sitney, Mekas, Stan Brakhage, Austrian
filmmaker Peter Kubelka, and writer Ken Kelman. Mekas justified
both the committee and its procedure, saying in the most prestigious
art world magazine that their choices were made "according to the
intuitions of some of the best minds making films and writing on
cinema today."[153] Mekas's statement of privileged curatorship reflects
the extent to which events had led him to reverse his initial champion-
ship of all independent films. Now within a united circle of political

allies, the choices made by Mekas and others were inscribed in Anthology Film exhibitions, catalogues, and auxiliary publications that included two books as *the* New York avant-garde cinema.

Clarke was not the only filmmaker angered by the committee's self-congratulatory rhetoric and practices. Numerous other filmmakers and participants of the underground film scene were being left out in the cold. Tomkins noted in passing that the situation itself was ironic since Mekas, "who was often criticized in the past for his 'permissiveness' in showing any film by any filmmaker should now be running a rigorously selective archive."[154] Amos Vogel volunteered another view, "There are really two Jonases—one very dedicated, the other a Machiavellian maneuverer, a history rewriter, an attempted pope. He has two passions: film and power. His greatest talent is to make people—some people—believe that he is what he is not."[155] Vogel's statement looks backward to a schism that developed between the two of them when the Film-Makers' Cooperative was founded. Vogel, as one of the other chief independent film distributors and exhibitors of the 1950s and 1960s, implies retrospectively that the dissension that may have been previously masked in public discourse was explicitly foregrounded after the founding of Anthology Film in 1970.

At one level, Anthology Film's beginnings may be seen as the last ritual of a New York avant-garde in the midst of being decentralized and swallowed up by the larger systems of museum and university film practices. At another level, group movement away from the discourse and practices of commercialism may be understood as an effort to garner a toehold of power among shifting institutional economic bases for avant-garde cinema. What is often lost in narratives of Anthology Film's ascendency is that it represented not simply a new organization's rise to power and accommodation of certain texts into elitist categories but a reconfiguration of powers already present in the avant-garde cinema. Anthology Film's appearance is most significant for the way that it represented a disruption of overtly political film practices and a recuperation of radical cinema potential into safe categories of conservative curatorship.

The significance of Clarke's position throughout the 1960s involved her dominant role in the larger struggles for institutional bases of an independent cinema. Clarke participated in the process by defining a far-reaching, artist-controlled independent cinema system that would be an economic alternative to Hollywood. She may have enjoyed only occasional, singular successes, but she ultimately contributed toward specifying and solidifying independent film's status among the arts, educational and commercial systems. Her films staked out a potentially radical cinematic politics toward representation that may only be fully reclaimed in the 1990s as critics more thoroughly interrogate the intersections of race, gender, and representation politics.

NOTES

1. Shirley Clarke, "Maya Deren," TS, Nov. 1966, Shirley Clarke papers, Wisconsin Center for Film and Theater Research, University of Wisconsin–Madison and the State Historical Society of Wisconsin, Madison.

2. Ibid.

3. Ibid. Quoted with the permission of Shirley Clarke.

4. Ibid. Quoted with the permission of Shirley Clarke.

5. Shirley Clarke, interview with author, Chicago, Illinois, 23 Sept. 1981.

6. Lauren Rabinovitz, "Choreography of Cinema: An Interview with Shirley Clarke," *Afterimage* 11, no. 5 (Dec. 1983): 10.

7. Clarke, "Maya Deren." Quoted with the permission of Shirley Clarke.

8. "The Expensive Arts: A Discussion of Film Distribution and Exhibition in the U.S.," *Film Quarterly* 13, no. 4 (Summer 1960): 31.

9. Shirley Clarke, interview with author, Chicago, Illinois, 24 Sept. 1981.

10. Shirley Clarke, diary, 1967, Shirley Clarke papers.

11. Elaine Tynan, Letter to Shirley Clarke, 6 June 1962, Shirley Clarke papers.

12. Shirley Clarke interview, 24 Sept. 1981. Quoted with the permission of Shirley Clarke.

13. Ibid. Quoted with the permission of Shirley Clarke.

14. See Nik Krevitsky, "Choreographer Workshop," *Dance Observer* 15, no. 9 (Nov. 1948): 122; Doris Hering, "Reviewers Stand," *Dance* 22, no. 12 (Dec. 1948): 35.

15. Shirley Clarke interview, 24 Sept. 1981.

16. Nancy Chodorow, *The Reproduction of Mothering: Psychoanalysis and the Sociology of Gender* (Berkeley: University of California Press, 1978), 51–52.

17. Ibid., 5–6.

18. Shirley Clarke interview, 24 Sept. 1981.

19. Ibid.

20. Gretchen Berg, "Interview with Shirley Clarke," *Film Culture*, no. 44 (Spring 1967): 52.

21. Rabinovitz, "Choreography of Cinema," 8.

22. Berg, "Interview with Shirley Clarke," 52.

23. Marjorie Rosen, "Shirley Clarke: Videospace Explorer," *Ms.* 3, no. 10 (Apr. 1975): 107.

24. Gideon Bachmann, "Interview with Shirley Clarke," MS, Nov. 1955, 22, Shirley Clarke papers. Quoted with the permission of Shirley Clarke.

25. According to Clarke, Buckley was a bullfight aficionado and sometimes

attended the spectacles with his friend Ernest Hemingway; Shirley Clarke interview, 24 Sept. 1981.

26. Shirley Clarke, interview with author, Chicago, Illinois, 26 Sept. 1981.

27. Ibid.

28. For a brief, but complete treatment of *Bells of Atlantis* in this context, see Stuart Liebman, "1949–1958," in *A History of the American Avant-garde Cinema*, ed. John G. Hanhardt (New York: American Federation of the Arts, 1976), 85–91.

29. One might note, however, that Deren herself used dancers superimposed over a starry sky and in reversed or negative image in *The Very Eye of Night*.

30. Howard Thompson, "Big Country in 'Loops,' " *New York Times*, 20 Apr. 1958, sec. 2, p. 7.

After the loop showed in Brussels, all but a few disappeared. Of the loops on which Clarke principally worked, nine are now stored in film archives but are not available for general screenings.

31. Shirley Clarke interview, 26 Sept. 1981. Quoted with the permission of Shirley Clarke.

32. Ibid., 23 Sept. 1981.

33. Ibid.

34. See, for example, Stuart Leibman, "1949–1958," 85; Henry Breitrose, "Films of Shirley Clarke," *Film Quarterly* 13, no. 4 (Summer 1960): 57.

35. Rabinovitz, "Choreography of Cinema," 8–9.

36. Howard Thompson, "The 16mm Honor Roll," *New York Times*, 29 Dec. 1957, sec. 2, p. 5.

37. "The Expensive Arts: A Discussion of Film Distribution and Exhibition in the U.S.," 31. The film was screened in its original 16mm form.

38. Ibid., 30–31.

39. Jonas Mekas, "A Call for a New Generation of Film-makers," *Film Culture*, no. 19 (1959); reprinted in *Film Culture Reader*, ed. P. Adams Sitney (New York: Praeger, 1970), 73–74.

40. P. Adams Sitney, *Visionary Film: The American Avant-garde, 1943–1978*, 2d ed. (New York: Oxford University Press, 1979), 148.

41. Irving Sandler's *The Triumph of American Painting: A History of Abstract Expressionism* (New York: Harper and Row, 1977) has since been regarded as the definitive work describing the development of Abstract Expressionism and its eventual descent into narcissism. For a more recent work that shows greater insight into the generative social mechanisms for Abstract Expressionism, see Max Kozloff, "American Painting during the Cold War," in *Pollock and After: The Critical Debate*, ed. Francis Frascina (New York: Harper and Row, 1985), 107–23.

42. Barbara Haskell, as quoted in Diana Crane, *The Transformation of the Avant-garde: The New York Art World, 1940–1985* (Chicago: University of Chicago Press, 1987), 25.

43. Crane, *The Transformation of the Avant-garde*, 29–30.

44. Shirley Clarke interview, 26 Sept. 1981.

45. While he also assisted on *Skyscraper,* Pennebaker simultaneously directed *Opening in Moscow* (1958), a film about conductor Leonard Bernstein's concert tour in the Soviet Union. Clarke coedited the film, and Ricky Leacock and Albert Maysles assisted Pennebaker. Such collaborative practices also strongly influenced Clarke's development as a documentary filmmaker.

46. Joyce Chopra said that untrained women got hired to take sound (which was considered of secondary importance) because the cinéma vérité filmmaker "wanted a nice girl" with whom to travel; Chopra, as quoted in Jan Rosenberg, *Women's Reflections: The Feminist Film Movement* (Ann Arbor, Mich.: UMI Research Press, 1983), 34.

47. Rabinovitz, "Choreography of Cinema," 9.

48. James Blue, "One Man's Truth—An Interview with Richard Leacock," *Film Comment* 3, no. 2 (Spring 1965): 18, emphasis mine.

49. Robert C. Allen and Douglas Gomery, *Film History: Theory and Practice* (New York: Alfred A. Knopf, 1985), 234.

50. Kozloff, "American Painting during the Cold War," 116.

51. Haskell, as quoted in Crane, *The Transformation of the Avant-garde,* 31.

52. Lawrence Alloway, as quoted in Kozloff, "American Painting during the Cold War," 118.

53. Shirley Clarke interview, 26 Sept. 1981.

54. Ibid.

55. Emile de Antonio, as quoted in Barbara Zheutlin, "The Art and Politics of the Documentary: A Symposium," *Cineaste* 11, no. 3 (1981): 16.

56. Frederick Wiseman, as quoted in Alan Rosenthal, *The New Documentary in Action: A Casebook in Film Making* (Berkeley: University of California Press, 1971), 70.

57. Stephen Mamber, *Cinema Verite in America: Studies in Uncontrolled Documentary* (Cambridge, Mass.: MIT Press, 1974), 138.

58. Ibid., 117.

59. Ibid.

60. George Bluestone, "The Intimate Television Documentary," *Television Quarterly* 4, no. 2 (Spring 1965): 52.

61. See, for example, Jeanne Allen, "Self-reflexivity in Documentary," *Cinétracts* 1, no. 2 (Summer 1977): 37–43; Richard M. Blumenberg, "Documentary Films and the Problem of 'Truth,'" *Journal of the University Film Association* 29, no. 4 (1977): 19–22; Annette Kuhn, "The Camera I: Observations on Documentary," *Screen* 19, no. 2 (Summer 1978): 71–83; Julia Lesage, "The Political Aesthetics of the Feminist Documentary Film," *Quarterly Review of Film Studies* 3, no. 4 (1978): 507–23; Bill Nichols, "Documentary Theory and Practice," *Screen* 17, no. 4 (Winter 1976–77): 34–48; Jay Ruby, "The Image Mirrored: Reflexivity and the Documentary Film," *Journal of the University Film Association* 29, no. 4 (1977): 3–11; Vivian Sobchack, "'No Lies': Direct Cinema as Rape," *Journal of the University Film Association* 29, no. 4 (1977): 13–18; Brian Winston, "Documentary: I Think We Are in Trouble," *Sight and Sound* 48, no. 1 (Winter 1978–79): 2–7.

62. Larry Gross, "Life vs. Art: The Interpretation of Visual Narratives," *Studies in Visual Communication* 11, no. 4 (Fall 1985): 10.

63. Penelope Gilliatt, "The Connection," *Sight and Sound* 30, no. 3 (Summer 1961): 145.

64. Jeanne Allen, "Self-reflexivity in Documentary," 42.

65. For example, see Louis Calta, review of *The Connection, New York Times,* 16 July 1959, 30, and Brooks Atkinson, review of *The Connection, New York Times,* 7 Feb. 1960, 11; H. B. Lutz, "Some Words on 'The Connection,' " *Village Voice* 4, no. 41 (5 Aug. 1959), 11; Jerry Tallmer, "Theater: *The Connection,*" *Village Voice* 4, no. 39 (22 July 1959), 9; and Jonas Mekas, "Theater: Look Out! Poets at Work," *Village Voice* 5, no. 11 (6 Jan. 1960), 5.

A sample of contemporary reviews includes Robert Brustein, "Junkies and Jazz," *New Republic* 141, no. 13 (28 Sept. 1959): 29–30; Harold Clurman, review of *The Connection, Nation* 189, no. 4 (15 Aug. 1959): 80; Henry Hewes, "Broadway Postscript: Miracle on Fourteenth Street," *Saturday Review* 42 (26 Sept. 1959): 27; Donald Malcolm, "Off Broadway: Drug on the Market," *New Yorker* 35, no. 34 (10 Oct. 1959): 126–28; David Newman, "Four Make a Wave," *Esquire* 55, no. 4 (Apr. 1961): 45–51.

66. For example, see the reviews of *The Connection* by Donald Malcolm, Robert Brustein, and Jerry Tallmer.

67. Newman, "Four Make a Wave."

68. Elayne Zalis, "Cross-examining the Lawmakers: *The Connection* (Play and Film) as Seen through Patriarchal Eyes," University of Iowa, 1986, 9–11.

69. Ibid.

70. Ibid., 16.

71. Donald Richie, "Letter from Cannes," *Nation* 192, no. 24 (17 June 1961): 527.

72. Ibid.; see "Strolling the Croisette," *Variety,* 10 May 1961, Shirley Clarke papers.

73. *Film Francaise,* as quoted in Richie, "Letter from Cannes," 527.

74. European Newspaper Clippings file, Shirley Clarke papers.

75. Clarke, as quoted in Richie, "Letter from Cannes," 527.

76. Mosk, "Cannes Film Fest Pictures," *Variety,* 10 May 1961, 19.

77. "The First Statement of the New American Cinema Group," *Film Culture,* nos. 22–23 (Summer 1961); reprinted in *Film Culutre Reader,* ed. P. Adams Sitney (New York: Praeger, 1970), 79–83.

78. Ibid., 81.

79. David E. James, *Allegories of Cinema: American Film in the Sixties* (Princeton, N.J.: Princeton University Press, 1989), 87.

80. "How to Get a Free Hand in American Film-making," *London Times,* 17 June 1961, C5.

81. Ibid.

82. Gideon Bachmann, "Vers un cinéma 'expressif,' " *Cinéma* 61, no. 56 (May 1961): 22; "The Connection," *La vie americain,* no. 16 (July 1961): 27–29; Gideon Bachmann, "Vers un nouveau cinéma americain: 'Connection' et la recherche du réel," *La gazette littéraire,* 12 Nov. 1961, 17.

83. Richie, "Letter from Cannes," 526.

84. Ibid.

85. Melinda Ward, "Shirley Clarke: An Interview," in *The American New Wave, 1958–1967*, ed. Melinda Ward and Bruce Jenkins (Minneapolis and Buffalo: Walker Art Center and Media Study, 1982), 20.

86. See New York State Board of Regents v. *The Connection* Company, 12 NY2d 779, (New York State Court of Appeals 1962). The legal documents cover the decisions and proceedings throughout 1961 and 1962 as reported in the Appellant's Brief, the Record on Appeal, and the Respondent's Brief.

87. Bosley Crowther, "Choice of Words: Let the Film-makers Pick Their Own," *New York Times*, 11 Feb. 1962, sec. 2, p. 1.

88. "Ban By-passed: 'Connection' at Judson Church," *The Village Voice* 7, no. 52 (18 Oct. 1962): 10.

89. Jonas Mekas, *Movie Journal: The Rise of the New American Cinema, 1959–1971* (New York: Collier Books, 1972), 61.

90. See, for example, Tim J. Kelly, " 'Connection' Compels, Repels," *Arizona Republic* (Phoenix), 16 Feb. 1962, 56, Shirley Clarke papers; Maggie Savoy, "Controversial Film Scores by Stressing Reality," *Arizona Republic*, 13 Feb. 1962, Shirley Clarke papers.

91. Eugene Archer, "Court Upsets State's Obscenity Ban on 'Connection,' " *New York Times*, 3 July 1962, Shirley Clarke papers; James L. Conners, "Appellate Okay of 'The Connection': But Will Circuits Risk Public Reaction?" *Variety*, 11 July 1962, Shirley Clarke papers; Arthur Schlesinger, Jr., "Pads, Preston and Politics," *Show*, Aug. 1962, Shirley Clarke papers.

92. Eugene Archer, "Woman Director Makes the Scene," *New York Times Magazine*, 26 Aug. 1962, 46.

93. Ward, "Shirley Clarke: An Interview," 20.

94. For example, Archer Winsten, " 'Connection' Bows at New Griffith," *New York Post*, 4 Oct. 1962, Shirley Clarke papers; William Specht, "Court Halts Showing of 'The Connection,' " *Film Daily*, 4 Oct. 1962, Shirley Clarke papers; Beverly Gary, "Film Director," *New York Post*, 18 Oct. 1962, Shirley Clarke papers; Jonas Mekas, "Movie Journal: Open Letter to the New York Daily Movie Critics," *Village Voice* 7, no. 51 (11 Oct. 1962), 13.

95. Lewis Allen, Letter to Investors in *The Connection*, 3 Nov. 1962, Shirley Clarke Papers.

96. Ibid.

97. Albert Bermel, "Young Lady with a Camera," *Escapade* 10, no. 5 (May 1967): 78.

98. Bosley Crowther, "The Connection," *New York Times*, 4 Oct. 1962, 44.

99. Many of the following insights and observations about *The Cool World* are the results of discussions with Todd Boyd during the spring and summer of 1989 as well as Douglas Loranger's presentation of the film for my class at the University of Iowa in the spring of 1989.

100. Noël Carroll, *"Nothing but a Man/The Cool World,"* in *The*

American New Wave, 1958–1967, eds. Melinda Ward and Bruce Jenkins, 41–42.

101. A Chicago audience at the 1983 Black Light Festival on black cinema at the Art Institute of Chicago expressed this opinion about *The Cool World.*

102. "The Sad Boppers," *Newsweek* 63, no. 16 (20 Apr. 1964): 114.

103. In this context, it is interesting that her final appearance is more thematically than literally set in relation to Duke. While the cops drive him away at the end of the film, his mother is leaning on the shoulder of a new boyfriend as they weave down the street outside her apartment.

104. Carroll, *"Nothing but a Man/The Cool World,"* 41–42.

105. "Conference on *The Cool World,*" transcript, 23 Oct. 1963, Shirley Clarke papers.

106. Ibid.

107. Ibid.

108. For a sample of reviews, see Hollis Alpert, "Mood Ebony," *Saturday Review,* 25 Apr. 1964, Shirley Clarke papers; "A Child of Mother Harlem," *Time,* 17 Apr. 1964, Shirley Clarke papers; Judith Crist, "The New Movies," *New York Herald Tribune,* 21 Apr. 1964, Shirley Clarke papers; Bosley Crowther, "Screen: Fighting to the Top in Harlem," *New York Times,* 21 Apr. 1964, 42; Robert Hatch, "Films," *The Nation,* 27 Apr. 1964, 447–48, Shirley Clarke papers; Gordon Hitchens, "The Cool World," *Film Comment* 2, no. 2 (Spring 1964): 52–53; Mike McGrady, " 'The Cool World' Is the Other America," *Newsday,* 21 Apr. 1964, Shirley Clarke papers; Richard Oulahan, "Low-budget Realism, Warts and All," *Life,* 24 Apr. 1964, Shirley Clarke papers; Harriet Polt, "The Cool World," *Film Quarterly* 17, no. 2 (Winter 1963–64): 33–35; "The Sad Boppers," 114; Andrew Sarris, "The Cool World—Review," *Village Voice,* 23 Apr. 1964, 16, Shirley Clarke papers; Jesse Walker, "Film Reviews: The Cool World," *Film Comment* 2, no. 2 (Spring 1964): 51–52; Archer Winsten, " 'The Cool World' at the Cinema II," *New York Post,* 21 Apr. 1964, 22, Shirley Clarke papers.

109. See, in particular, Ann Geracimos, "What Makes Harlem Go," *New York Tribune,* 12 May 1964, Shirley Clarke papers; Leroy McLucas, "Shirley Clarke Shooting 'The Cool World,' " *Film Culture,* no. 27 (1962–63): 37.

110. See, for example, Shirley Clarke, "The Cool World," *Films and Filming* 10, no. 3 (Dec. 1963): 7–8; Harriet Polt, "Interview with Shirley Clarke," *Film Comment* 2, no. 2 (Spring 1964): 31–32.

111. Ibid.

112. During this time period, Clarke was also working on a documentary for public television broadcast, *Robert Frost: A Lover's Quarrel with the World.*

113. Shirley Clarke, "Statement: Whys and Wherefores of The Cool World," TS, 1964, Shirley Clarke papers. Quoted with the permission of Shirley Clarke.

114. Shirley Clarke interview, 26 Sept. 1981.

115. Ibid.

116. Shirley Clarke, as quoted in Susan Rice, "Shirley Clarke: Image and Images," *Take One* 3, no. 2 (Nov.–Dec. 1970): 21.

117. Fred Wiseman, Letter to Shirley Clarke, 1969, Shirley Clarke papers.

118. Ibid., 1965, Shirley Clarke papers; Shirley Clarke, Letter to Fred Wiseman, 29 Sept. 1969, Shirley Clarke papers; Shirley Clarke, Letter to Fred Wiseman, 23 Aug. 1970, Shirley Clarke papers.

119. "Talk of the Town," *New Yorker*, 39, no. 30 (14 Sept. 1963): 33.

120. Robert Hughes, Letter to Shirley Clarke, Apr. 1964, Shirley Clarke papers; Gibson A. Danes, Letter to Shirley Clarke, 14 May 1964, Shirley Clarke papers.

121. Shirley Clarke interview, 26 Sept. 1981. Quoted with the permission of Shirley Clarke.

122. Clarke, Letter to Fred Wiseman, 23 Aug. 1970; Shirley Clarke interview, 26 Sept. 1981.

123. Clarke, Letter to Fred Wiseman, 23 Aug. 1970; Rice, "Shirley Clarke: Image and Images," 21.

124. Crane, *The Transformation of the Avant-Garde*, 33.

125. Alan Solomon, former director of the Jewish Museum, as quoted in Calvin Tomkins, "Moving with the Flow," *New Yorker* 47, no. 38 (6 Nov. 1971): 59.

126. J. Hoberman and Jonathan Rosenbaum, *Midnight Movies* (New York: Harper and Row, 1983), 70.

127. Although Clarke was a member of the Coop's board of directors, she was nominally active in the organization.

128. Amos Vogel, "Brakhage, Brecht, Berlin, Eden West and East," *Village Voice* 10, no. 10 (23 Dec. 1965), Shirley Clarke papers.

129. Two brief but detailed discussions of *Chelsea Girls* may be found in Hoberman and Rosenbaum, *Midnight Movies*, 70–73; David E. James, *Allegories of Cinema*, 70–74.

130. Calvin Tomkins, "All Pockets Open," *New Yorker* 48, no. 46 (6 Jan. 1973): 44.

131. Mekas, *Movie Journal*, 278.

132. Tomkins, "All Pockets Open," 45.

133. David C. Stewart, *Film Study in Higher Education* (Washington, D.C.: American Council on Education, 1966), 166.

134. Mekas, *Movie Journal*, 343.

135. Tomkins, "All Pockets Open," 44.

136. Film-Makers Cooperative, "Film Income Sheet: *The Connection*," 1967, Shirley Clarke papers.

137. Nora E. Taylor, "Finding a Market for 'Personal Cinema,' " *Christian Science Monitor*, 14 Sept. 1968, 10.

138. Betty Kronsky, "Jason OutJasons All Reviewers—This One Too," *Village Voice* 12, no. 52 (12 Oct. 1967): 33–34.

139. Parker Tyler, *Underground Film: A Critical History* (New York: Grove Press, 1969), 40.

140. For a discussion of *David Holzman's Diary*, see "Jim McBride," in *Autobiography: Film/Video/Photography*, ed. John Stuart Katz (Toronto: Art Gallery of Ontario, 1978), 62; David E. James, *Allegories of Cinema*, 286–89.

141. Film-Makers Distribution Center, "*Portrait of Jason* Summary Report," 1967, Shirley Clarke papers.

142. Ibid.

143. Tomkins, "All Pockets Open," 45.

144. Ibid., 46.

145. Ibid.

146. Jonas Mekas, Letters to Shirley Clarke, 1970, Shirley Clarke papers.

147. Rosen, "Shirley Clarke: Videospace Explorer," 108.

148. Tomkins, "All Pockets Open," 46.

149. Ibid., 47.

150. Rabinovitz, "Choreography of Cinema," 10.

151. Shirley Clarke interview, 23 Sept. 1981.

152. P. Adams Sitney, ed. *The Essential Cinema: Essays on the Films in the Collection of Anthology Film Archives* (New York: New York University Press and Anthology Film Archives, 1975), v-xii.

153. Jonas Mekas, "Letter to the Editor," *Artforum* 10, no. 1 (Sept. 1971).

154. Tomkins, "All Pockets Open," 48.

155. Ibid., 37.

6

Joyce Wieland and the Ascendancy of Structural Film

Joyce Wieland first met Shirley Clarke in 1963 when Wieland was a young woman starting out in the New York City art world. Instead of frequenting the places where she would most likely meet other painters, Wieland was drawn to Jonas Mekas's midnight screenings at the Grammercy Arts Theatre. Each week, people brought in both finished and unfinished films, some of them little more than idiosyncratic home movies. Mekas democratically projected each submission, and then the small audience discussed, argued, and fought over the film. Wieland was affected not so much by what she saw on the screen as by what was happening around her. The communal spirit at the informal, relaxed shows made Wieland feel like she was still at home in Toronto.[1] The heady atmosphere created the impression that, in independent filmmaking, the best interests of the artisan-producers motivated the practices of an entire system.

Clarke, whose experimental films were already a success and who had helped to initiate organizational practices for the New American Cinema, was one of the first who personally assured Wieland that she was welcome in this community as a filmmaker as much as an observer. It impressed Wieland that the director of *The Connection,* a woman who had controlled the almost all-male cast and crew of a feature film and who knew everyone at Mekas's screenings, should seek out a shy newcomer for expressions of comradeship, "She was so sympathetic, and she really was encouraging. . . . I was terrified of the art scene, and something in me couldn't get it together to make anything for that scene. . . . But with the underground filmmakers, it was loose. You could make mistakes."[2] Soon, Wieland was bringing new "bits of film" that she had made to the Grammercy, "It was like having a home. . . . We had a place where things could be relevant and shown. . . . It would be like coming to church. The audience was a family of filmmakers."[3]

Wieland's "family" shortly included many filmmakers—Ken and Florence Jacobs, George and Mike Kuchar, Hollis Frampton, Betty and Graeme Ferguson, Barbara Rubin and Jonas Mekas, as well as Shirley Clarke. When she finished her most ambitious and personal film of the early 1960s (*Water Sark*), she showed it privately to Clarke. Clarke liked the film so much that she helped Wieland launch it with a positive critical review for the Film-Makers' Cooperative catalogue.[4] Two years later when Clarke decided to make a documentary on the Soviet poet André Vosnesensky, she hired Wieland and Barbara Rubin as her crew.[5] In this way and others, Clarke was the role model and friend to Wieland that Deren had been to her.

Like Clarke and Deren before her, Wieland became a well-known woman filmmaker in the downtown Greenwich Village world of the avant-garde cinema. Like both Clarke and Deren, she made experimental and documentary films that addressed the conditions of contemporary alienation. She, too, analyzed the politics of representation and worked from a position of investigating her own marginalization and, like Deren's and Clarke's experiences, Wieland's films were not necessarily understood for these strategies when they first appeared.

But unlike Deren and Clarke, Wieland assumed a role solely as a filmmaker-producer within the New York art world. She relied upon organizational structures already established as the means to disseminate and promote her art. Her position as an artist of the avant-garde cinema was constituted not through the multifaceted roles that her predecessors sought and occupied but according to spheres of specialization in artistic practices. In this context, the most politically radical, gender-specific features of her films were the most suppressed in existing discourses of contemporary critical aesthetics, whereas Wieland herself always understood her work within terms of sexual difference. Both the increasing narrowness of the theoretical and critical discourse surrounding the New York filmmakers in the latter half of the 1960s as well as Wieland's limited power as a woman filmmaker to participate in that discourse ultimately led her away from the New York avant-garde cinema. As she increasingly rethought her social role as an artist and adopted Deren's and Clarke's model, she applied her expanded sense of an artist's activities not to "improving" the New York avant-garde but to defining a unified network of independent film practices outside what had become the established avant-garde center. She took Deren's and Clarke's models for the woman filmmaker out of New York City and spread them beyond the United States.

Joyce Wieland: The Young Woman as a Canadian Painter

By the time she arrived in New York City in 1963, Wieland had already developed a reputation in Toronto as a woman who made paintings that flaunted social conventions. One Toronto art critic reviewing her first show in 1959 likened Wieland to cartoonist-humorist James Thurber.[6] But more often than not, Wieland had shocked and angered the parochial Toronto art world. The critics reacted hostilely to the graphic sexual imagery in her sometimes autobiographical and often capricious paintings about women's sexual and social experiences.

Wieland came to artistic maturity in a city undergoing a transition in its attitudes and practices regarding contemporary art. The importance of New York City's postwar emergence as a world art center overshadowed all other independent art practices in the Canadian regional capital. While Abstract Expressionism conquered critics and curators on its home front in the United States, it was also exported to Europe and Canada. Since it had been dominated in the 1950s by American economic and cultural colonization, Toronto emulated "things American"; it capitalized on New York City's geographic proximity investing in and mimicking Abstract Expressionism.[7]

Local critics as well as the increasing number of new galleries drew public attention to the young Abstract Expressionist artists of Wieland's generation early in their careers. Art critic Barrie Hale described the phenomenon by which Toronto promoted its own Abstract Expressionists, "Something of the storybook romance of the young painter struggling in his atelier, thinking, thinking, working, working, the enormous pressures of his exquisite sensibilities exploding in mad bohemian parties, had invaded the Toronto imagination. . . . The young artist—as iconoclast, as innovator, as romantic seeker and increasingly as public figure—had invaded the consciousness of [the] city."[8] In a community filled with "boosterism," Wieland exhibited between 1960 to 1963 her work of the past decade.

Wieland's earliest drawings and paintings, done in the early and middle 1950s in the studio in which she lived alone, were most often reflections on her family and childhood. They exhibited the combination of humor, sentimentality, and rebellion against convention that is representative of all her subsequent paintings and films. But in this case, they expiated a bittersweet childhood and established the importance of autobiographical themes. Whereas many artists began their careers with autobiographical subjects but shunned self-referential topics once they achieved mature styles, Wieland made what is personal a point of celebration throughout her career. The personal was, perhaps, initially important to Wieland because she was orphaned when she was nine and has dim memories and only a few recollections of a carefree childhood.[9] Wieland's father was a British music hall performer who deserted his first wife and children when he met a sixteen-year-old runaway girl in London; they left for Canada after their two children were born.[10] Joyce was born in Toronto on June 30, 1931.

The small family's fortunes went badly in Canada. Wieland's father died in Toronto in 1938, and her mother's death followed in 1940. Once her parents died, Wieland's older brother departed, and her eighteen-year-old sister Joan took a factory job to support Joyce and herself. The two girls lived in a series of downtown Toronto rooming houses, and Joyce helped with such odd jobs as shoveling snow, selling scratch sheets at the racetrack, and drawing pin-ups for local boys.[11] Such Dickensian circumstances separated Wieland from other school children her own age and led her to find solace in her drawings and illustrations.

With encouragement from her sister, Wieland studied art when she attended Toronto Central Technical High School from 1946 to 1949. She learned from women artists unable to get college teaching posts in the years immediately following World War II because returning members of the armed forces received preferential job treatment. At a time when North American culture embodied ambivalent attitudes toward career women as well as toward artists in general, Wieland's teachers and sister comprised her adult role models.

But Wieland had trouble being taken seriously as an artist. When she apprenticed at an advertising company after she graduated from high school, she spent most of her time washing brushes and getting coffee.[12] When she worked for Graphics Animation, an animated film company composed of former National Film Board of Canada filmmakers and young Toronto artists, she felt that if she showed her ignorance when doing something new she would either be replaced or treated condescendingly.[13]

Wieland's status as a serious artist was further compromised by the fact that she was more likely to be known as the wife of a major artist than for her own work. In 1956, Wieland married Michael Snow, a painter with whom she worked at Graphics. Wieland's marriage meant the end of her own studio because Wieland and Snow could not afford a home and two studios.[14] Her move home symbolized the beginning of her twenty-year deference to Snow's career as she herself confessed, "I was on my way in a sense to becoming an artist's-wife type artist."[15]

Not untypical for women coming-of-age in the late 1950s, Wieland assumed the woman's traditional role in her marriage, thereby splitting her identity, energy, and time among her roles as a homemaker, wife, and artist. Snow, freed from any domestic responsibilities and obligations, had already established his reputation as Canada's most promising young painter by the time Wieland received her first public recognition as an artist three years later. When Snow also overshadowed Wieland's importance as an avant-garde filmmaker a decade later in New York City, Wieland had to cope all over again with the frustration of being remembered primarily as an artist's wife.[16] Wieland is an exemplary case of Virginia Woolf's artist without "a room of her own," illustrating how such circumstances and socially inscribed conditions of male privilege have excluded women from becoming "authors."[17] Like countless other women, Wieland had to work at her art part-time, interrupted and distracted by domestic responsibilities, but she produced a body of work in spite of this.

Snow and Wieland, however, did play major supporting roles in each other's careers. Snow, older and better educated, introduced Wieland to new intellectual currents and responded encouragingly to her work.[18] Wieland reciprocated by introducing Snow to Canadian nationalist issues and getting him involved in Canadian artists' political organizations. Wieland has always acknowledged Snow's influence but likes to discuss it less often than do her critics.[19] Conversely, Snow and his critics rarely mention or acknowledge Wieland's influence on him.[20]

Because Toronto art dealers were eager to develop local talent, Wieland received careful consideration and, in a relatively brief period, she achieved fame as an important contemporary artist. After her first one-woman show in 1960, Wieland signed with Avrom Isaacs's Isaacs Gallery, one of Toronto's leading dealers for contemporary art. Like the New York City gallery system, Toronto's art world tended to support only those artists associated with a couple of leading galleries, and once the Isaacs Gallery picked up Wieland, it established her among the Toronto avant-garde elite. Between 1960 and 1963, Wieland exhibited in Toronto, Winnipeg, and the United States. Her drawings, paintings, and collages were bought by individual and corporate collectors as well as by museums and colleges. In this situation, Wieland encountered less discrimination than many of her American contemporaries who were similarly married to more famous artists and could not get art dealers to look at their work or to represent them. Unlike Lee Krasner, Elaine De Kooning, and even Helen Frankenthaler, Wieland was not so eclipsed by a more famous husband as she might have been starting out in New York City.

The style of Wieland's paintings and drawings specified the importance of intimate points of view, women's identities, and the relationship between personal and collective Canadian experience. *Laura Secord Saves Upper Canada* (1961), for example, is an Abstract

Expressionist painting that Wieland said resulted from her early memories of school.[21] It literally employs the written gestures, colors, and artifacts found in an elementary school classroom. A complementary blue and orange impasto are the ground for a Union Jack flag, a toy airplane, and white figures that resemble scrawls on a blackboard. By also referring to the Canadian patriot Laura Secord who walked miles in 1812 to warn the British that the Americans planned to invade Canada, *Laura Secord* intertwines personal memories of childhood innocence with the collective memories of Canadian and women's histories.

When Wieland began painting the more intangible, self-proclaimed subject of women's wombs and biological fertility cycles, her canvases grew in scale. Large ovoid shapes filled the centers of paintings that the artist classified as "sex poetry."[22] She retrospectively said that the subject matter belonged to a period in her life when she was coping with her inability to bear children.[23]

Beginning in 1960, these paintings were lightly colored and executed by staining or soaking the paint into untreated canvas. Feminist critics such as Lucy Lippard claimed more than a decade later that this style of painting was a uniquely female expressiveness within Abstract Expressionism.[24] Lippard argues that "central-core imagery," like that which organizes much of Wieland's work from this time period, exists throughout the works of several leading women abstractionists. Using Helen Frankenthaler's stained landscapes as her most notable example, she claims that this pictorial structure is a historical means for disguising uniquely female experience or content in an idiomatic rendering of Abstract Expressionism.[25] While the particulars of her Feminine categorization have been contested, Lippard offers a purposeful critical argument for recognizing difference between women's and men's Abstract Expressionist productions.

One may use Wieland's *Balling* (1961) as an illustrative example. The painting's title describes large concentric circles that define a pink field, two smaller globes flanking the pink area, and a small circular center. As a slang term for sexual intercourse, the title also refers to the painting as a representation of an erect penis viewed extremely close up. But, as a former curator of the Art Gallery of Ontario points out, the painting is composed of "huge, amoeba-like shapes [which] are hermaphroditic, open to interpretation as womb and penis."[26] The vantage point offered to the spectator lacks any sense of depth, thereby alluding to phallic pleasure without representing phallic proportions. For example, overlapping concentric circles rendered flatly in a spray of green paint concentrate dynamic energy in the painting's core. An arrow pointing up to a circle in the left-hand corner and an arrow

pointing down to a circle in the right-hand quadrant further stabilize
the central area itself as the spatial core of pleasure. The very act of
stain painting itself soaks the image into the canvas rather than building up layers of paint through accretion. *Balling* subverts a traditional
pornographic representation of the penis as a powerful weapon and
remaps erotic potential through "feminized" vocabulary. The diffused
tints of pinks and greens (colors also associated with spring flowers)
are clichéd colors associated with feminine sensuality and delicacy. The
concentration of tension around a centered ovoid thereby becomes an
almost iconic representation of the womb.

Although it may be tempting to categorize such manifest "feminine"
content as subconsciously feminist or belonging to an Eternal Feminine, the labels themselves are ultimately more problematic than productive. Wieland's paintings rely upon vocabulary associated with culturally constructed notions of womanliness, that is to say, values about
femininity formed within patriarchal structures of discourse. As Kay
Armatage has pointed out, recent feminist critical theory would claim
that they instead offer "an approach to sexuality which is clearly prefeminist, particularly in [their] absorption with phallic pleasure."[27]
The very term *feminism* here refers to a historically constituted set of
social relations, ideas, and practices associated with the resurgence of
the women's movement in the late 1960s and 1970s that these paintings
predate. Their significance rather lies in the way they both inscribe a
poetics of difference within Abstract Expressionism and refer to the
artist herself as "Other" within the Toronto art world.

The reception of Wieland's work pivoted on her stature as a woman
artist. Critics wrote more about her presence as a professional artist
than about the aesthetic issues that were usually the subject of dominant critical discourse. For example, Barrie Hale's articles about Wieland are preoccupied with her gender and issues of conventional
feminine behavior. Even his favorable newspaper review of her work
appears under a headline identifying Wieland as "Artist, Canadian,
Soft, Tough, Woman!"[28] When critics did write about Wieland's artistic
style, they said that her symbolic depiction of male and female sexual
anatomy was shocking. Perhaps unwittingly adding fuel to the fire,
Wieland herself responded within the confines of these terms, "If all
I wanted to do was shock, I'd just go down to the street and expose
myself."[29] It may be as much because of her gender as in spite of it
that Wieland acquired a reputation as a local celebrity.

When Wieland, like her contemporaries, reintroduced figuration
in her paintings from 1962 to 1964, the political candor of her work
became even more explicit. The heyday of Abstract Expressionism

had faded, and most artists' styles evolved into the vocabulary of newly fashionable Pop Art. North American Pop artists covered their canvases with recognizable images of popular culture—like product package design, comic strips, pin-ups—as a means for celebrating and satirizing the brutality of contemporary culture. Much of Pop Art's commercial success rested on the fact that the public felt more comfortable with pictorial content manifested in recognizable representation. But Wieland simply transferred and translated her former preoccupation to the Pop Art aesthetic: the penis became her iconic trademark for satirical commentary. Now, more easily recognizable phallic images of rising and falling cigarettes, airplanes, and hot dogs were interspersed with graphic depictions of the penis.

Wieland's drawings, paintings, and assemblages became the targets of even greater critical discomfort. Expressions of outrage occurred in Toronto, a town famous for its prudery.[30] One story about a man who strolled into the Isaacs Gallery during one of Wieland's exhibitions drives the point home. The man did not so much express his displeasure at the paintings but at the idea that "members of the more delicate sex" should be allowed in the vicinity of such vulgarity.[31] He was particularly embarrassed because a woman was standing near him. When he discreetly explained his views to this woman and suggested that she leave the room, he did not think it was funny that he was talking to the artist.[32]

Wieland's tendency to shock the male critics and audience alike frequently resulted in her critical dismissal. One critic, who said that Wieland had a "strange and sick" sense of humor, refused to discuss her work in serious critical terms, "There are parts of the body that one simply doesn't expect to see singled out and painted in such aroused form all over the canvas."[33] Even one of Wieland's earliest and staunchest supporters among local art critics expressed nervousness about the work as well as about the artist, "She comes on strong, she does, certainly as a woman, and as an artist."[34] Only occasionally was a critic as untroubled by a woman's audacity as the *Toronto Daily Star* reporter who said, "Not only is this show a marvelous nose thumb at pomposity and fatuousness in art and society. It indicates, too, that Miss Wieland has found some very personal and original answers to the good old problems of time, space and the picture frame."[35]

Wieland's Pop Art canvases are painterly storyboards divided into a series of squares in which action occurs sequentially. Some are horizontally arranged like comic strips, others are vertical formats that imitate the look of the filmstrip or animator's flip-book (not so surprising for someone who had formerly worked at Graphics Animation).

In *Nature Mixes* (1962), for example, Wieland's allusion to spring flowers in the colors of *Balling* is made explicit as a pink hand framed by a green background metamorphosizes frame by frame into a flower and then into a penis. *Nature Mixes* is a wry vision that asserts cinematic mutability is a metaphor for the organic integration of the world.

Despite the mixture of positive and negative critical reactions to her work, Wieland was happy in Toronto. She herself later claimed that she preferred the "folksy" environment of the Toronto art scene in 1963 to the more cosmopolitan art capital of New York City.[36] She admitted to being terrified of the intense competition, pressure, and high financial stakes of the New York art gallery system.[37] Snow, however, felt that Manhattan would provide a better environment for artistic growth as well as for more prestigious critical attention, so Wieland accompanied her husband to New York City in 1963.[38]

Wieland's new life in the congested urban environment of downtown Manhattan initially frightened her, and it led to a personal preoccupation with themes of disaster. As a Canadian outsider, she was unaccustomed to the degree of violence she generally experienced in American urban culture.[39] The public assassinations of President John F. Kennedy and Lee Harvey Oswald occurred shortly after her arrival. Surrounded by grotesque tragedies, Wieland introduced a disaster motif into paintings and assemblages that were bolder and more exuberant than her earlier work. Although she had introduced nosediving airplanes into her filmstrip sequence paintings in Toronto, her New York paintings reduce numbers of accidents to artlessly drawn comic strips. Boats sink, airplanes fall, and ocean liners crash, hinting at the way contemporary media have saturated and alienated social sensitivity to violence. More important, however, Wieland equates the social situation with a sexual one. The rising and falling phallic airplanes in her paintings or the smashed toy jet, red plastic heart, and lipstick-stained coffee mugs in the assemblage *Cooling Room, No. 2* (1964) make an apparent analogy between sexual icons and modern, technologized death on a large scale.[40]

Wieland and Structural Film

Once Wieland had become part of the regular crowd at Mekas's Film-Makers Showcases, she and Snow were also often at Ken Jacobs's weekly screenings in his loft under the Brooklyn Bridge.[41] Watching new 8mm movies made by Jacobs and others, Wieland began working in the more "primitive," home-movie format. In *Patriotism, Part II* (1964), for example, Wieland adapts her painterly themes and vocabulary to create a Pop Art 8mm film. She employs live-action, stop-motion techniques so that hot dogs march across a bed and a man's body in time to a John Phillip Sousa march. The finale links phallic and patriotic signs as icons of political domination when a row of marching American flags wrap themselves around the hot dogs.

In contrast to the vision of a world ruled by the phallus that she was developing in films and paintings, Wieland also cinematically imagined one small space where there was no such domination. In *Water Sark* (1965), she represents a woman's familiar domestic space as the site for feminine self-discovery. In an autobiographical diary of the house-wife at her kitchen table, a domestic altar is a world of aesthetic beauty—exciting colors, tones, textures, compositions. Using mirrors, prisms, glasses of water, and magnifying glasses as refractory media, Wieland filmed herself filming the objects around her. Her emphasis on the images' physicality, sensuality, and spirituality legitimizes and ultimately ritualizes a woman's cinematic self-discovery in the same manner that Stan Brakhage and others celebrated male self-identification in the late 1950s. But at the very moment Wieland was reworking an established model of filmmaking for her mystical celebration of woman as an introspective subject, the dominant aesthetic direction of avant-garde cinema was shifting.

By 1965, a new style had emerged in the New York avant-garde community, a style that capitalized on Andy Warhol's highly publicized cinematic experiments from 1963 to 1965. Later known as "structural films" when P. Adams Sitney first used the label in 1969, the new movies assumed a rigorously intellectual and self-reflexive stance on the formal processes of filmmaking.[42] With a force unequaled by any other contemporary avant-garde film, Warhol's films had attacked the past decade's romantic films of self-discovery. *Kiss, Sleep,* and *Blow Job*—each constructed of a few takes from a static position extended over long periods of time (*Sleep* was more than six hours long)—seemed to insult the Modernist insistence that art was a pure expression of the filmmaker's subconscious. The films, by showing the activities that the titles describe, instead posed as a kind of anti-art.

Beyond the small community of filmmakers where they were first shown, Warhol's films became celebrated. In the uptown world of the New York art galleries and museums, their fame brought new attention to the independent film community as a whole. The films also outraged and scandalized the general public, most of whom had never seen the movies in question (let alone any avant-garde films). But people heard or read about Warhol's movies in the media, which gave them widespread coverage. Warhol's extended static imagery was so

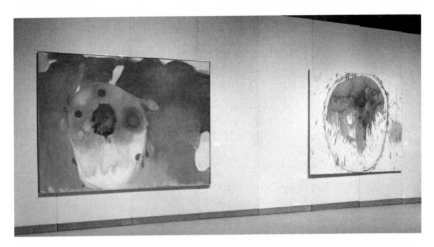

Installation view of Joyce Wieland retrospective, Art Gallery of Ontario, Toronto, April 17–June 28, 1987. *Left: Time Machine Series* (1961), in the collection of the Art Gallery of Ontario. *Right: Balling* (1961), in the collection of the National Gallery of Canada. Photography by Brenda Dereniuk. Photo courtesy of the Art Gallery of Ontario, Toronto.

Water Sark (1965), directed by Joyce Wieland. A kitchen table: the domestic altar as a world of beauty. Photo courtesy of Joyce Wieland.

Rat Life and Diet in North America (1968), directed by Joyce Wieland. Gerbil draft resisters on the lam.

Installation view of *True Patriot Love/Véritable amour patriotique* (1971), The National Gallery of Canada, Ottawa. *Left: 109 Views* (1970–71), in the collection of York University, Toronto. *Center: I Love Canada/J'aime Canada* (1970), in the collection of the MacKenzie Art Gallery, Regina, Saskatchewan. *Right:* duck pond. Photo courtesy of the Isaacs Gallery Ltd., Toronto.

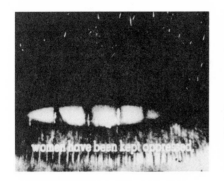

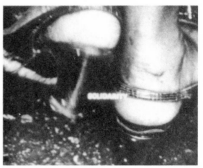

Pierre Vallières (1972), directed by Joyce Wieland. Photo courtesy of Joyce Wieland.

Solidarity (1973), directed by Joyce Wieland. Photo courtesy of Joyce Wieland.

The Far Shore (1976), directed by Joyce Wieland. The painter Tom McLeod. Photo courtesy of Joyce Wieland.

The Far Shore. Eulalie: her spiritual isolation expressed in visual terms. Photo courtesy of Joyce Wieland.

The Far Shore. Eulalie and Tom. Photo courtesy of Joyce Wieland.

The Far Shore. Eulalie and Tom. Photo courtesy of Joyce Wieland.

Céline Lomez (Eulalie) and Joyce Wieland on location during the shooting of *The Far Shore*. Photo courtesy of Joyce Wieland.

Joyce Wieland directing the camera crew of *The Far Shore*. Photo courtesy of Joyce Wieland.

Photo of Joyce Wieland. Photo courtesy of Joyce Wieland.

radical that it alienated audiences. Restless viewers shifted their attention to other stimuli around them—the materials, conditions, and
processes of the image, projection, and viewing environment. Patricia
Mellencamp has described the viewer's experience, "By reminding us
that our eyes must work . . . that the text was not located in the film
but was a process with, not for us, these works engaged in numerous
ways film's material apparatus, including the disruption of the comfortable place of the spectator at the movies."[43] Warhol made his films
so painstakingly self-conscious that they suggested ways that material
processes could become their own content.

Such an approach departed from Deren's concept of cinematic
form based on the image's mimetic properties. Structural filmmakers
displayed the processes and construction of the cinematic image rather
than uniformly displacing them onto the pattern of a narrative. Structural films investigated the physical properties of film itself as a flat
material making use of light, projection, printing procedures, and
the illusion of movement. They emphasized the tensions among the
physical materials, the spectator's perceptual processes, and the emotional or pictorial realities cinema has traditionally represented. The
didactic goal of such self-reflexive addresses was to be an alternative
to Deren's tradition of expression based on verisimilitude, mimesis, or
pictorial illusion.[44]

Many of the short films that Wieland made between 1965 and 1968
admitted issues of concern to the structural filmmakers. The four-
minute-long *1933* (1967) is monochromatically tinted loops of the
street below Wieland's window over which the numbers "1933" are
superimposed on and off; repetitions and interspersed white leader
disrupt visual, spatial, and narrative continuities. *Sailboat* (1967) is
similarly a short (three-and-a-half minutes) film of repetitive water-
scapes in which a sailboat attempts to glide along the horizon, and the
word *sailboat* is superimposed on the screen. *Catfood* (1968) is more
Warholian in style but more playful than Warhol in fashion. It offers
thirteen minutes of different long takes that provide varying close-up
views of Wieland's cat eating a fresh fish.

1933, Sailboat, Catfood, and *Rat Life and Diet in North America* (1968)
legitimized Wieland's position in discourses promoting structural film
in New York City. Even *Artforum,* the most prestigious North American
arts periodical, asserted Wieland's importance as a structural filmmaker.[45] P. Adams Sitney assigned Wieland a place among his list of
leading structural filmmakers in the 1969 article that gave identity to
structural film as a style of filmmaking.[46] Such critical prominence,
in addition to the economically stabilized apparatus for avant-garde

cinema, facilitated film rentals in colleges, museums, and film societies. Wieland's short films were shown at important museums and film festivals not only in New York City but subsequently in Great Britain, Belgium, and Germany.[47]

Wieland's position as a leading structural filmmaker in the United States also enlarged her artistic reputation in Canada. Between 1967 and 1970, the Toronto daily newspapers frequently profiled Wieland.[48] Information on Wieland's personality, projects, and New York films regularly appeared in the Canadian film magazine *Take One*.[49] Canada's leading art periodical, *artscanada*, reviewed each of Wieland's new films from 1967 to 1970.[50] They unanimously express pride in a Canadian who was famous in New York City while she still maintained ties to the Canadian art scene.

Wieland's Experimental Films, Woman's Discourse, and Feminist Film Theory

However helpful such discursive placement may have been to Wieland's career, the structural film label narrowed Wieland's critical reception to the confines of formalist-centered concerns. Critics ignored other features—the political dimensions of the subject matter, the domestic interactions, the role of the female body as the site of enunciation, the disruption of linear narrative, and authoritative point of view as the organizing logic. Only recently have Canadian feminist critics such as Leila Sujir begun to argue that Wieland's films "tell not only of intellectual matters, but physicality—the body as matter, perceiving through the body . . . a language which comes out of the body, a language in the feminine."[51] In this context, Wieland's work represents an example of what French feminist theorists Hélène Cixous and Luce Irigaray call *l'écriture féminine*. Wieland's films from the middle and late 1960s that were ignored or marginal to earlier critical discourses may assume new significance in the international feminist arena of the 1980s and 1990s.

It is important in this regard then that Wieland's experimental films of the 1960s be repositioned and reevaluated within such a textual system of women's cinema. It is doubly important for Canadian feminism that has been marginalized within Western feminist film theory, where critical preoccupations have neglected how an ongoing state of economic colonialism might materially affect women's roles and lives.[52] Canadian feminists, who better appreciate the importance of synthesizing national social identities with feminist symbols because they have been doubly silenced from speaking about themselves, have already begun the less than unified task of interrogating Wieland's films as both Canadian and feminine.

Whereas Wieland's early film *Barbara's Blindness* (1965) (made in collaboration with Betty Ferguson) was altogether dismissed among New York critics in the 1960s because it did not fit into the structural film category, Toronto filmmaker-writer Anna Gronau included *Barbara's Blindness* (as well as *Ritual in Transfigured Time* and Marie Menken's *Glimpse of the Garden,* made in 1960) in a 1984 Banff Centre show of women's avant-garde films. She praises *Barbara's Blindness* for the way it subverts the narrator's privileged control of the "look," or male gaze.[53] Here, a found-footage film made from a classically styled educational movie about a girl's blindness has been intercut with clips from adventure films. When the male voice-over narrator praises God for the girl's restored vision, the ironic conclusion is that the object Wieland and Ferguson intercut for her to see is an atomic bomb blast. In one sense, the film is a Pop Art collage that condemns the U.S.'s power to pose a nuclear threat to the entire world; in another sense, it goes further to challenge the authority of "who speaks" and "to dismantle hegemonic narrative structures."[54]

Hand Tinting (1967) is another example of a film marginalized in structural film criticism of the 1960s and 1970s that is productive for feminist film discourse of the 1980s and 1990s. It initially received some praise for its deconstruction of cinema's formalist and material features whereas the images' latent content—mostly African-American girls at a job training center—went largely undiscussed. The four-minute film is composed of cut-away shots that Wieland filmed for a proposed documentary on a West Virginia job training center. Wieland dyed this leftover footage, added flashes of other footage, and scratched and perforated the film itself with her sewing needles. Recent allusions to *Hand Tinting* incorporate into feminist critical discussion the importance of tools and methods of working particular to women's crafts.

The movie is comprised of looped and reversed images of the girls dancing, swimming, and talking so that a repetitive or loop effect results in actions that recur but are never completed. Their incomplete movements and gestures become isolated rhythms of social rituals. Lacking spatial depth and temporal completion, the repetitive actions negate the illusion of solid space created in documentary cinema. Although both Deren and Clarke used slow motion and repetition, they did so to single out movement from the background and to heighten the expressive flow of movement itself.

Destroying movement as a reference system contained within solid space, Wieland studies incomplete, repetitive gestures to deconstruct the girls' actions themselves. In the terms of structural film, what remains is a tension between the image as a material object and its pictorial value as facial and bodily referents for women of color. But what is signified is the artificial construction of fragmented subjects— perhaps itself a feminist analytic metaphor for African-American women's position within the Xerox job training center as well as in white, patriarchal society. Toronto critic Kass Banning has argued for a psychoanalytic possibility—that the disappearance and reappearance of the images of women in the film leads to a replay and reevocation of "the primordial experience of loss and separation from the maternal body."[55]

Wieland's best-known structural film, *Rat Life and Diet in North America,* likewise may be reevaluated as a woman's discourse that has potentially further-reaching radical aims than those of structural cinema. Lippard responded to how the film's position within structural film criticism suppresses its most distinctive features, "I thought the message was pretty straightforward, but the avant-garde, ill at ease with political emotion, was able to interpret it with typical ambiguity."[56] The movie is, loosely defined, an animal parable like those by Beatrix Potter. *Rat Life* tells the story of gerbil draft resisters in the United States who break out of jail, elude their cat jailers, and escape to Canada, where they start a cooperative organic farm only, in the end, to be attacked again.

Rat Life reintroduces Wieland's humorous sense of play and exploration of intimate spaces close to the body. Sequences show the gerbils loose amid the dirty dishes of a finished supper while they are on the lam. Later in the film, they nibble cherries during the cherry festival that is celebrated when they have won their freedom. The magnified images intensify the sensuous colors, surfaces, and textures of food, crockery, and cloth. The effect is similar to that of Dutch still life paintings or to the more recent Photo-Realist still lives by Audrey Flack.

While continuous close-ups may have been necessary to scale the gerbils as actor protagonists, they also keep action centered close to the camera eye. The space is further flattened through frame superimpositions of titles and red crosses. (They are reminiscent of commercial packaging designs like those Wieland learned during her apprenticeship at Graphics Animation.) Frame flashes of black leader film and other insert shots temporally undermine realism. The results celebrate the formal beauty of the miniature drama on the kitchen table that becomes accessible only when it is magnified.

Wieland's whimsical tale also examines and deconstructs the concept of narrativity as a lexicon for storytelling. Narrative development occurs through the codes of popular children's books—anthropomorphic heroes whose desires motivate action, simple words juxtaposed on images, streamlined cause-and-effect sequences, and brightly colored representational graphics with little illusionistic three-dimensionality. Thus, through the codes of another popular domestic idiom, Wieland frees her narration from the need for detailed explanation or strict cause-and-effect progression. *Rat Life* entertains highly didactic purposes, making possible the structural examination of cinematic materials, the deconstruction of hegemonic narrative structure, identification with the victims of political oppression, and the articulation of an intimately defined domestic space close to the eye and body.

But *Water Sark* has received the most attention as the subject of woman's discourse. Leila Sujir analyzes *Water Sark*'s enunciation of female pleasure or *jouissance* (total joy or ecstasy in one's sense of wholeness), "There is the discovery of the body and the construction of the self through a play of movement. . . . The movement of the camera is intimate, close to the body, moving with a body and out from it, making a self portrait."[57] Kay Armatage similarly defines *Water Sark* as a "practice of image construction through which she is able to operate the feminine over the male body in a very literal displacement of the phallic."[58] As Armatage points out, Wieland's play with investigating her own upper body and particularly her naked breasts as well as the image fragments of filming herself through the use of mirrors and prisms "resonate enormously with the texts which constitute the body known as *l'écriture féminine*."[59] By tracing the feminine body as camera movement across the ground and contours of her human body, Wieland literalizes *l'écriture féminine* Cixous and Irigaray define as woman's discourse.

Conceptual Art in New York City

By the late 1960s, people all around Wieland were expressing their anger at the United States military involvement in Southeast Asia. In New York City, Wieland lived among a social group of artists characterized by its free-spirited romanticism, its antagonism to traditional American mores and values, and its allegiance to left-wing political philosophies. In an environment in which college students, left-wing radicals, and artists openly debated American foreign policies as well as the politics of art, a Canadian expatriate grew increasingly furious not only about American intervention in Southeast Asia but also about United States exploitation in her home country.

Since the early 1900s, the United States policies of foreign corporate development and investment in Canada (as well as in other countries) had become internationally recognized as "economic imperialism" or "economic colonialism." Such colonization worked against cultural as well as economic national unity in a country already split by British and French colonial loyalties. But when worldwide attention focused increasingly on the United States intervention in Vietnam, Canadians who identified with these victims of American imperialism helped to support intensified Canadian nationalist activities. While political protests became more vigorous in both Canada and the United States, artists in New York City produced a number of activities that promoted direct interrelationships between art, artisanal production, and political engagement. Among such practices, Conceptual Art became prominent as an intellectual response to North American cultural events.

Conceptual Art was the legitimate artistic heir to the Happenings of the early 1960s and to the activities of the Fluxus movements in Germany a few years earlier. What unified Conceptual Art was its attempt to deprive works of their aura in order to expose and subvert their function as objects of commodity exchange. By opposing traditional media like painting and sculpture, Conceptual Art often relied on more ephemeral forms as an act of political resistance that could not be economically recuperated by corporate investors in art and the war. Conceptual Art was often events, performances, or linguistic and cultural analyses. Some artists used other nontraditional materials and places to circumvent the environment of the contemporary art world. Everything from city streets to rural wastelands to the human body became the literal ground for physical transformation. The result was unsuitable for individual acquisition or consumption; it could not be reduced to a monetary equivalent. In any case, the artist's idea rather than the finished product signified artistic activity and the essence of Conceptual Art. As art critic Suzi Gablik said, "The intention of such works has been to remain relatively free from the realm of consumerism, the exigencies of the market, and fluctuation of supply and demand. [But] in changing the very nature of art . . . they have exacted a fundamental adjustment in our ideas about structure, permanence, durability, and boundaries."[60] Conceptual Art attempted to avoid the creation of objects for the museums and galleries that trafficked in art objects as commodities for the corporate benefactors of museums and the Vietnam War.

Conceptual Art's shift from artisanal production to artistic practice as well as its need for visual documentation of events allowed a new kind of liaison and merger with filmmakers and filmmaking activities. By the time Conceptual Art became discursively prominent in New York City, the avant-garde cinema had become increasingly bound to the same institutions as the larger artistic community. The Museum of Modern Art (MOMA) had launched its Cineprobe program, a series of screenings devoted to independent filmmakers. The Whitney Museum of American Art likewise inaugurated a New American Film-makers screening program in 1970. Social networks among all kinds of artists were already in existence and intensified through artists' collaborations in anti-Vietnam War activities. Conceptual Art was not only the first art movement of the 1970s but the first explicitly multimedia movement of the decade.

But Conceptual Art was just as quickly recuperated into the flow and trade of art objects. Videos, films, and photographs of events as well as books and catalogues replaced the art "object" as the definitive trace of an idea. They instead became the commodity objects of exchange. By the time Christo completed his massive *Valley Curtain* in 1972—a Conceptual Art hanging of a large-scale, bright orange curtain across a Colorado mountain valley—his drawings, plans, and models were numbered and sold. In addition, Albert and David Maysles made a film of the events (*Christo's Valley Curtain*), books were published, and numbered swatches of the curtain itself were subsequently put on sale.

Wieland briefly participated in a series of Conceptual Art events that tied political statements to performance and agitprop theatre. Aided and abetted by Canadian expatriates in Manhattan as well as by the Minimalist and Conceptual artists Donald Judd and Sol LeWitt, Wieland organized as Conceptual Art events a quilting bee, a large party for Prime Minister Pierre Trudeau, and a demonstration at the Canadian Embassy in Manhattan.[61] Wieland and her Canadian co-organizer Mary Mitchell even named their activities "Les Activistes Culturels Canadiens" as a theatrical means to protest the United States domination of Canada. Because many of the people involved were newsworthy Canadian celebrities, Canadian newspapers attached importance to what they labeled as "classic non-events" or "material tokens of idealistic Canadianism."[62] The activities of "Les Activistes Culturels Canadiens" demonstrated the degree to which Conceptual Art could be forged out of the blur that resulted between public and private interaction when the press lent credence to the moment.[63]

Reason over Passion (1969): Structural Film as Conceptual Art

At the same time Wieland was involved in such expressions of anti-art, she was also making a feature film, *Reason over Passion*. As an extension of Conceptual Art and structural film concerns, *Reason over Passion* demonstrates the way the visual media—selected and edited images—substitute for first-hand experience of the subject they represent. Largely comprised of Canadian landscapes shot with a hand-held camera from a moving car or train and then rephotographed from a moviola, *Reason over Passion* presents the soothing, lulling clichés of the travelogue documentary. As referents to an encoded, picturesque unity more sophisticated than the children's book, the images provide the basic material of Canada's struggle for national identity and unity, "The sound of the Scottish bagpipes combines with the movement of the sea. The coupling of that with journey and with public signs of Canada—the anthem, the flag, the political convention, the faces of political figures, in particular, Trudeau's face—gives us an evocation of place and draws our attention to the movement of time: film time and historical time."[64] Among the postcardlike impressions, Prime Minister Pierre Trudeau functions as a Canadian icon in much the same way that selected Canadian images do. The Prime Minister, whose face signified to the rest of the world the myth of a unified Canada, is shown in freeze-framed close-ups (reminiscent of the technique in segments of *Hand Tinting*) accompanied by grinding machine noises.

The narrative means by which the film operates has received critical attention, but not as an early example of feminist practice. From its initial reception, the movie has been called meditative because it allows the spectator to freely construct meanings from massive amounts of discontinuous, fragmented poetic material.[65] But the fact that narrative multiplicity may also be seen as a feminist strategy for cinematic organization has largely gone unnoticed. Sujir does note, however, that the film's denial of closure—its "refusal to give destination or completion" may be seen as a component of feminine language.[66] Furthermore, the film's foregrounded enunciation of "reason over passion" is itself the object of an investigation that questions and challenges the primacy of rational logic and language as a mode of patriarchal epistemology.

Wieland's illusionistic fragments physically challenge their own verisimilitude and their ability to explain reality. The graininess of the rephotographed footage reduces the precision of depth illusion, making the images ineffective as photographic representations of reality.

Superimposed subtitles heighten the images' function more as flat
backgrounds for a written text. The title superimpositions, themselves
nonsensical permutations of Trudeau's famous "reason over passion"
slogan, add neither contextual meaning nor any informational explanation of the pictures.[67]

An electronic beep sounded at regular intervals further alienates
the viewer from the isolated visuals and, by its measured regularity,
emphasizes the slow progression of the film. In other words, the sound
builds into the parade of landscape shots a rhythmic measurement of
the phenomenon of time passing while one watches a movie. Wieland
heightens one's self-awareness with many structural tricks from her
earlier works—especially repetition, slow motion, speeded-up motion,
and jump cuts. The film's self-reflexive treatment of time leads to a
contrast between viewing duration and the actual time represented by
travel across Canada.

By dislocating the familiar codes and structures of travelogue documentaries, the film relies upon structural strategies to isolate itself from
any experience independent of the cinema. The contrast between the
opening and closing shots underscores the point. In the opening,
Atlantic waves rolling in on Canada's eastern coast dynamically signify
unspoiled land embraced by the sea. The film ends with a similar
image, though this time it is a postcard of the British Columbia coast.
The card also depicts sea bordering land, but as a landscape reduced
to one frozen image, the postcard is a tangible object for consumption.
Reason over Passion ultimately deconstructs the material processes of
images and their roles in ideology.

The Death of the Avant-garde in New York City

Wieland's nationalist rhetoric and political emotionalism became
increasingly difficult to contain inside the aesthetically focused discourses of American avant-garde cinema. The new cinema system had
supplanted a discourse of political art practice with one of intellectual
aesthetic theory. Increasingly the object of avant-garde film discourse,
the filmmakers themselves emphasized the visual theories that their
films mobilized, addressing cinematic practice purely as ontological
investigation. Once the filmmakers enjoined this discourse, Wieland's
attempts to participate resulted in admonishment: "I was made to feel
in no uncertain terms that I had overstepped my place, that in New
York my place was making 'little films.' "[68] Wieland became an outsider
to the very group of structural filmmakers with whom she had initially
been defined.

As the New York avant-garde cinema was absorbed into established museums and universities, these institutions reversed the nonselective programming base that had first attracted Wieland to the film community. A smaller, more restrictive group of films and a star system of filmmakers were becoming valorized in the museums and universities. Critic J. Hoberman has observed, "By the early 1970s, almost all of the major filmmakers (and a host of minor ones) had come in from the cold—a protected species, like academic poets—to spawn a new generation of university-trained, tenure-seeking filmmakers, film theorists, and film critics."[69] Both Snow and Hollis Frampton were among the first beneficiaries of such an effort, a circumstance that made Wieland's marginalization particularly painful since she had worked side by side with both men since the beginning of their filmmaking efforts.[70]

The New York filmmakers' admission to the institutions, critical organs, and aesthetic categories of the New York art world reflected a climate of art consumption as commodity rather than of the political turmoil going on around them. The same practices and discourses that initially gave Wieland prominence now promoted structural film as a Modernist activity engaged in purely intellectual, apolitical pursuits. Structural film became known as a cinematic correlative to the Minimal abstract paintings that had recently gained widespread acceptance. This well-known argument was initially put forward by Peter Wollen in his landmark essay "The Two Avant-Gardes."[71] But what is significant about the purely discursive alliance is that by 1970 Minimal Art was no longer the vanguard of contemporary painting.

By the late 1960s, Minimal Art became viewed more as the exponent for a corporate establishment that represented to the New Left all that was wrong with America. The art of Frank Stella, Kenneth Noland, Ellsworth Kelly, Larry Poons, and Jules Olitski allowed no gestures, no shapes, no spaces that would refer to concrete experiences in their self-referential studies of chromaticism, form, structure, and materials. Critic Max Kozloff claimed that their refusal to allow anything to interfere with the efficient plotting of art's structures became so overwhelming that efficiency itself became the pervasive ideal.[72] When such gigantically modeled expressions of self-sufficiency became the emblems of corporate boardrooms and banks as well as of museums, the linkage made the message clear that this art now signified the managerial class's dream of a new order.

The discursive appropriation of Minimal Art as a model for the philosophic concerns of structural film may have helped confer legitimacy to avant-garde cinema's position in the museum and university, but it also made New York experimental film the object of harsh criticism from abroad. Critics charged that structural film activity, as an extension of the formalist concerns of Minimal Art, was apolitical in an age when art had a moral obligation to try to effect political change. Synthesizing Marxist theories, certain critics reasoned that because an "apolitical position" presumed no ideological clash with dominant values, it was in and of itself a politically recuperative act for dominant ideology.[73] In a decade in which the growing body of film literature was dominated by theories and criticism from France and England, the changing discursive framework in which structural film was received narrowed the structural film program to one tied solely to formalism.

No single event contributed more to this narrowing of focus than the founding of Anthology Film Archives in 1970. The formation of Anthology Film as a repository for self-acclaimed "monuments of cinematic art" and for the values incumbent in these films privileged formalist "art for art's sake." The practices by which such films were selected for the archives, the collective ideology of the five men in power, and the discursive value of canonization itself rested exclusively on cinema as a formalist activity. Although these were the efforts of a small band trying to preserve their privileged position in practices now controlled by the larger institutions of the arts, the event itself represented the degree to which the dominant discourse could no longer admit the variety that had been one of independent film's hallmarks before institutionalization.

Wieland's films, like those by Clarke and others, were excluded from the Anthology Film Archives collection. When the announcement of the first selected films was made, Wieland was far away on a temporary teaching assignment at the Nova Scotia College of Art and Design. By the time she and Snow returned to New York City in early 1971, Wieland said she no longer felt the need to live and work among this community.[74]

The days of the underground film were finished. New York's most prestigious art museums and periodicals were now the centers for avant-garde film activities. *Artforum* had even devoted an entire issue to avant-garde cinema. Film-Makers Distribution Center had folded and, out of its ashes, the rigorously selective Anthology Film Archives had arisen. Whereas Mekas's *Movie Journal* columns had previously framed independent cinema against a backdrop of American political and cultural issues, his columns of 1970 retreated into a romantic celebration of individualized personal genius, using as examples

Gerard Malanga, Andrew Noren, Stan Brakhage, Bruce Baillie, Ed Emshwiller, Hollis Frampton, Ken Jacobs, and Jack Smith.[75] Inasmuch as Mekas's columns were a bellwether for independent cinema promotion throughout the previous decade, he also sounded something like a death knell in 1970. "As we all know, the underground film scene in New York today is at its low ebb."[76] Ken and Flo Jacobs had already left New York City because he had a teaching position at Harpur College in Binghamton, New York. Shirley Clarke had almost disappeared from sight. Marie Menken and Willard Maas had died within a few days of each other in late 1970 and early 1971. Hollis Frampton and George Kuchar took teaching posts in upstate New York and California, respectively. Wieland's friends Betty and Graeme Ferguson had returned to Canada in 1970, where Graeme Ferguson was developing the Imax film system.

In the spring of 1971, Wieland made two last public appearances within the New York avant-garde cinema. She screened and discussed *Reason over Passion* at Millennium Film Workshop, and her outline for a fictional narrative film set in Canada appeared in *Film Culture*.[77] Both her public appearance and her written prose illustrate that her commitment to *Canadian* content had solidified, and they demonstrate that Wieland's presence in New York City was unnecessary and perhaps even detrimental to developing nationalist themes within a Canadian syntax.

No longer willing to withstand her position among the New York avant-garde as both female and Canadian Other/Outsider, Wieland doubly reclaimed her identity and moved back to Toronto in 1971. Coinciding with the upsurge of new feminism and the dissipation of her nucleus for an avant-garde community, Wieland's change of heart and address resembles not so much the simultaneous politicization of many women artists in the early 1970s as the rebellions waged by Clarke and Deren against their marginalization in the avant-garde. Deren had responded to her environment by carving out a singular, exoticized position for herself fashioned after forms of Haitian culture, and Clarke either submerged herself in the African-American and Beat subcultures of the 1960s or periodically retreated alone into protracted depressions and psychosis. In all three cases, the women's positions as women artists in a small, intense, and fiercely competitive community relegated them to ambivalent receptions and antagonistic relations among their peers, "living among the enemy," as Lucy Lippard calls it.[78] But Lippard also concludes that Wieland's "exposure to and work within the structuralist discipline undoubtedly had a benign effect on her art, rather like Eva Hesse's contemporary response to the minimalism she adopted primarily as an armature for her own emotive expressiveness."[79]

In this regard, Wieland was shaped and touched by her participation in the New York avant-garde without being conquered by it. Her involvement in the New York avant-garde cinema had taught her not only how to situate her work within existing structures but also the politics of how those structures work. Putting in motion the change she later characterized as "the beginning of having her own life," Wieland set out for Toronto to mobilize a new nationalist, feminist avant-garde based on the New York organizational model of the early and middle 1960s.

NOTES

1. Lauren Rabinovitz, "An Interview with Joyce Wieland," *Afterimage* 8, no. 10 (May 1981): 9.

2. Ibid.

3. Ibid.

4. Ibid.

5. Joyce Wieland, "North America's Second All-woman Film Crew," *Take One* 1, no. 8 (1967–68): 15; the documentary was never finished.

6. "A Singular Spirit," *Toronto Daily Star*, 28 Feb. 1959, Joyce Wieland clippings file, Isaacs Gallery, Toronto, Canada.

7. Two benchmark examples of the ways that Toronto nurtured a climate for the acceptance of Abstract Expressionism include the 1954 group of Canadian artists named the Painters Eleven who began holding annual group exhibitions of their abstract paintings and the large number of locally organized traveling shows of contemporary American work. For a more detailed discussion on the exportation of Abstract Expressionism to both Canada and Europe, see Max Kozloff, "American Painting during the Cold War," in *Pollock and After: The Critical Debate*, ed. Francis Frascina (New York: Harper and Row, 1985), 115–16.

In addition, the expansion of galleries devoted to contemporary art, the rising number of individual art collectors, and the emergence of an auction market for Canadian contemporary art formed the nucleus of an economic organizational structure for Canadian Abstract Expressionism. The Gallery of Contemporary Art and Avrom Isaacs's Greenwich Gallery devoted themselves exclusively to the sale and exhibition of contemporary abstract art. The American-dominated media extolled Abstract Expressionism and a new middle-class of eager collectors provided money. More Canadians were soon imitating the New York School paintings with "home-grown" products that fed a booming market.

8. Barrie Hale, "Son of Toronto Painting 1953–1965," *artscanada* 30, no. 1 (Feb.–Mar. 1973): 57.

9. Joyce Wieland, interview with author, Toronto, Canada, 15 Nov. 1979.

10. Ibid.

11. Ibid.

12. See Sandra Paikowsky, *Joyce Wieland: A Decade of Painting* (Montreal: Concordia University and Concordia Art Gallery, 1985), 3; Joyce Wieland interview, 16 Nov. 1979.

13. Joyce Wieland, interview with author, Toronto, Canada, 16 Nov. 1979. George Dunning, later known for directing *Yellow Submarine*, hired Wieland in 1955, and she worked for Graphics Animation until the company declared bankruptcy in 1958.

Wieland learned animation techniques at Graphics with a group of renegade artists who experimented with the materials when they weren't working on the commercial assignments. A favorite pastime was making short parodies of their clients' television commercials with leftover film stock. Wieland's personal attempt at cinematic parody resulted in her first film, *Tea in the Garden* (1956). Made with her co-workers, her four-minute parody of a Salada Tea commercial introduced her to filmmaking as a cooperative activity.

14. Joyce Wieland interview, 15 Nov. 1979. I cannot help but add here that on the date of this interview at Wieland's and Snow's home—when Wieland some twenty-three years later did not yet have her own studio outside the home—the interview was interrupted while Wieland dealt with the domestic emergency of replacing a broken refrigerator and with several telephone calls to Snow who, working at his studio, could not be disturbed.

15. "Kay Armatage Interviews Joyce Wieland," *Take One* 3, no. 2 (Nov.–Dec. 1970), 24.

16. Snow's film *Wavelength* (1967) won critical acclaim, international experimental film awards, and a place in film history that made Snow one of the most important formalist filmmakers of the 1960s and 1970s.

17. Virginia Woolf, *A Room of One's Own* (New York: Harcourt, Brace and World, 1957). For an excellent interpretation of Woolf's essay in relation to Foucault's work on authorship and gender division, see Peggy Kamuf, *Signature Pieces: On the Institution of Authorship* (Ithaca, N.Y.: Cornell University Press, 1988), 145–73.

18. Joyce Wieland, interview with author, Toronto, Canada, 14 Nov. 1979.

19. Ibid.

20. None of the many articles devoted to Snow and his work mention Wieland other than to indicate that she was his wife or that she participated in the two films that they made together. Regina Cornwell's book-length treatise on Snow, *Snow Seen: The Films and Photographs of Michael Snow* (Toronto: Peter Martin Associates, 1979), is the most complete auteurist study to date on Snow, and it, too, only mentions Wieland in the above two contexts.

Although each independently maintained an artisanal career, Wieland and Snow occasionally worked together. They coproduced two films (*A Salt in the Park* in 1959 and *Dripping Water* in 1969), and they cooperatively made movies or art objects as gifts for friends. Wieland sometimes acted and assisted in Snow's films, and Snow played musical instruments for Wieland's film soundtracks.

21. Joyce Wieland interview, 16 Nov. 1979.

22. Paikowsky, *Joyce Wieland: A Decade of Painting,* 3.

23. Ibid.

24. Ibid.; also see Lucy Lippard, *From the Center: Feminist Essays on Women's Art* (New York: E. P. Dutton, 1976).

25. Ibid.

26. Marie Fleming, "Joyce Wieland, A Perspective," in *Joyce Wieland,* ed. Philip Monk (Toronto: Key Porter Books, 1987), 32.

27. Kay Armatage, "The Feminine Body: Joyce Wieland's *Water Sark,*" *Canadian Woman Studies* 8, no. 1 (Spring 1987): 84.

28. Barrie Hale, "Joyce Wieland: Artist, Canadian, Soft, Tough, Woman!" *Toronto Telegram,* 11 Mar. 1967, Joyce Wieland file, National Gallery of Canada, Ottawa, Canada.

29. Ibid.

30. Paikowsky, *Joyce Wieland: A Decade of Painting,* 3.

31. Michelle Landsberg, "Joyce Wieland: Artist In Movieland," *Chatelaine* 49, no. 10 (Oct. 1976): 110.

32. Ibid.

33. Robin Green, Review of Joyce Wieland exhibit, 1963, Joyce Wieland clippings file, Isaacs Gallery.

34. Hale, "Joyce Wieland: Artist, Canadian, Soft, Tough, Woman!"

35. Review of Joyce Wieland exhibit, Isaacs Gallery, *Toronto Daily Star,* 23 Nov. 1963, Joyce Wieland clippings file, Isaacs Gallery.

36. Joyce Wieland interview, 16 Nov. 1979.

37. Ibid.

38. Ibid.

39. Ibid.

40. For a more detailed analysis of this work, see Fleming, "Joyce Wieland, A Perspective," 44–61; Marguerite Pinney, "Joyce Wieland Retrospective, Vancouver Art Gallery," *artscanada* 25, no. 3 (June 1968): 41; Anne Montagnes, "Myth in Many Media: Joyce Wieland," *Communiqué,* no. 8 (May 1975): 36–39.

41. At one of Jacobs's informal parties, Wieland's and Snow's Canadian pal Bob Cowan urged a pair of Bronx twins to show their 8mm home movies. George and Mike Kuchar's vulgar parodies of Hollywood melodrama were such a hit that Mekas soon added them to the midnight bills at the Grammercy. Several years later, Wieland's good friend George Kuchar created *Knocturne* (1967–72), a trash epic just for Wieland, and starred her in it. She had already played the "Muse of Cinema" in Jacobs's super 8mm feature *Sky Socialist* (1965–67). These filmmakers depended upon each other for help, for ideas, and for fun in making candidly frank, uninhibited, improvised movies on shoestring budgets.

42. P. Adams Sitney, "Structural Film," *Film Culture,* no. 47 (Summer 1969): 1–10; reprinted in *Film Culture Reader,* ed. P. Adams Sitney (New York: Praeger, 1970), 326–48.

43. Patricia Mellencamp, "Receivable Texts: U.S. Avant-garde Cinema, 1960–1980," *Wide Angle* 7, nos. 1–2 (1985): 77.

44. For further discussion of structural film in this regard, see Peter Wollen, " 'Ontology' and 'Materialism' in Film," *Screen* 17, no. 1 (Spring 1976): 7–23; reprinted in *Readings and Writings: Semiotic Counter-Strategies*, Peter Wollen (London: New Left Books, 1982), 189–207.

45. Manny Farber, "Film," *Artforum* 8, no. 5 (Jan. 1970): 28–29. A year and a half later, Regina Cornwell's essay, "True Patriot Love: The Films of Joyce Wieland," *Artforum* 10, no. 1 (Sept. 1971): 36–40, was a full-scale discussion of Wieland's films and paintings.

46. Sitney, "Structural Film"; he elaborates further in *Visionary Film: The American Avant-garde, 1943–1978*, 2d ed. (New York: Oxford University Press, 1979), 369.

47. Wieland's films showed at the Museum of Modern Art in New York City in 1968; the National Theater in London in September 1968; the World Festival of Experimental Film in Knokke-le-Zoute, Belgium, in December 1968; and the 1969 Oberhausen Film Festival.

48. Simultaneously, Wieland continued to show paintings and quilts in Canada, and these exhibits culminated in a 1968 Vancouver Arts Gallery retrospective that established Wieland's place as Canada's leading contemporary female artist.

For a sample of the profiles, see Barrie Hale, "Joyce Wieland: Artist, Canadian, Soft, Tough, Woman!"; Kay Kritzwiser, "The Spirit of '67: Art with Derring-Do," *Toronto Globe and Mail*, 30 Dec. 1967, Joyce Wieland file, Isaacs Gallery, Toronto, Canada; "Joyce Thinks Canada Is Last Hope for Rats and People," *Toronto Globe and Mail*, 8 Mar. 1969, Joyce Wieland file, Midwest Film Center, School of the Art Institute of Chicago, Chicago, Illinois.

49. For a sample of articles by or about Joyce Wieland's life in New York City, see Joyce Wieland, "North America's Second All-woman Film Crew," 14–15; Bob Cowan, "Letter from New York City," *Take One* 2, no. 6 (July 1969): 25–26; Bob Cowan, "New York Letter," *Take One* 1, no. 10 (July 1968): 29.

50. See Richard Foreman, "New Cinema Festival at Jewish Museum," *artscanada* 24, no. 2 (Apr. 1967): 9–10; Manny Farber, "Films at Canadian Artists '68," *artscanada* 26, no. 1 (Feb. 1969): 28–29; Manny Farber, "La raison avant passion," *artscanada* 26, no. 4 (Aug. 1969), 45–46.

P. Adams Sitney's "There Is Only One Joyce" in *artscanada* 27, no. 2 (Apr. 1970): 43–45, is still one of the most often reprinted articles on Wieland's experimental films.

51. Leila Sujir, "A Language of Flesh and Roses," in *In Search of the Far Shore: The Films of Joyce Wieland*, ed. Simon Field (London: Canada House, 1988), 3–4. Quoted with the permission of the author.

52. For a further discussion of this issue, see, for example, Kass Banning's criticism of my earlier work on Wieland and of Lucy Lippard for failing to acknowledge the difficulties inherent in an analysis of the female Canadian artist and for unproblematically inscribing her into an ahistorical feminist

aesthetic. While such was not my intention, I found Banning's discussion of the paradoxical relationship feminists in colonized cultures (and more especially Third World cultures) encounter with international feminism dominated by American and European political, intellectual hegemony instructive in reevaluating my assumptions and argument; Kass Banning, "The Mummification of Mommy: Joyce Wieland as the AGO's First Living Other, *C Magazine*, no. 13 (Mar. 1987): 32–38.

53. Anna Gronau, "Avant-Garde Film by Women: To Conceive a New Language of Desire," in *The Event Horizon: Essays on Hope, Sexuality, Social Space, and Media(tion) in Art*, ed. Lorne Falk and Barbara Fischer (Toronto: Coach House Press and Walter Phillips Gallery, 1987), 164.

54. Ibid.

55. Kass Banning, "Textual Excess in Joyce Wieland's *Handtinting*," *CineAction!* no. 5 (Spring 1986): 14.

56. Lucy Lippard, "Watershed: Contradiction, Communication and Canada in Joyce Wieland's Work," in *Joyce Wieland*, ed. Philip Monk (Toronto: Key Porter Books, 1987), 3.

57. Sujir, "A Language of Flesh and Roses," 3. Quoted with the permission of the author.

58. Kay Armatage, "The Feminine Body," 84.

59. Ibid., 86.

60. Suzi Gablik, *Has Modernism Failed?* (New York: Thames and Hudson, 1984), 42.

61. Wieland claims that she and Mitchell fabricated additional events for the sake of press attention; Joyce Wieland interview, 16 Nov. 1979.

62. See Barrie Hale, "Getting in Style with Pierre Elliott Trudeau: A Manhattan Quilting Bee," *Toronto Daily Star, Star Weekly Magazine*, 15 June 1968, Joyce Wieland file, National Gallery of Canada; Barry Lord, "Canadian Artists in N.Y. Bravely Waving Our Flag," *Toronto Daily Star*, 7 Mar. 1970, Joyce Wieland file, National Gallery of Canada.

Mary Mitchell was a Canadian playwright living in New York City. Wieland executed a video clip for her play *Enactment*, which was shown in 1967 at LaMama, a New York theater for experimental works.

63. See Hale, "Getting in Style with Pierre Elliot Trudeau"; Bernadette Andrews, "A Woman Honors Canada in Display at National Gallery," *Toronto Telegram*, 2 July 1971, Joyce Wieland file, National Gallery of Canada.

64. Sujir, "A Language of Flesh and Roses," 3. Quoted with the permission of the author.

65. George Lellis, "La raison avant la passion," in *Form and Structure in Recent Film*, ed. Dennis Wheeler (Vancouver: Vancouver Art Gallery/Talon Books, 1972).

66. Sujir, "A Language of Flesh and Roses," 3.

67. Not only has Wieland formally inverted the message of the phrase that came from a famous speech by Canadian Prime Minister Pierre Trudeau, but Wieland and Hollis Frampton (who assisted her with the permutations) arrived at the combinations with the aid of a computer, the ultimate tool for reasoning.

They logically, systematically created garbled polysyllables that became pho-netically interesting in and of themselves.

68. "Interview with Joyce Wieland," 24.

69. J. Hoberman, "After Avant-garde Film," in *Art after Modernism: Rethinking Representation,* ed. Brian Wallis (New York: New Museum of Contemporary Art, 1984), 65.

70. Wieland and Frampton began a film together in 1967; Wieland finally completed the film after Frampton's death in 1984 (*A and B in Ontario*).

71. See Peter Wollen's essay "The Two Avant-gardes," *Studio International* 190, no. 978 (Nov.–Dec. 1975): 171–75; reprinted in Peter Wollen, *Readings and Writings: Semiotic Counter-Strategies* (London: New Left Books, 1982), 92–104.

72. Kozloff, "American Painting during the Cold War," 121.

73. See Jean-Louis Comolli and Jean Narboni, "Cinema/Ideology/Criticism (1)," *Screen* 12, no. 1 (1971); Peter Gidal, ed. *Structural Film Anthology* (London: British Film Institute, 1978).

74. Joyce Wieland interview, 16 Nov. 1979.

75. A sample of his 1970 columns are collected in *Movie Journal: The Rise of a New American Cinema, 1959–1971* (New York: Collier Books, 1972).

76. Ibid., 401.

77. Joyce Wieland, "True Patriot Love: A Canadian Love, Technology, Leadership and Art Story," *Film Culture,* no. 52 (Spring 1971): 64–73.

78. Lippard, "Watershed," 4.

79. Ibid., 6.

7

After the Avant-garde: Joyce Wieland and New Avant-gardes in the 1970s

On July 2, 1971, the National Gallery of Canada in Ottawa looked more like a county fair than a typically dignified art exhibit opening. Large-scale quilts, knitted wall hangings, embroideries, and hooked rugs filled the museum's main floor. Bottles of specially distilled perfume were displayed, and the perfume's scent filled the galleries. Twenty-eight ducks splashed in a children's plastic swimming pool and a brass marching band performed. Journalists and guests mingled with each other while eating slices of one of the displayed objects—a huge, iced cake made from sixty dozen petits four glacés and forty pounds of fruitcake. Joyce Wieland's retrospective, *True Patriot Love/ Véritable amour patriotique*, was underway.

After being disappointed with the way the New York independent cinema had failed to sustain a significant alternative to bourgeois values, Wieland was reborn as a feminist and nationalist who was also Canada's most famous woman artist being feted at the prestigious National Gallery. It is ironic that, because she had been a New York City artist, the Canadian arts community now regarded her as an established leader in the art world. But instead of basking in institutional legitimization and public celebrity, Wieland waged a continuous war over the course of the next decade against institutional oppression of women, artists, and native peoples as well as against society's destruction of the environment. In her art and in a range of supporting activities, Wieland acted as a champion for the leading cultural protest movements of the 1970s—feminism, ecology, and Eskimo and other tribal rights. Beyond the scope of the New York independent cinema, Wieland applied the artistic models for representation as well as for economic and political organization that she had learned in the cinema network of the early and middle 1960s, but she expanded them into a system for how filmmaking may participate in cultural activism and political agitation.

Unlike either Deren or Clarke, who appeared to work for the elimination of gender and racial differences within culture, Wieland celebrated sexual difference as a source of moral value. Her feminism is based in a woman-centered perspective that developed in the early and middle 1970s. Rather than consider women's differences from men as a source of inferiority, a woman-centered analysis regards sexual difference as a matter of pride and confidence. It presupposes the centrality, emotional importance, and political necessity of women's sphere and a separate women's culture. Describing her development in this direction, Wieland said in 1972, "I got into looking around in history for female lines of influence. I read the lives and works of many, many women, salonists, diarists, revolutionaries, etc. I started to invent myself as an artist. . . . Eventually women's concerns and my own femininity became my artist's territory."[1] Nurtured by the recent work of feminist historians who studied, in particular, women's biographies and the nineteenth-century culture of domesticity, Wieland is exemplary of many feminist artists who, in the 1970s, began to create alternative spaces where women could withdraw from the world built by men for the sake of their personal and collective development.

True Patriot Love: Woman-centered Feminism

When the National Gallery decided in 1971 to hold a one-woman show by a living artist for the first time, Wieland made the occasion of her individual entrance into "the Canadian academy" a collective celebration of women's sphere in art history. Instead of simply displaying her own past work, she searched out prizewinning craftswomen whose work she had seen at county fairs and commissioned them (using her $7,000 Canada Council grant that was earmarked for the show) to execute pieces that she designed. *Flag Arrangement* was four knitted Canadian flags; *Wolfe's Last Letter* and *Montcalm's Last Letter* were embroidered photographic reproductions of the British and French military commanders' letters; *The Great Sea* was two hooked rugs; and *Arctic Day, 101 Views, The Water Quilt,* and *Spring Tree* were quilts on ecological themes. By hiring women who otherwise practiced their art as a leisure activity, Wieland attempted to legitimize the place of women's domestic craft heritage within the arts institution.

At a time when art museums generally ignored crafts, Wieland's celebration of women's needlework was an unprecedented effort to raise the public's consciousness about Canadian women and their tradition in the arts. In addition, the show included quilts that Wieland had made alone or with her sister during the past four years. As Lucy Lippard has noted, "The quilt has long been used as a metaphor for women's networks and collaboration."[2] Wieland challenged the notion of the artist as a single creator whose professional status is based on a discourse that defines artists through their participation in arts institutions and the gallery system.[3] She offered, instead, an alternative that subverted women's traditional, hierarchical place among creative expressions and celebrated it as radical both in art and artistic process.

Wieland, who had been using her homes as studios for almost twenty years now, capitalized on her domestic environment. She had been making quilts, embroideries, and pocketed plastic and cloth wall hangings since 1965, and before that she had used cloth, bric-a-brac, and household articles in collages and assemblages. She introduced women's domestic needle arts in her large-scale wall pieces to reshape traditional signs of domestic oppression into political celebrations of women's artistic heritage and women's interrogation of state politics. Kay Kritzwiser wrote, "Look at those deceptive plastic pockets. They're gaudy and slick, but when you pull out the little pillows stuffed into them, you are made aware of Vietnam and national greed and wanton destruction of the earth."[4] The best known of Wieland's quilts from this period are two brightly colored, simply designed bedcovers that serve as banners for the appliqued letters "Reason Over Passion" and "Raison Avant Passion." For the first time, women's collaborative expressions became linked to state politics.

But the show puzzled many of the nation's journalists, and reporters blasted *True Patriot Love*'s focus on domestic objects and collective process. "Is it art?" one critic asked Wieland during a radio interview.[5] Others not only said women's crafts were unsuitable in an art museum but added that women's "quilting bees" were hardly valid artistic activity.[6] The Ottawa daily newspaper even went so far as to attack the show on its editorial page.[7] The sudden harsh critical reaction was evocative of the kinds of things critics said when Wieland was starting out in Toronto in the early 1960s.

Wieland's celebration of sexual difference threatened the Romantic, masculine tradition of artistic creativity as an exclusive male privilege. The Ottawa newspaper editor worried over this and the possible side effects of *True Patriot Love:* "Suburban housewifes could hardly miss the point of it all: why not whip up some instant art of your own, just like Joyce? It's easy, and it's fun."[8] As Kritzwiser aptly noted, "Wieland at her most innocent is Wieland at her most wicked."[9] *True Patriot Love* demonstrated that women could not only challenge their marginalization by the art world and take pride in the techniques, materials, and artisanal processes associated with the feminine but they could also use their tradition as propaganda against patriarchy.

After the Avant-garde: New York City

Wieland's disaffection with the film world of New York City and her rejuvenation in feminist nationalism was not unlike the situation of many artists in the early 1970s. New York City's arts had become so thoroughly entrenched in bureaucracy, commercialism, and professionalism that critic Harold Rosenberg declaimed the community's dissipation as a site for cultural critique and resistance, "Instead of being . . . an act of rebellion, despair or self-indulgence, art is being normalized as a professional activity within society."[10] Suzi Gablik supports his point of view, making an even more elaborate case for "the death of the avant-garde," "Success and security now play such a central role in the American imagination . . . that even artists have learned to strive along an imposed scale of careerist values, mapping out their lives like military strategists. If early capitalism led to the formation of ascetic tendencies, late capitalism has spawned a more acquisitive and exploitative form of individualism, together with an art more oriented toward production and profit."[11] Others have noted that although Conceptual Art may be seen as an opposition to this formation of the New York art world, its anticommercial tendencies had the impact "of a beanbag hurled against cement."[12] Individual artists, too, recognized a sense of something collectively lost as the art world was restructured in the early 1970s. Robert Mangold's personal statement may be exemplary: "I left New York, very disillusioned, in 1970. For one thing, I felt there was a kind of commercialism taking place that I found offensive. I felt the need to put distance between me and the art world. Things were happening that somehow seemed so divisive, and everyone was jealous of everyone else."[13] Mangold not only duplicates Wieland's exact sentiments but echoes her theme of displacement and loss. A certain kind of avant-garde with which artists and critics identified had ended.

The rhetorical figures of professionalism, careerism, and commercialism that run through all these statements may also be seen another way. They suggest symptoms of what has now been generally described as a paradigmatic shift from Modernism to Postmodernism. Gablik defines the paradigmatic terms: "If modernism was ideological at heart—full of strenuous dictates about what art could, and could not, be—postmodernism is much more eclectic, able to assimilate, and even plunder, all forms of style and genre and circumstance, and tolerant of multiplicity and conflicting values."[14] The Modernist avant-garde that Gablik describes had been ideologically unified since World War II through its position of radical alienation. But in the early 1970s, it had become an umbrella for pluralist concerns all competing for success measured in terms of the marketplace. In this context, what later became labeled as Postmodernist traits began to dominate—a preoccupation with object production and surface styles, the rejection of the artist's moral stance and the leveling of Modernist art's heroic purpose:

> Central to avant-gardism were the concept of alienation and protest and the assumption that art must be something more than the production of superfluous luxury products. . . . What began before World War I as a burning involvement of artists in the future of their societies . . . had subsided by the mid-1970s into acknowledgment that art would never change the world. . . . It was this loss of hope, more than anything else, that transformed the avant-garde from an ethical into an aesthetic movement.[15]

The idea of art—as well as an avant-garde—that Deren, Clarke, Wieland, and others embraced as a subversive activity became subsumed to the production of art's value as an exchange commodity.

A major component of such an ideological shift was the avant-garde's economic reorganization in the early 1970s. The large New York museums like MOMA and the Whitney experienced budget deficits that contributed to abrupt changes in policy and curatorial staff. Private funding had diminished while operating costs increased. As a result, acquisitions declined considerably at the Whitney, and exhibition policy, labor relations, and public relations all became increasingly directed toward financial and administrative goals rather than those of art professionals.[16]

The major consequence was that museums became more oriented toward governmental agencies, corporations, and the general public. In this regard, the director of the Guggenheim Museum was quoted as saying, "Our plan is to . . . enlist the support of a growing membership; play as hard for the government dollar as we can, and seek corporation support."[17] The statistics bear out this statement: corporate sponsorship of the arts in general rose from $23 million in 1963 to $463 million in 1979, and by the end of the 1970s, few New York museum exhibitions were produced without corporate support.[18] Since they were dependent on corporate patronage and governmental grants, the big museums programmed for the largest possible attendance figures to demonstrate to these agencies the breadth of their public appeal and their ability to sell enhanced public images of industry and the state.

These economic pressures affected not just the types of art and movies that museums promoted but also the relationships between the large museums and the small, informal network of artist organizations. Museums concentrated on fewer, more bankable artists recycled through an ever-tightening circle of organizations. The exclusionary practices that Wieland and Clarke had experienced in the avant-garde cinema system was indicative of something larger being played out across the New York art world as a whole.

After the Avant-garde: Feminism and the Arts in New York City

But in the Postmodern era, art produced by women generally retained an oppositional position to the central institutions and networks of artistic activity. Whereas most artists who had participated in the political activism of the late 1960s dropped back into the mainstream within a few years, women artists rarely had such positions in which to drop back. Instead, they regularly allied with the women's movement of the early 1970s. They perpetuated the anger, social concern, and radical analyses that were so widespread a few years earlier. As Lucy Lippard said, their experiences in the antiwar movement had especially taught them "a lot about how the art world runs, about the relationships between artists' power and institutional power, and about the interrelationships between cultural institutions and those controlling the world."[19]

The situation reflects feminism's growing impact as a widespread cultural movement. Modern feminism had been revived in the 1960s as a reform movement for women's rights through such organizations as the President's Commission on the Status of Women in 1961, various state commissions that followed, and the 1966 founding of NOW, the National Organization for Women. The passage of the Equal Rights Amendment became, in the 1970s, the central issue on which NOW and other groups focused their efforts. *Ms.* magazine, which served as a popular forum for the circulation of feminist goals, practices, and ideas, supported the campaign. Betty Friedan's *The Feminine Mystique* provided the intellectual foundation for the realization that the source of women's subordination was in the social construction of sexual difference. But this movement was largely a liberal reform effort, dominated by white, professional women over the age of thirty.

In the late 1960s when younger, more radical women became angry over their second-class treatment in the anti-Vietnam protest movement, they responded more militantly to growing concern over women's position in society. As experienced political organizers in the civil rights movement and members of Students for a Democratic Society and other student groups of the New Left, they reevaluated both their own subordination within the Left and the Marxist theories that ignored gender issues in favor of class ones. By the early 1970s, they were developing a critique of Western culture and its continuous oppression of women. They focused on how women's rights had been ignored on such issues as lesbianism, rape, gender identity, abortion, and child care. Such groups as the Redstockings, WITCH, and the New York Radical Feminists became part of a vanguard movement in the early 1970s for advocating challenges to patriarchy itself. Shulamith Firestone, a cofounder of the New York Radical Feminists, elaborated their philosophy for oppression and change in *The Dialectic of Sex: The Case for a Feminist Revolution* in 1970. Demanding revolutionary change through a fundamentally altered society, Firestone and others advocated the formation of consciousness-raising groups as a means to relate individual problems to larger patterns of social discrimination. By meeting in small groups and examining the lives of individual group members (the personal is political), radical feminists hoped to construct an ideology that would reconstruct women's social roles.

While consciousness raising highlighted women's oppression, it also began to validate women's experiences as a source of pride and confidence. What had appeared as defects increasingly became viewed as elements of strength. Feminist writers like Adrienne Rich and Susan Griffin urged that "female experience ought to be the major focus of study and the source of dominant values for the culture as a whole."[20] By the middle 1970s, the terms of radical feminism gradually shifted toward favoring a woman-centered analysis that would focus on female experience. The development of woman-centered curricula across the country and the growth of women's studies as an intellectual discipline are exemplary of feminist reorganization and cultural intervention in the 1970s.

In the art world, women artists participated in these political agendas and formed specialized groups to meet their individual needs and to express their shared demands as women artists. Women Artists in Revolution began in 1969 to protest widespread sexual discrimination and women's subordination. During 1970 and 1971, the Ad Hoc Women Artists' Committee picketed and took legal action against the

Whitney Museum of American Art for its exclusion of women artists from its annual exhibition of contemporary American art. Articles about women's art began to appear that addressed not only the content of the art but women artists' lowly positions as social subjects in the New York art community. Feminist alternative galleries like A.I.R. Gallery provided new sites for displaying women's art outside established galleries and museums. By 1975, three publications devoted to feminist art (*Feminist Art Journal, Heresies,* and *Women Artists Newsletter*) were being published.

Independent cinema in New York, likewise, felt these effects. After the picketing and discrimination suits filed against the Whitney, the museum ran a special program in 1973 of more than fifty new documentaries and experimental films by women. The New York Cultural Center ran a week-long special program of women's experimental films in the same year. The First International Festival of Women's Films in 1972 provided a showcase for women's cinema that was organized and programmed by women. In 1972, two feminist cooperatives (New Day Films and Women Make Movies) for film distribution and production began full operation in Manhattan. By 1975, Iris Films and Women/Artist/Filmmakers also offered distribution and marketing services for films made by women.

The vast majority of filmmakers served by these organizations, however, were women who made their first films after 1969. Although the First International Women's Festival included Gunvor Nelson and Storm De Hirsch, it primarily featured the work of a younger generation of women filmmakers, women who had recently graduated from art or filmmaking schools. The films—both experimental and documentary—incorporated personal elements of autobiography or dealt with gender issues for the purpose of consciousness raising and social transformation. They were part of the broader movement that emphasized the political as personal by documenting how social events and beliefs affect individual women's lives.

Although the same issues were being explored by Wieland and others of her generation, they had not previously been the main subject, as such, of cinema discourse. Thus, Carolee Schneemann's *Fuses* (1967) was excluded from the First International Festival of Women's Films even though the film is an autobiographical diary. The film, which graphically details the filmmaker's sexual relationship with her male lover as well as images of female genitalia, domesticity, and sensuous landscapes, had been critically positioned within the aesthetics and social outrages of the New York avant-garde cinema of the late 1960s. Schneemann was a well-known participant among Manhattan

Happenings, experimental theater, and multimedia performances. Her self-proclaimed interest in creating "sensory arenas" and her detailed, graphic depiction of various sexual acts seemed to keep her outside critical discourse and practices being built up around groups of feminist filmmakers in the early 1970s.

Hundreds of other young women filmmakers, however, now participated in a newly defined network of social resistance. Films like *I Am Somebody* (1970), *Janie's Janie* (1971) and *Joyce at Thirty-four* (1971) showed everywhere from women's film festivals and gallery screenings to feminist consciousness-raising groups to the educational film circuit of schools, clubs, and churches. Most of the films draw their strategies largely from the realist tradition and particularly from cinéma vérité approaches to filmmaking in the 1960s. Objecting to this practice, radical feminist Claire Johnston first chided this movement, largely documentary in nature, as an inadequate liberal feminism, "Any revolutionary must challenge the depiction of reality; it is not enough to discuss the oppression of women within the text of the film: the language of the cinema/depiction of reality must also be interrogated, so that a break between ideology and text is affected."[21] Johnston argues that a feminism of resistance—a countercinema—must confront within the films the language of representation so as to expose how realism has falsely constructed women. She argues, by extension, from the critique of cinéma-vérité practices that Clarke had made a decade earlier.[22]

There were at least a few women filmmakers, including Michelle Citron, Sally Potter, and Laura Mulvey, who were able to span the newly emerging network of feminist cinema, the radical aesthetics of Johnston's countercinema and the institutionalized discourse of intellectual film theory. But Yvonne Rainer, in particular, became the most critically acclaimed figure among avant-garde as well as among feminist cinema discourse. Like most feminist filmmakers of the 1970s, Rainer made her first films at the beginning of the decade. She was, however, already prominent in the New York avant-garde as a Judson Dance Theater dancer-choreographer and a performance artist whose multimedia work had received significant praise from Manhattan arts critics (including Jonas Mekas). In fact, Rainer herself acknowledges that she was better known in the art world than in the dance world.[23]

If this were simply a biographical narrative of lineage, one could claim that Rainer is the heir to Deren's, Clarke's, and Wieland's positions as token "successful" women filmmakers within the dominant practices of the New York independent cinema. Rainer, like Deren and Clarke, made the transition from participation in the dance world to film. But Rainer, as a subject of critical discourse, illustrates the shift in the avant-garde that so displaced Clarke and Wieland that they and others of their generation could no longer actively produce within its structures. Rainer's films of the early 1970s—*Lives of Performers* (1972) and *Film about a Woman Who...* (1974)—are cool, ironic psychodramas that draw on autobiographical material but self-reflexively analyze the characters' experiences as women as well as the specifics of their cinematic presentation. The films express an auto-critique of the filmic mode of representation for specifically feminist purposes.

Rainer's analysis of women's bodies and lives as the site of visual and linguistic meanings engages the same theoretical issues as the other most institutionally valorized experimental films of the early 1970s. Consigned to intellectual and aesthetic discourse, the structural film of the late 1960s evolved into a poststructural mode, that is to say, films that emphasized the relationship of image to language. While theorists wrestled in print with the contradictions among cinema theories that defined film as a purely visual form, filmmakers likewise confronted ways that linguistic as well as visual components define what is cinema. Engaged in an intertextual dialogue, scholars and filmmakers addressed issues of how meaning is conveyed through narrativity, language, processes of spectator identification, and pleasure. Played out in classroom spaces and journal pages, the ideas in such films as Michael Snow's *Rameau's Nephew by Diderot (Thanx to Dennis Young) by Wilma Schoen* (1973–74) and Hollis Frampton's *Poetic Justice* (1971) were central to an intellectual discourse articulated outside the films by the filmmakers as well as by scholars. Noël Carroll gave cohesion to this field when he dubbed the poststructural films the "new talkies."[24] The journal *October* validated the claim when it devoted an entire issue to the new talkies in 1981. It covered film theoretical developments in language and film, signification, and sexual difference; individual articles were devoted to Marguerite Duras's *India Song*, Yvonne Rainer, Hollis Frampton, video artist Martha Rosler, and Hans-Jürgen Syberberg.

Rainer's films as well as the filmmaker's own verbal discussion of her films were comfortably situated within this discourse. Rainer's films and her aesthetic concerns received attention no less than four times in *Artforum* between 1970 and 1974; she was interviewed in the avant-garde arts magazines *Avalanche*, and she authored a book (*Work 1961–73*) published by a major university press.[25] Alluding more frequently to contemporary semiotics, psychoanalysis, and film theory than to other art objects or events, the arguments are about language

and signification, spectator identification and alienation, sexual difference and representation. They are made in professional terms: they
rely upon the authority of contemporary European thinkers and re-
quire that the reader be already familiar with post-1968 theoretical
discourse. Such criticism works to ally the filmmaker and the films
with an elite independent film culture.

Rainer was also the object of critical attention in the new feminist
art journals with an audience extended beyond that of independent
cinema. But even in some of these periodicals, most notably *Camera
Obscura* in 1976, Rainer's articles as well as the magazine as a whole
adopt the discourse of elite film culture and address a specific professional audience. The result is that while Rainer as an authorial subject
was identified with both the elite independent film culture of the
early 1970s and with an emergent feminist cinema, the discourse that
contained Rainer was fiercely tied to continental critical theory and
addressed to a specialized group of scholars and artists—feminist and
otherwise. Whereas feminist cinema in the 1970s generally specified
aims of social transformation and addressed a broader audience of
intellectuals, artists, and activists in the women's movement, Rainer's
cinema remained largely within the rarified arena of the new talkies.

The issue here is not to dispute Rainer's feminist analyses but to
suggest how they became known as such among audiences in the
early 1970s. As profoundly important as Rainer's work has been for
independent cinema and particularly for feminist film theory and
criticism in the 1970s and 1980s, her reception has been largely formed
within a space dominated by professional intellectual interests. Inasmuch as Rainer achieved a kind of centrality to the Postmodern cinema
that was unequalled by any of her predecessors, she did so in an arts
system whose position of activist resistance had shrunk while New
York City's role as an international art leader had changed.

After the Avant-garde: The Continent beyond
New York City

By the early 1970s, New York's art and film institutions were no
longer able to so thoroughly dominate the North American arts. Although arts activity had always taken place outside New York City,
other arts centers were only now taking over some of the functions
that the New York art world had controlled for twenty years. For
example, filmmakers such as James Broughton, Stan Brakhage,
Freude Bartlett, Scott Bartlett, Kenneth Anger, Bruce Baillie, and
Bruce Conner had lived and worked outside New York throughout
the 1950s and 1960s. Enclaves of filmmakers in a number of cities

supported each other, attended community screenings, and participated in film and arts journals that were analogous to New York City's activities. Freude Bartlett and Baillie had organized cooperative distributing companies based in northern California (Serious Business, Inc. and Canyon Cinema). Most of the organizations devoted to distribution, exhibition, and critical evaluation, however, had remained in New York City, and they centralized, consolidated, and controlled arts practices and discourse there.

But in the early 1970s, New York's economic retrenchment and narrowing focus on contemporary art made it impossible for the art system to display, consume, and evaluate the increasingly larger numbers of art works being produced throughout the country. Contributing to the economic problems of New York City museums, the National Endowment for the Arts (NEA) revised its award policies and now attempted greater dispersal of federal funds throughout the United States. While former sources for revenue dried up in New York, regional museums in the U.S. competed more successfully for both NEA and corporate funds. Regional centers enjoyed unprecedented economic support, and their rise in power displaced New York City's function as the single gatekeeper to artistic success and prestige.

Among feminist art practices, the situation was more aggravated. Women artists' groups in New York City largely fought the discriminatory traditions of major institutions and created marginal spaces in which to produce, exhibit, and discuss women's art. But their projects, which often seemed aimed at breaking down the doors, suggested that they took their direction and identity from their efforts to gain admission to established centers of the New York art world.

Many of the most exciting developments in women's art in the early and middle 1970s occurred outside New York City. They were more often grounded in the woman-centered analysis or perspective that was increasingly dominating radical feminism. In California, Judy Chicago began the first women's art program in 1971. In 1972, the Feminist Art Program (headed by Chicago and artist Miriam Schapiro) at the California Institute of the Arts built *Womanhouse,* a widely acclaimed and discussed exhibition of woman's domestic environment.[26] In 1973, a coalition of feminist art groups opened the L.A. Woman's Building, an administrative, studio, and exhibition space for women artists. Feminist cooperative galleries, alternative presses that supported women's art journals and newsletters, and women's bookstores existed in every other major city. Some critics felt that working outside the New York environment actually emboldened feminist art because it would not be defined in relation to the practices of the New York mainstream, "The less an alternate structure is in competition with the commodity art world, the better."[27] The network that supported feminist art was not so clearly a hierarchy dominated by New York interests as had been the case in the art world at large for the past two decades.

The independent cinema mirrors these structural changes. Regional film centers became established across the United States and Canada and hosted important seminars, film programs, premiere screenings, and critical activities. Both the San Francisco Bay area in northern California and Chicago provided important institutional bases for independent film activities beginning in 1971 with the founding of the Pacific Film Archives at the University Art Museum in Berkeley and the Midwest Film Center at the School of the Art Institute of Chicago. Film festivals, which featured independent as well as commercial films, had spread across the continent and occurred annually in every major city and on numerous college campuses. These efforts, as well as others, received new support from revised federal funding programs in both the United States and Canada so that they could afford expanded cinema programs that would rival those of the New York City museums.

Decentralization also occurred because of the intensified role that universities played in independent film culture. In the first half of the 1970s, the number of North American schools offering undergraduate and advanced degrees in cinema multiplied so rapidly that several educators have suggested film studies was the fastest growing discipline in advanced education. Whereas some two hundred colleges offered courses in film in 1967, more than one thousand colleges offered curricula in cinema studies by 1977.[28] At the same time, the American Film Institute surveyed one hundred fifty schools offering degrees in film.[29] By the end of the 1970s, the university and art school were not only the chief sources for film culture but were also the primary economic support and organizational refuge for the avant-garde filmmaker. Since 1970, the number of avant-garde filmmakers who held faculty positions had grown steadily (e.g., Ed Emshwiller, Hollis Frampton, Ernie Gehr, George Kuchar, Stan Brakhage, Paul Sharits, Shirley Clarke, and Stan Vanderbeek were among those who had moved into university or art school teaching positions in the 1970s).

Supporting the boom in cinema studies, universities during the 1970s also became leading sites for avant-garde film criticism and promotion as well as for production and exhibition. Although *Film Culture* had been a singular periodical devoted to independent cinema in the 1960s, new periodicals such as *Afterimage, October, Wide Angle,*

The Velvet Light Trap, Millennium Film Journal, and *Jump Cut* constructed what was vanguard in the 1970s as they covered independent film activities and acquired international circulations. Many of these journals received support from academic institutions. The institutional consolidation of film studies also necessitated scholarly production about cinema (professors have to write to retain their faculty positions), and publications about independent film increased while being further absorbed in intellectual journals and established arts magazines.

After the Avant-garde: Toronto as a New Avant-garde Center

Toronto was, in many respects, an exemplary city for how such changes reorienting independent film made it a focal center for an avant-garde. Such prestigious institutions as the Art Gallery of Ontario now ran weekly film screenings that included avant-garde films. Local universities, including the University of Toronto and York University, had stepped up programs for film culture. The number of cinema studies courses increased and film majors multiplied. *Take One,* the Toronto-based film magazine started in 1968, also undertook more scholarly projects under the auspices of its editor, Peter Martin, and during the 1970s published a series of books on Canadian cinema.[30]

Local organizations modeled after the film cooperatives of the early and middle 1960s were also beginning to grow. The Funnel, a small, nonprofit organization reminiscent of Mekas's Film-Makers Cinematheque, held informal screenings and talks by experimental filmmakers in a storefront theater. Two local collectives for independent production and distribution modeled after the Film-Makers' Cooperative were finally in full operation. *Cinema Canada* began monthly publication as a nationalist film magazine.

Inasmuch as Toronto may serve as a model city for art and cinema practices in a changing North American structure, the city also exhibits significant features that differentiate its status from U.S. urban arts environments in the 1970s. Toronto had not merely been another satellite to New York arts culture, it was also an important center for Canadian national arts culture. Artists' collectives concerned with issues of national art and radical art practices had operated in Toronto throughout the century: the Artists Union (1936–37), the Progressive Arts Clubs in the 1930s, the Art Students' League in the late 1920s, and the Group of Seven (1913–24).[31] Wieland herself said, "The difference between [art in] Canada and the United States is that the States never had that kind of working socialist movement that grew from small seeds as in this country."[32] Such models of cooperative artists' organizations became revitalized during the resurgence of nationalism in the late 1960s and early 1970s.

But because of the relationship to New York City arts built up over the last twenty years, Toronto rather contradictorily contained an artistic identity marked by both national self-definition and its "Otherness" to New York and American arts culture. Almost symbolically duplicating women's contemporary position in an arts world structure, Toronto in the 1970s represented tendencies to define a Canadian-identified alternative to American arts values while simultaneously defining itself against and in relation to those values. If, as larger patterns demonstrate, descriptions of arts activities in the 1970s can no longer focus on New York City in isolation, Toronto may be the single most important city for encapsulating and articulating tensions between a Postmodern arts economy and political resistance to dominant definitions and categories.

Joyce Wieland and the Toronto Avant-garde

The expressions of a nationalist spirit growing among Toronto's artists and filmmakers occurred not only in public statements and critical discourse but also in the development of a new structural framework for political arts activities. Wieland assumed a position of leadership within this evolving network of alternative organizations. She became a key figure in the local chapter of the national artists' union, Canadian Artists' Representation (CAR). CAR, begun in 1968 by Ontario artists Jack Chambers and Greg Curnoe, represented the hope that an organization structured like a labor union could improve the artist's economic status.

In early 1972, Wieland and the Ontario branch of CAR, CARO, demanded that the Art Gallery of Ontario (AGO) rescind its appointment of a U.S. citizen as its chief curator and end its policy of using public funding on non-Canadian art. After a series of staged protests, petition campaigns, and private lobbying efforts throughout 1972, the museum agreed to a compromise. The Art Gallery of Ontario promised to include artist representation in the museum's future policymaking decisions, and it elected Wieland to its board of trustees. Although Wieland felt AGO's move was only a token gesture of acquiescence, she nevertheless celebrated with the other CARO members the museum's concession that the artist has a right to shape museum governance policies.[33]

Wieland's year-long term on the board of trustees was a stormy one.

When the museum planned an exhibit funded by a private corporation that held South African investments, Wieland opposed a corporate sponsor that supported the apartheid government. Alone among the artists scheduled to be included in the exhibit, Wieland withdrew her work from the show and notified CARO, who picketed outside the museum. Board members, angry over Wieland's posture and the increasingly public threat of CARO, opposed further election to its body of any artists when Wieland's one-year term ended.

Wieland instead helped CARO rechannel its political energies for a new primary target—the public. In a series of 1973 art shows, lectures, fundraisers, and performances, Wieland and CARO championed the Cree tribe's lawsuit against the province of Ontario. They opposed the province's proposed dam construction in James Bay because it would flood tribal lands, ruin the region's ecological balance, and force six thousand people to relocate their homes. Under Wieland's leadership, CARO became more than a labor coalition for individual artists' rights. It instead represented an alternative political advocacy program that, through artists' works and collective presence, could educate the public about pressing Canadian problems.

Pierre Vallières (1972)

While she simultaneously participated in CARO's political protests and worked in other media, Wieland made two new short films as part of her larger artistic program. *Pierre Vallières* and *Solidarity* (1973) tackle contemporary Canadian political issues and create sympathy for the oppressed—in one, a Québecois separatist who is a political prisoner, in the other, laborers who are striking against a factory owner. The two films remain aesthetically rooted in structural cinema but have a popular accessibility that is not evident in any of Wieland's earlier work.

Pierre Vallières is a forty-five-minute interview that Wieland and two other women conducted with the revolutionary Pierre Vallières. His activities supporting Quebec's secession from Canada had made him an outlaw and a folk hero. Wieland's film concentrates on a single physical detail of the man, Vallières's moustached mouth. The visual image of the moving mouth fills the entire screen while the soundtrack is composed of Vallières's monologues on what he sees as Canada's two primary colonized groups: women and the Québecois.

Drawing on a cinéma vérité rhetorical style, the film focuses on a political oral narrative spontaneously presented in response to an interviewer's questions. But though one expects from cinéma vérité that the character will unknowingly reveal some deeper truth about himself, the single image of the speaker's enlarged mouth does not initially seem well-suited for character analysis. This rather typical Wieland point of view is a highly unusual practice in cinéma vérité, but it is a recurring feature of structural films. The image of Vallières's mouth resurrects the structural technique of extensively examining a single image to reveal something about how it conveys meaning.

In its magnified state, the large pulsating mouth—two pink, moist lips; coarse, black hair; a graceful tongue;—has a physical similarity to female genitalia. If a linkage between mouth/lips and vagina is already symbolically inherent, the particular point of view here makes it visually explicit. But the image further inverts classic psychoanalytic interpretations of female sexuality as negative, unformed, and passive and instead highlights the strong, sensuous movement of the lips. As Lucy Lippard said, "Unlike the passive 'movie star mouths' of Warhol or Wesselmann, [Wieland's] are active; they have something to say."[34]

The same image also imparts an important cultural significance. The discolored, crooked teeth framed by the two lips and moving tongue suggest the speaker's origins in the working class. The cultural hero here is ostensibly the colorful individual Pierre Vallières, but Wieland has so individualized a single detail that it becomes an emblematic icon for sexual and political power. The man's mouth is a social poetics about the interconnectedness between the individual, feminine sexuality, and political power.

Solidarity

Wieland's next film, made a year later with Judy Steed, is also ostensibly a documentary. *Solidarity*'s material images are from a workers' strike at the Dare food plant in Kitchener, Ontario. Like *Pierre Vallières*, it has a close-up viewpoint accompanied by political speeches that emanate from the image's field (diegetic sound). In this case, however, the closely examined objects are the feet of various picketers at a demonstration; the soundtrack is made up of the electronically amplified speeches from the stage. The political conditions of Canadian working women is the thematic topic.

In *Solidarity*, Wieland has finally found an alternative for creating spatial depth without depicting it pictorially in a realist cinematic manner. The moving camera and edited series of feet affirm a great spatial field without defining any continuous geographic space. Whereas Vallières's voice acoustically marked an off-screen space as an extension of the limited, static frame, *Solidarity*'s electronically amplified speeches and crowd reactions only allude to an ambiguous space beyond the magnified frame. Wieland has produced an imaginary terrain filled with feet, women's strong voices, and radical messages.

Solidarity is reminiscent of Wieland's earlier experimental films in that its magnified details are so isolated from any depth of field and are seen so closely that colors, textures, and shapes become interesting features in and of themselves. The numerous mud puddles against which the feet are viewed are more evocative of *Water Sark*'s celebration of light-reflected surfaces almost ten years earlier than of *Pierre Vallières*. But like *Pierre Vallières,* the magnified images have important cultural connotations. In this case, the feet—sandaled, high-heeled, bare, black, white—reinforce the sense of crowd diversity and, more important, underline the multiplicity of ethnic, age, class, and racial groups composing the demonstration. It seems appropriate that Wieland, who loves puns and ironies, may claim credit for progressing in a short span of time from watching what a leader says to concentrating on what the people's feet do.

Toward a Feminist, Nationalist Cinema: *The Far Shore* (1976)

At the same time she was making *Solidarity* and *Pierre Vallières* and participating in the loose network of Toronto activist art organizations, Wieland was also writing and trying to finance a feature-length film for a popular audience. In what seems to be a paradoxical move, she attempted a breakthrough to the commercial cinema. Wieland wanted to make a feminist film with Canadian ideological issues on a large scale. It was an extension of her woman-centered position that female experience and representation should provide the dominant values for the culture as a whole.

Although Wieland had witnessed Clarke's failure to achieve a successful alternative commercial cinema in New York, she expected that the same practices might work in Canada where, at the time, any Canadian-made film was, by definition, alternative cinema. As Wieland's art dealer, Avrom Isaacs, observed, "Anyone else [but Joyce] would have known that you couldn't raise the money [to make a movie] . . . and they wouldn't have tried."[35] Few Canadian films could secure enough investors to be completed, and even fewer reached the public. In the early 1970s, Canadian commercial film production was practically nonexistent, although Canada was the single largest foreign market for American films.[36] Booming box office revenues in the first half of the 1970s had no effect on Canadian film production. Such a

stalemate occurred because two multinational corporations (Famous
Players Limited and Odeon Theatres Limited) owned or controlled
more than 66 percent of the commercial cinemas in Canada while nine
distributors acted as agents for American companies and controlled
more than 90 percent of commercial theatrical film rentals.[37] This
effectively reserved the exhibition outlets for American features, virtually guaranteeing that without access to the theaters, few Canadian
features would attract investors.

A new wave of optimism regarding the future of a Canadian film
industry and new economic incentives had an ameliorating effect in
the middle 1970s. A small number of commercial Canadian films were
beginning to make an international breakthrough. The success of such
films as *The Apprenticeship of Duddy Kravitz* (1974) and *Lies My Father
Told Me* (1975) seemed to indicate the emergence of a Canadian film
industry that would break the market monopoly of Hollywood films.
When the Canadian government closed a tax loophole that gave private investors a more sizable tax write-off for films that were nonreturn
investments, it halted investment interest in the failure of Canadian
cinema. In 1975, both Famous Players and Odeon Theatres agreed
to support the emergent Canadian film industry with a voluntary
exhibition quota and an investment program.

Wieland's fund-raising efforts for her film benefited directly from
such changes. Like other hopeful commercial projects, Wieland's
film received public funding from the Canadian Film Development
Corporation, the national agency that promoted Canadian commercial filmmaking, but she required more than limited federal support
to complete production and gain access to the exhibition network.
With the changed atmosphere in 1975, she was finally able to get
the necessary production funds from Famous Players, and the
corporation's backing assured her entrance into the commercial
exhibition network.

Wieland's film participated in this boom because, in its guise as a
period melodrama, it appeared to be an ideal commercial vehicle—an
apolitical, sentimental story about a pair of star-crossed lovers, one
Québecois, the other English-Canadian. Even though investors were
nervous that the film's producers were two women who had never
made a feature film, it met their need for a Canadian story while the
script did not stray too far from Hollywood generic conventions. *The
Far Shore*, however, invokes social analysis through the heroine's discovery that legally, economically, and psychologically, marriage robs
a woman of her independence and right to self-determination. Adopting melodramatic form for a feminist statement, *The Far Shore* both

depicts the way the bourgeois family entraps the individual and critiques the nuclear family as the basic social model of patriarchal culture.

The precredit sequence shows the heroine, Eulalie, being courted by her future husband in her native Quebec in 1919. Amidst a country landscape of flowers and tall grasses on a sunny summer day, Eulalie expresses great love for her surroundings, whereas her male companion, Ross, stiffly explains in English and broken French that he only beholds land to be improved scientifically. Eulalie and Ross represent simplified aspects of bicultural, bilingual Canada, an identification that is cemented when the young girl accompanying them serves as go-between for Ross's marriage proposal and he is unable to understand Eulalie's acceptance in French.

Ross's and Eulalie's wedding and postnuptial auto trip to Toronto are set against a lush musical score during the credit sequence. The dramatic action begins when Eulalie enters her husband's bourgeois home in Toronto. She discovers there that he truly only wanted a "housewife," a woman who could be a domestic and social ornament. Psychologically and culturally isolated, Eulalie meets one kindred spirit in her new surroundings, the landscape painter residing on her husband's estate. The painter Tom McLeod is modeled on Canada's most legendary artist Tom Thomson, a master of Canadian wilderness scenes who mysteriously disappeared on an Ontario lake in 1917. Thomson also figured prominently in the formation of the Group of Seven, Canada's first organized supporters and producers of a nationalist art.

Drawn together by their mutual respect for the unspoiled beauty of nature, Eulalie and Tom express the possibility of a union based in love for the arts, closeness to the land, and uncomplicated romantic passion. But when Tom refuses to compromise his ideals by serving as Ross's guide on a northern Ontario mining expedition, he leaves the estate, and Eulalie is lonelier than ever. Later, on a camping trip with her husband and his friends in northern Ontario, Eulalie again meets the artist. Dissatisfied with her marriage and the way of life that her husband represents, she takes an ax to Ross's rowboat, jumps fully clothed into the icy northern lake, and swims to join Tom camped across the water.

Ross and a friend subsequently make a futile search for the couple, who are enjoying a passionate reunion. But in the finale, the friend spies the couple in their canoe and fires two gunshots at them. The last images are the overturned canoe, the artist's dead body, and Eulalie's hat floating on the water.

Feminist Melodrama as a Woman's Discourse: *The Far Shore*

The crises of domestic melodrama are personal and emotional as distinct from the primarily social and behavioral conflicts of westerns, science fiction films, or horror movies. The possibilities for broad spatial action are, therefore, more limited in domestic melodrama than in certain other genres. The genre must depend upon states of mind expressed or externalized into visual terms. British film scholar Thomas Elsaesser has described the process as a sublimation of the dramatic values into the mise-en-scène.[38] He further explains how the symbolic significance of the objects that fill the mise-en-scène produce a criticism of the patriarchal systems of familial relationships, "The setting of the family melodrama almost by definition is the middle-class home, filled with objects, which surround the heroine in a hierarchy of apparent order that becomes increasingly suffocating. . . . [It] also brings out the characteristic attempt of the bourgeois household to make time stand still, immobilise life and fix forever domestic property relations as the model of social life and a bulwark against the more disturbing sides of human nature."[39] Elsaesser concludes that the family melodrama introduces through the mise-en-scène a claustrophobia that visually undermines the family as a structure for a woman's individual fulfillment.

In the best Hollywood family melodramas, for example, those by Vincente Minnelli or Douglas Sirk, individual crises that threaten the stability of the family unit always lead to a reconciliation that reenforces the authority and self-containment of the family. The films' visual emphasis on the trappings and designed spaces of the bourgeois home suggests that it is the materialistic values of American society rather than the antagonism of other characters that keep the protagonist frustrated in the family unit and unable to achieve his or her individual desires. In such films as *The Magnificent Obsession* (1954), *All That Heaven Allows* (1955), *The Cobweb* (1955), and *Home From the Hills* (1960), Sirk and Minnelli amplify the contradictions between the family's inability to accommodate individual fulfillment and the plots' contrived endings that artificially reconcile differences without resolving the initial problems. This presentation subverts the narrative values of closure and patriarchal authority upheld by Hollywood classical cinema and results in a Hollywood-styled format characterized by its own internal contradictions.[40]

Elsaesser's argument is an important consideration for a discussion of *The Far Shore* because such internal generic contradictions of family melodrama are a dominant issue of the film's expression. *The Far*

Shore's imagery emphasizes environmental textures, colors, shapes, and slow rhythms, heightening the expressiveness of setting, decor, objects, and gestures. Long takes, limited camera movement, and editing patterns further contribute to elongated scenes with little dramatic action and to abbreviated or concentrated scenes with great dramatic action. The expressiveness of the mise-en-scène is more important than narrative events or characterization, and it serves the idea of spatial and material entrapment in the family as *The Far Shore*'s primary theme.

But while maintaining the characteristic structure of family melodramas, Wieland disrupts even further the Hollywood-styled discourse that, through the system of the "suture," encourages the spectator to identify with fictional representation as a reflection of his or her subjectivity. The process of cinematic suture occurs through narrative and formal articulation, most notably in the relationships among individual shots. For example, the shot–reverse shot paradigm of classical Hollywood cinema offers the viewer a pattern of images whereby the controlling gaze of the cinematic apparatus is displaced onto a character within the narrative so that the representation of his individual subjectivity becomes privileged as the speaking subject of the text. This displacement from the initial image's promise of plentitude and signification of a speaking subject is part of a larger system of cinematic organization known as classical continuity editing. Together with the effacement of the work done by the cinematic apparatus, the Hollywood film constructs a system of absences and negations through which coherence and plentitude emerge.

Hollywood narrative similarly relies on a series of structuring absences. It promises the eventual disclosure of something not yet revealed by repetitively inscribing what is lacking or missing and by disturbing the original stability only so that it can be restored at the end. In other words, the stabilized order represented at the film's outset is broken (the revelation of a lack), which initiates spectator desire for a return to the imaginary coherence and abundance first offered. The narrative progresses through a series of delays until ultimately it does return to its point of origin, thus compensating the spectator for the perceived loss and provisionally suturing or mending what has been lost. *The Far Shore* may promise just such a narrative trajectory in its initial, somewhat classically composed scenes of a marriage proposal, a wedding, and a honeymoon that is disturbed once the honeymoon is over. But the film, nevertheless, undermines the possibility of resolution and a return to order.

The Far Shore does not, in the formula of Hollywood domestic melodrama, effect closure wherein the woman returns to the space within conventional bourgeois boundaries. *The Far Shore* instead concludes with Tom's visible death and an on-screen marker of Eulalie's disappearance. Until this last moment, the possibility for a conventional resolution existed either through Tom as Eulalie's more suitable partner in a liberal marriage or through Tom's death and Eulalie's subsequent return to her husband. But Eulalie's disappearance beyond the boundaries of the frame ruptures melodramatic closure. Although she is rendered "absent," Eulalie is beyond the screen space established by the film and escapes to the invisible wilderness that Wieland labels "the far shore." In this context, Eulalie cannot be reintegrated into any determined closure and cannot be reinscribed into women's social roles within patriarchy.

The Far Shore's punctuation with silent film techniques that are contemporary with the story's time period also disturbs the smooth operation of classical cinema storytelling. For example, the increasing tempo of crosscutting between Eulalie and Tom in one canoe and their pursuers, Ross and his friend, in another canoe, cites D. W. Griffith's use of parallel action. Griffith's convention for conveying a climactic pursuit may seem an homage easily accommodated within Wieland's formal system. But the reference itself becomes excessive when accompanied here by a musical cliché for silent film chases. Rendered here as an anachronism for representation of a pursuit, the scene itself becomes a parody of silent film chases that calls attention to the apparatus as the speaking subject, an obvious rupture during the movie's most important dramatic action.

The mise-en-scène, in its attempt to serve both a narrative function and a conscious metaphoric one, similarly relies upon such an extended play of painterly homage that it, too, ruptures the effacement of the means for constructing realism. Employing dramatic expressionistic light to intensify color, the mise-en-scène imitates a baroque painterly illusionism, functioning simultaneously as a visual correlative for the intense emotional crises of the heroine and a photographic summary of European and Canadian art history. Interior scenes reproduce the look of Dutch and Italian Masters while the lake wilderness scenes photographically mimic famous Canadian painters' interpretations. The movie's lighting and textural effects in certain scenes are even reminiscent of Jean-Baptiste Siméon Chardin or the Canadian landscape artists of the Group of Seven. Wieland exploits a common technique from her structural films whereby images themselves contradict the notion that they represent photographic material of a natural world.

For example, repetitive cutaway close-ups of carpets, paintings, and embroideries that bridge changes of scene and time may all be leitmotifs intertwining Eulalie's and Tom's identification with artistic activity as the means for spiritual redemption. But these close-ups are so magnified that the shots emphasize the material qualities of the images, their texture, hue, reflection of light, and formal arrangements. The close-ups ultimately undermine their function within an illusionistic story and point instead to their own abstract expressionism.

At the formal level, *The Far Shore* does not rely upon classical Hollywood editing. There are no establishing shots nor is there fragmentation of the visual perspective to suture the spectator into a visual field of plentitude. There are single long takes and the extended visual perspectives of Eulalie and Tom as character subjects without any recourse to the absent reverse field that affixes their positions as such.

For example, cutaway close-ups that introduce new scenes run counter to the Hollywood convention of wide establishing shots that orient the spectator to an implied three-dimensional space. A night scene of Eulalie occupying her time alone begins with an extreme close-up of an embroidered fish on which a hand sews. The shot serves Eulalie's subjective point of view without articulating this position in a conventional shot–reverse shot pattern. The embroidered fish symbolically refers to the water and water/life motif that links the painter Tom to Eulalie throughout the film, and the image also reinforces the role of art itself as both a structural and symbolic motif of unity.

When the extended scene introduced by the embroidery close-up ends as Eulalie's husband Ross begins to rape her, the film cuts from a medium long shot of the grappling couple to an extreme close-up of another fish, one that Tom is painting onto a shop window. (Ross's sexual activity is a violent attempt at domination in the form of rape, and his professional activity also rapes the land and water to build sewers, bridges, and dams that will exemplify men's mastery over their environment.) The motif not only joins Tom and Eulalie as artists against Eulalie's husband but also repeats the process of inscribing a subject's point of view while withholding the identity of that subject as a character within the film. The image of the partially formed fish, lacking definition and the suggestion of modeling, is initially unable to indicate any cinematic space or even a natural object. It momentarily breaks the smooth flow of the story and links locales and characters only through the image's poetic properties.

In another example, Eulalie listens to her husband lecturing his employees, and the visual field first offered is her point of view of a richly patterned carpet. The extended duration of the close-up as the first shot in the scene fixes the image as a representation of an art object and as a self-referent, undermining its service to the illusionism of the narrative. The accompanying voice of Eulalie's husband Ross relays information about engineering's role in building the future. It comes from an off-screen space that cannot be acoustically or visually (diegetically) identified as an extension of the on-screen space. Sound and image operate as discrete elements, establishing an antagonism between contemplating objects as art and the scientific approach of dominating and mastering nature. The information that this perception—both literal and thematic—is fixed in an individual character source is so delayed that the subsequent revelation (a move to an establishing objective point of view that centrally frames Eulalie staring at the carpet) becomes the scene's climax. In effect, the film asks that the process of suture with Eulalie become a key issue rather than a transparent or assumed position.

An extended scene between Tom and Eulalie in Tom's cabin midway through the film further illustrates how these formal processes are articulated along the story's trajectory. In this scene, the characters take turns holding a magnifying glass up to their lips and silently mouthing texts to each other. The image is reminiscent of Wieland's extreme close-up of lips in *Pierre Vallières*. A detail within the close-up, the mouth (Wieland's personal motif for women's strength and power) literally becomes magnified cinematographically, producing a visual pun on the cinema's iris effect. The scene's lack of any accompanying soundtrack further displaces emphasis onto the visual organization and interrupts the kind of flow on which classic narrative cinema time is based.

After the silent mouthing, which occurs in real time, several days and weeks elide into roughly the same amount of screen time. The depiction of elapsed time is inverted again as Tom and Eulalie sing an entire folk song together in real time. Although these different depictions of time occur within the same geographic space in the narrative, the sequences convey little new narrative information or insight into character; instead, they operate more as pure poetic devices. They thus exemplify a creative mix of experimental and narrative techniques that undermine the film as a conventionally naturalistic story.

When the claustrophobic entrapment of Eulalie's marriage has reached crisis proportions, the film achieves its formal climax. In Eulalie's bedroom, a close-up iris shot of Eulalie fades completely to a white disc framed in red. It then slowly dissolves to a canoe crossing a lake within the white disc and then irises out so that the landscape image fills the entire frame. As a simple narrative transition, the highly unusual shot connects Eulalie to the wilderness landscape through which Tom now glides in his canoe. The midway red-and-white formal abstraction of the extended dissolve also symbolically links Tom and Eulalie with the colors of the Canadian flag. But, at more abstract levels, the subject of the transition is its transcendence into a cinematic art object. The constriction visually portrays Eulalie's psychological claustrophobia with Ross, and the dilation symbolically foreshadows the psychological release she will feel when she joins Tom in the wilderness. Since Eulalie's point of view has organized the progression, it also suggests a subjective sexual daydream—her internal visual point of view, a visual field of multiple images. The activity of the technique makes female orgasm the power that here controls and unifies the construction of the image.

The Public Reception: The Making and Unmaking of *The Far Shore*

In the context of marketing and publicizing a commercial film to a broad audience, *The Far Shore* did not articulate the importance of simultaneously comprehending both Hollywood and experimental levels of discourse, prompting serious problems for reading the film. Generic formulas (melodrama and otherwise) and experimental cinema have traditionally posed markedly different sets of demands upon the spectator. Popular commercial movie audiences were not generally familiar enough with the way Wieland's previous films drew upon structural film strategies to disrupt the illusion of realist narrative, nor were they accustomed to frequent disruptions and disturbances to a system for coherence they understood as pleasurable. Independent cinema followers were not comfortable with Wieland's wholesale adoption of a discourse so enmeshed in popular codes and so removed from a "pure" experimental discourse of low budgets, antinarrative or narrative deconstruction, and formal or phenomenological aesthetics. Like Deren's and Clarke's films, *The Far Shore* was contained within dominant discourses of either classical or independent cinema, which presented problems for understanding the film's representation and critique of gender identity. In the case of *The Far Shore*, Wieland's two largest potential audiences were so unprepared for the intertextual familiarity necessary for reading the film that the film ultimately frustrated and alienated much of its audience.

By publicizing and promoting the film project since 1970, Wieland had helped to shape reception for the film without directing expecta-

tions to its intertextuality. Canadian magazines and Toronto's daily
newspapers had closely followed the film's evolution through all its
preproduction and production phases.[41] Even such a small production
detail as the Thomsonesque paintings used in the film as Tom
McLeod's work became the subject for a newspaper feature.[42] But
the public discourse that cohered during the years in which she was
constantly trying to find backers situated the film within rhetoric that
promoted the act of making the film itself over the film's radical
strategies.

A large amount of press coverage on the making of a Canadian
feature film was not unusual in the cultural climate of Canada in
the middle 1970s. Movie reviewer and culture critic Robert Fulford
observed in 1974, "In any art . . . the art object is what counts, the
everything else is what doesn't count. The everything else includes
financing, promotion, prize-giving, reviewing and conversation at the
party after the premiere. . . . In the Canadian cinema the order is
reversed: the *everything else* is what people talk about, worry about,
write articles about."[43] The self-promotion of Canadian cinema was not
only more important than the individual product but wholly consistent
with the avant-garde model that Wieland had learned in New York in
the 1960s.

Even in this context, *The Far Shore* and Wieland received more
attention than was usual because Wieland's case stimulated its own
dramatic narrative for the newspapers. Wieland's six-year struggle to
find investors allowed the press to write a romantic story of the virtuous
Canadian artist-heroine trying to create a major work of art about
Canada without the corrupting influence or money of the American
business community. Some of the periodic newspaper accounts that
describe Wieland going door-to-door in downtown Toronto skyscrapers or Wieland battling with the Canadian Film Development Corporation surround her with an aura more like *The Perils of Pauline* than a
contemporary film producer.

The film's commercial career, however, was brief and troubled. By
marketing the film herself, Wieland had no energy left after making
the film. She was also naive about distribution and exhibition practices.
As a victim of inexpert marketing and of the limited access individual
Canadian filmmakers have to theatrical outlets, *The Far Shore* got only
limited trial commercial runs at Famous Players theaters in Toronto
and Ottawa. The film opened and closed quickly in both cities, where
audiences and critics alike saw the film as "a confusing mix of humor
and soap."[44] Among the popular audiences that were unprepared for
the radical formal strategies, the art crowd that felt the film was a

paean to commercialism, and the nationalists who thought *The Far Shore* purveyed an apolitical, sentimental federalism, the film had few champions.

The film's showing failed to interest other commercial distributors or exhibitors, and Wieland pursued the alternative exhibition route— the film festival. But after the audience at the 1976 Edinburgh Film Festival reacted hostilely to the film, Wieland grew discouraged and dropped that strategy. Wieland was in attendance at the festival that had warmly received her earlier films, and she felt betrayed when the audience chided her for employing popular conventions and a romantic aura.[45] After being rejected by the audience that had formerly championed her, Wieland completely divorced herself from any international community of independent filmmakers.

Since the film's initial release in 1976, *The Far Shore* has intermittently played at other film festivals, college campuses, art museums, and film societies. It was not until 1978, however, that the film even had a United States booking.[46] *The Far Shore* has been relegated to the same kind of elitist network in which Wieland's other films participate while it enjoys none of the artistic prestige such a network confers. Without a marketing campaign to give the film widespread commercial appeal and without a critical or theoretical framework to promote the film to intellectuals, *The Far Shore* instead became obscure.

With all these detractors, *The Far Shore* got lost and its potential as a feminist film went largely unnoticed. But the greatest strengths of *The Far Shore* are exactly those strategies that were problematized by the film, alienating audiences when it was first released. The significance of *The Far Shore* as an effort to understand the dynamics of a radical feminist film form was particularly noted by feminist theorist-filmmaker Laura Mulvey.[47] *The Far Shore* invokes the value of simultaneous cognition and disruption of linear narrativity and illusionist spectacle as direct means for the inauguration of a feminist discourse.

The Far Shore represents a kind of "mid-life summing up" in Joyce Wieland's career, since it was released the year she turned forty-five. She had been working on the film since *True Patriot Love*, released the year she turned forty.[48] In many respects, the film is less a summary of Wieland's position than a synthesis of her art and life up to that point. It is especially possible to see the film this way once one remembers art critic Harold Rosenberg's dictum, "If art went backwards, it would be handicraft and if it went forward, it would become media."[49] Wieland's work in the 1970s, and particularly *The Far Shore*, incorporates these polarities as well as the two poles of cinema discourse, the seeming opposites of commercial and experimental cinemas.

The varied nature of Wieland's art in the 1970s—quilts, a feature film, experimental documentaries, political activism, perfume, and even a cake—has prevented many critics from arriving at any statement unifying her place among the art worlds of Canada, the United States, feminism, and cinema. Some have even blamed Wieland for not being an artist easily pigeonholed or categorized, labeling her work "an untidy array,"[50] as one critic proclaimed, "Cloudcuckoolands will interest the curator or scholar who someday tries to put together all the pieces of Miss Wieland's various, unusual career."[51] The implication is that "to make a mess" is to introduce chaos rather than to court efficiency, to be sloppy and disorderly rather than to be tidy and ordered, in short, to be irrational rather than rational. Such a monumentally patronizing statement admits and reiterates a number of points: the continued anger against a woman artist who challenges patriarchy; the dismissal of feminine regimes as the articulation of art and the world; the castigation and relegation of Woman as Other to the irrational.

But as one shifts to feminist discourse in the 1970s and 1980s, Wieland's position as an artist and filmmaker should be reevaluated. Lucy Lippard's response that cloudcuckoolands do interest her begins to frame a perspective whereby the critical terms themselves redefine what constitutes artistic expression, process, and purpose.[52] Lippard was not the first to reclaim Wieland's importance for the transformations of art and cinema into the 1980s, but she has argued the case most eloquently, "Women artists are often *accused* of being synthesizers, as though synthesis were not the ultimate ingredient of transformation. The patronizing implication that men innovate, erecting the poles of thesis and antithesis, and women come along afterwards and smooth off the edges in synthesis is outdated. It is the synthesizers . . . who open the gates to new fields so that the innovators can dash ahead—for a while."[53] Wieland's chief contribution has been one of synthesis: she bridges the avant-garde model of postwar experimental cinema and the socialist tradition of Canadian nationalist art. She adapted these for feminist purposes in the 1970s, renegotiating political systems and representation strategies to remake the power structures of society and to imagine within them a powerful discourse of the feminine.

NOTES

1. "Kay Armatage Interviews Joyce Wieland," *Take One* 3, no. 2 (Nov.–Dec. 1970), 24.
2. Lucy Lippard, "Watershed: Contradiction, Communication and Canada

in Joyce Wieland's Work," in *Joyce Wieland,* ed. Philip Monk (Toronto: Key Porter Books, 1987), 10.

3. For a more detailed account of *True Patriot Love/Véritable Amour Patriotique* in this regard, see Lauren Rabinovitz, "Issues of Feminist Aesthetics: Judy Chicago and Joyce Wieland," *Woman's Art Journal* 1, no. 2 (Fall 1980–Winter 1981): 38–41.

4. Kay Kritzwiser, "Wieland: Ardent Art for Unity's Sake," *Toronto Globe and Mail,* 25 Mar. 1967, Joyce Wieland file, National Gallery of Canada, Ottawa, Canada.

5. William Ronald, as quoted by Adele Freedman, "Joyce Wieland's Re-emergence: The Arctic Light at the End of *The Far Shore,*" *Toronto Life,* June 1980, 184–85.

6. Kathleen Walker's "The Artist as Patriot," *Ottawa Citizen,* 23 Oct. 1976, Joyce Wieland file, National Gallery of Canada, sums up the critical reviews for *True Patriot Love.* But, for especially pointed examples, also see Anthony Westell, "Abusing American Won't Save Canada," *Toronto Daily Star,* 10 July 1971, Joyce Wieland file, National Gallery of Canada; Ashley Blackman, "Joyce Wieland at the National Gallery," *Ottawa Citizen,* 29 July 1971, Joyce Wieland file, National Gallery of Canada.

7. Tom Rossiter, "Wieland vs. Picasso," *Ottawa Citizen,* 7 Aug. 1971, Joyce Wieland file, National Gallery of Canada.

8. Ibid.

9. Kritzwiser, "Wieland: Ardent Art for Unity's Sake."

10. Harold Rosenberg, as quoted in Diana Crane, *The Transformation of the Avant-garde: The New York Art World, 1940–1985* (Chicago: University of Chicago Press, 1987), 45.

11. Suzi Gablik, *Has Modernism Failed?* (New York: Thames and Hudson, 1984), 60.

12. Peter Schjeldahl, as quoted in ibid., 55.

13. Robert Mangold, as quoted in ibid., 61.

14. Gablik, *Has Modernism Failed?* 73.

15. Ibid., 73–74.

16. Crane, *The Transformation of the Avant-garde,* 127.

17. Ibid., 128.

18. Gablik, *Has Modernism Failed?* 66.

19. Lucy Lippard, "Trojan Horses: Activist Art and Power," in *Art after Modernism: Rethinking Representation,* ed. Brian Wallis (New York: New Museum of Contemporary Art, 1984), 350.

20. Hester Eisenstein, *Contemporary Feminist Thought* (Boston: G. K. Hall, 1983), 47. Eisenstein credits the term *woman-centered analysis* to feminist historian Gerda Lerner; Eisenstein, *Contemporary Feminist Thought,* 155.

For a sample of Rich's work in this regard, see Adrienne Rich, *On Lies, Secrets, and Silence: Selected Prose, 1966–1978* (New York: W. W. Norton, 1979); Adrienne Rich, *Of Woman Born: Motherhood as Experience and Institution* (New York: W. W. Norton, 1976). For representative work by Griffin, see *Woman and Nature: The Roaring inside Her* (New York: Harper and Row, 1978).

21. Claire Johnston, "Women's Cinema as Counter-cinema," in *Sexual Stra-*

tegems: The World of Women in Film, ed. Patricia Erens (New York: Horizon Press, 1979), 139–40.

22. Both Julia Lesage and E. Ann Kaplan have responded to Johnston's claim and offered tempered versions of her argument. By comparing *Joyce at Thirty-four* to *Janie's Janie,* Kaplan argues that the latter does allow for raised consciousness, is subversive, and resists dominant female placing. She says that the film "shows a woman aware of the economic and class structures that formed her and [she makes] . . . a deliberate, and decisive, break with those structures. . . . As a working-class figure who speaks roughly and is not elegantly turned out, Janie's image is subversive. As an unabashedly militant, determined woman, who is ready to fight, Janie's representation resists dominant female placing." Kaplan and Lesage both conclude that certain examples of feminist realist films achieve a "limited" resistance to hegemonic codes of cinema, accomplishing a great deal both ideologically and visually. E. Ann Kaplan, *Women and Film: Both Sides of the Camera* (New York: Methuen, 1983), 130. See also Julia Lesage, "The Political Aesthetics of the Feminist Documentary Film," *Quarterly Review of Film Studies* 3, no. 4 (1978): 507–23.

23. The Camera Obscura Collective, "Yvonne Rainer: An Interview," *Camera Obscura,* no. 1 (Fall 1976): 85.

24. Noël Carroll, "An Interview with a Woman Who. . ." *Millennium Film Journal,* nos. 7–9 (Fall-Winter 1980–81): 37.

25. Stephen Koch, "Performance—A Conversation," *Artforum* 11, no. 4 (Dec. 1972); Lizzie Borden, "Trisha Brown and Yvonne Rainer," *Artforum* 11, no. 10 (June 1973); Annette Michelson, "Yvonne Rainer, Part One: the Dancer and the Dance," *Artforum* 12, no. 5 (Jan. 1974); Annette Michelson, "Part Two: Lives of Performers," *Artforum* 12, no. 6 (Feb. 1974): 30–35. See also Willoughby Sharp and Lisa Béar, "The Performer as Persona: An Interview with Yvonne Rainer," *Avalanche* (Summer 1972): 53; Yvonne Rainer, *Work, 1961–73* (New York: New York University Press, 1974).

26. For a more complete discussion of *Womanhouse,* see Judy Chicago, *Through the Flower: My Struggle as a Woman Artist* (Garden City, N.Y.: Anchor Books, 1977), 104–32. Chicago's autobiography itself serves as a good example of argument for a woman-centered perspective, and it argues from a position of consciousness-raising rhetoric. By highlighting her individual experiences of discrimination, Chicago hopes that other women will see widespread social patterns of injustice. In her discussion of her own consciousness raising to feminism, she presents herself as a role model in an effort to achieve solidarity with others.

27. Lucy Lippard, *From the Center: Feminist Essays on Women's Art* (New York: E. P. Dutton, 1976), 99.

28. Robert C. Allen and Douglas Gomery, *Film History: Theory and Practice* (New York: Alfred A. Knopf, 1985), 27–28.

29. Ibid.

30. A list of the Toronto publisher's books includes *The Handbook of Canadian Film,* 2d ed., by Eleanor Beattie, 1977; *The War for Men's Minds,* by Gary Evans, 1978; and *Canadian Film Reader,* by Seth Feldman and Joyce Nelson, 1977.

31. Barry Lord, *The History of Painting in Canada: Towards a People's Art* (Toronto: N. C. Press, 1974), passim.

32. Joyce Wieland, interview with author, Toronto, Canada, 11 Mar. 1980. Quoted with the permission of Joyce Wieland.

33. Ibid.

34. Lippard, "Watershed," 8.

35. Avrom Isaacs, as quoted in Michelle Landsberg, "Joyce Wieland: Artist in Movieland," *Chatelaine* 49, no. 10 (Oct. 1976): 110.

36. Eleanor Beattie, *The Handbook of Canadian Film*, 3.

37. Ibid., 15.

38. Thomas Elsaesser, "Tales of Sound and Fury: Observations on the Family Melodrama" *Monogram*, no. 4 (1974): 7.

39. Ibid., 12–13.

40. D. N. Rodowick, "Madness, Authority, and Ideology in the Domestic Melodrama of the 1950s," *The Velvet Light Trap*, no. 19 (1982): 40–46.

41. See, for example, "Kay Armatage Interviews Joyce Wieland," 23–25; Bill Auchterlonie, "Joyce Wieland, Filmmaker—*The Far Shore* in Progress," *Art Magazine* 7, no. 24 (Jan. 1976): 6–11; Michelle Moses, "A Glimpse of 'The Far Shore,' " *Cinema Canada*, no. 23 (Nov. 1975): 41–43.

42. James Purdie, "The Best Tom Thomson Faker in the Whole World," *Toronto Globe and Mail*, 12 July 1975, Joyce Wieland file, Midwest Film Center, School of the Art Institute of Chicago.

43. Robert Fulford, *Marshall Delaney at the Movies: The Contemporary World as Seen on Film* (Toronto: Peter Martin Associates, 1974), 77.

44. Review of *The Far Shore, Canadian Wire Service*, 9 Aug. 1976, Joyce Wieland file, Midwest Film Center, School of the Art Institute of Chicago.

45. Joyce Wieland, interview with the author, Toronto, Canada, 15 Nov. 1979.

46. The film had its U.S. premiere at the Midwest Film Center, School of the Art Institute of Chicago, in March 1978.

47. Laura Mulvey, "Feminism, Film, and the Avant-garde," *Framework*, no. 10 (Spring 1979): 3–10.

48. Lippard, "Watershed," 2.

49. Ibid., 6–7.

50. John Bentley Mays, "Wieland: Strong Overshadows Sweet," *Toronto Globe and Mail*, 23 Apr. 1983.

51. Ibid.

52. Lippard, "Watershed," 7.

53. Ibid.

8

Afterward: Women Sneaking around Museums

On one of the first sunny days of spring in 1987, Joyce Wieland was standing on the sidewalk outside her downtown Toronto warehouse studio. She had not outwardly changed much in the fifteen years since she had moved back to Toronto. Now that she was in her mid-fifties there were a few more lines in her face, and her round eyes seemed wider and deeper. In front of her, two friends were trying to wedge one of her over-sized, half-finished canvases into her car, the Volkswagon she had finally bought as an acquiescence to a modern woman's independence. When they were unable to make the painting fit, Joyce studied the problem, "I know. We'll hitchhike." As one of the two friends holding up an end of the painting, I paused for breath. This was even crazier than trying to get the painting in the car.

Here we were—invited speakers for Joyce Wieland's 1987 retrospective at the Art Gallery of Ontario (AGO), an event so big that one could not open any Canadian magazine without seeing something about Joyce in it. So, here we were—Joyce, Leila Sujir, and I—dignified women standing on a street corner trying to figure out how we were going to get the show's last painting from Joyce's studio to the museum across town. My questions of absolute practicality—"Why doesn't the museum staff transport this thing?" "Why didn't they do this weeks ago?" "How come we're doing this?" "Who do you think is going to stop to pick up three women and a six by seven foot painting?"—all went unnoticed. After a decade of studying, interviewing, and writing about Wieland, I couldn't help but think, "Here I am in another mess that could only be cooked up by Joyce!"

So there we stood with our thumbs out. Joyce was patient and optimistic. Leila seemed used to this sort of thing, having previously worked with Joyce. I thought we would be there for hours and that this small, simple task was about to take over my entire scheduled time in Toronto. A woman in a pick-up truck stopped nearby to make a delivery. Joyce ran over and asked if she would drive us and our painting to the museum. The woman said that she had other deliveries but would come back when she was finished. I merely accepted this as a rather polite refusal to three crazy women. We waited a little longer. It was a nice day, so I didn't entirely mind.

Then the woman in the pick-up returned. She was happy to help us load the painting. I felt guilty for ever having doubted her, for ever having doubted Joyce, for ever having doubted what we were trying to do. Leila rode in the back to steady the painting, Joyce followed in her car, and I sat with the driver. She and her lover were planning a motorcycle trip through the midwestern United States, and when she found out I was from Iowa, we had plenty to discuss. When we were stopped somewhere in downtown traffic, she handed me her business card: "Dyke Moving Co." Was it purely coincidence that two feminist critics and Canada's best-known woman artist were being rescued by a lesbian separatist mover?

We wound up and down one-way streets through rush-hour traffic, having a great time waving and winking at each other. We lost Joyce in the traffic but made it unscathed to the AGO's loading dock. The three of us in the truck brought the painting through the museum's back door. The staff willingly accepted the painting, but not us. We had to leave. Leila kept insisting that we were with Joyce—after all, we were their guests for the retrospective—but without Joyce there, it was to no avail. The guard did not believe that movers could also be critics. The only way we would get into the museum was as paying customers.

So we said good-by to our mover friend and went around to the front door. Leila again tried to persuade the ticket takers that we were museum guests, the evening speakers who were now supposed to help Joyce install the last painting on the second floor. She gave up; we paid our admission and were let into the museum.

While this momentary event—perhaps forgotten in the minds of all its participants except one—is neither a public symbol nor a woman's ritual, it is, nonetheless, an example of women's community just as representative of its time as Deren's baby shower was two decades earlier. Deren and Clarke could no more have hitched a ride with a feminist truck driver to get to a nationally prominent woman's art show than we would have considered a baby shower a progressive way to organize our own space. In the late 1980s, the cultural impact of feminism is widespread enough that feminists can—and, as the example demonstrates, do—spontaneously join together for a common purpose. Women participating in major arts institutions and women

having access to publications (in which to tell this anecdote) are neither
singular nor surprising. But, ours is still a very fragile network that
supports feminist activity and viability. It is a cultural system not
without current tensions.

Why were we out there on that street? Was it simply that the AGO
did not care enough to provide Wieland with additional labor and
transportation after it had already moved the rest of her paintings?
Or should one argue that, once admitted into the academy, Wieland
simply did not know the professional rules of the system? Was Wieland's decision to add a half-finished painting, made after seeing the
entire exhibition, a feminist's effort at resisting patriarchal enshrine-
ment? Did the museum staff regard Wieland's request for one more
painting, made after the show's opening, as a feminine whim? Can I
imagine any male artist being left on his own to transport and install
a painting in what was being touted as the biggest show of the year?

As a matter of fact, Wieland's entire show came about because she
demanded it, fought for it, and organized it. The critical discourse
saluting Wieland that surrounded the show's opening does not fully
address the ambivalence with which Wieland and women in general
are still regarded in cultural institutions. The back doors as well as the
front doors remain closed to women much of the time. Wieland got
in but only because she spent a great deal of time and energy—as well
as money—campaigning to be let in. We were unwelcome as laborers
at the loading dock, and we were turned away or simply not credible
as "art authorities" at the front door, but as paying customers, we
could gain entrance and then sneak into the back corridors and staff
offices.

After *The Far Shore,* Wieland had been so discouraged that she quit
making films. She retreated from the public eye and, during a rough
period both professionally and personally, she tried to find a way back
from the profound depression she experienced. During this time,
her marriage to Michael Snow ended. While working at home, she
designed quilts for her sister to execute and she painted two self-
portraits. In November 1978, Wieland flew to Cape Dorset in the
Arctic to work in an Eskimo print shop. She was rejuvenated by the
mystical sense of light she experienced in the Arctic and produced a
series of lithographs.

When she returned home to the new downtown studio and house
that she occupied alone, Wieland worked almost continuously for two-
and-a-half years on a series of small, colored pencil drawings. She
had become newly interested in the religious significance historically
attributed to color and light, "I began again to see in a different way,

seeing light broken down on the paper I was working on. . . . I found the image in the light on the paper."[1] She began to create her own mythology in weightless figures and animals who float intertwined in ethereal, prismatic clouds, waves, or gardens. In these drawings, Venuses and cherubs rule over air, water, land, and nature; they cavort or sexually mingle with other creatures. Calling upon the play of color and light she found in Chardin and Tiepolo, the small, oval-shaped drawings are feminine in their soft colors and mystical humanism, as well as aggressively feminist in their female bodily centered eroticism and hedonism. They resulted in a 1981 Isaacs Gallery show entitled *The Bloom of Matter*. The critics offered a somewhat mixed reception, some claiming that Wieland's "softness" and sentimental charm "booby-trapped" this work just as they did *The Far Shore*.[2] But the show was well attended and all the drawings sold quickly.

In the 1980s, Wieland extended the themes and techniques of the drawings to small circular or oval paintings. Gradually, the canvases grew larger and more preoccupied with images of figures confronting catastrophe and struggle. The mythological creatures of the beautifully serene, light-filled environments became companions or antagonists for self-portraits of the artist. Marie Fleming said about *Paint Phantom* (1983–84), "The figures wrestle in a surrealist space, towering over diminutive trees and mountains beside a wholly visible moon, its brightened crescent shining for and on a strip of earth below. . . . The figures are lit by some unknown source that makes the layered colour shimmer and the skin look opalescent, and that stains the clouds with an intensity of hue analogous to the fury of the struggle."[3] Combining allegory and catharsis, such paintings as *The Artist on Fire* (1983) and *Paint Phantom* rely upon boldly handled, dramatically colored images of fire and physical confrontation as universal symbols for the woman artist's fight and transformation.

Beginning in 1984, Wieland went to work organizing and directing a complete retrospective of her art and films. Besides completing several new paintings for the show, she finished three films that had been shot more than a decade earlier. She also reedited two earlier 8mm films (*Peggy's Blue Skylight* and *Patriotism, Part II*) and transferred them to 16mm.

Her renewed enthusiasm for filmmaking began when Hollis Frampton died of cancer in the spring of 1984 and his widow asked Wieland to complete a film Frampton and Wieland had begun together in 1967.[4] *A and B in Ontario* (1984) is a kind of playful hide-and-seek between the two filmmakers in which they use cameras and their individual fields of vision to "tag" and capture each other. *Birds at*

Sunrise (1985) is a microscopic study of the birds photographed outside Wieland's living room window in 1972. Its magnified point of view, structural interventions, and allegorical overtones are reminiscent of *Rat Life and Diet in North America.*

The 1987 retrospective at the Art Gallery of Ontario vindicated Wieland for *The Far Shore*'s failure to achieve national popularity and prestige, for the many times she had been professionally overlooked, and for the lack of critical attention over the last decade. Much was made of the fact that this was the first time the AGO had devoted an entire show to a living female artist, surely more of a rejoinder to the museum's sins of omission than a cause for celebration. The show was widely reviewed and, not unexpectedly given Wieland's past, Wieland herself was most frequently the subject of articles and editorials. But in the context of her retrospective, this time around she became the personification of Canadian art, "Wieland is the antithesis of that paragon of reason over passion, the powerful North American man— she is female and Canadian, and her art is a fascinating public record of her quest to affirm that in the case of Canada, thinking patriotism is a positive and life-enhancing act (Canadians have to be taught to love their country; Americans have to be taught not to), and that is the case of her own person, self-embracing affection is a positive and life-enriching attitude."[5] In many respects, what Wieland had suffered and struggled for as a woman artist repetitively marginalized in her own country as well as in the United States was now read as a sign of her validation as a living symbol of Canadian art. One newspaper critic even called her "an all-round cultural heroine."[6]

But Wieland persisted in being a difficult subject for easy consumption within the arts economy of 1980s Toronto. Even her status as martyred victim and survivor could not be so easily recuperated. In their rush to claim Wieland for intertwined nationalist and feminist concerns, the critics still expressed some misgivings. Kass Banning's article in a Toronto arts magazine asked why a major arts institution was now willing to embrace feminism and nationalism.[7] Banning insisted that Wieland's work, largely accomplished in previous decades, as well as her critical validation by U.S. feminist writers made Wieland a "safe" celebratory figure.[8] Banning as well as the *Canadian Art* reviewer complained that Wieland's discursive position within American feminist arts criticism reflected a contradictory tension for Wieland's nationalism.[9] They, instead, reveal a more deeply disturbing contradiction among Wieland's Canadian critics—feminist and otherwise—who did not take Wieland so seriously until American feminists did, and American-bashing has become a way to disclaim competing discourses in which Wieland was and continues to be contained. The fact that Wieland herself has refused to disavow her position in American feminist arts discourse and requested two retrospective catalogue essays by American critics who had championed her work did not help matters. It is important, though, not to be naive and to recognize that Americans have a long history of Canadian colonization that, with the Toronto art world's desire for American approval, provide a much larger cultural contradiction in which all discursive interplay must be situated.

Only a few years before Wieland's reclamation within Canadian arts, Shirley Clarke similarly achieved a vindication of her own. In December 1981, Anthology Film Archives held a retrospective of Clarke's work. As a peacemaking gesture that mended the rift between Mekas and Clarke, the show featured Clarke and screenings of all her films and more recent video pieces. Clarke, in turn, donated copies of her films to the organization barely surviving on a ragged budget. Like Wieland, she had made it into a canon, but she, too, had been included at least partially because she literally paid an "admission fee" to the museum.

During the 1970s and early 1980s, Clarke had worked primarily in video. In these years, video art had expanded because of the increasing availability and affordability of portable, synchronized-sound video cameras and playback systems and because of the support of museum and university video art programs. Clarke first worked in the medium in the 1970s when she received a Museum of Modern Art grant to explore video. For a few years afterward, she made hundreds of short tapes and a series of audience-participation pieces. In the middle 1970s, she began to make video dance pieces that, in many respects, are a reapplication of her ciné-dance ideas. *Trans* (1978), *OneTwoThree* (1978), *Mysterium* (1978), and *Initiation* (1978) are filled with layered imagery, varied scales of objects within the frame, and afterimage traces of richly colored, shadowy lines that elongate and distort objects and figures. These pieces reiterate the commitment to abstraction in dance that Clarke had expressed twenty-five years ago.

In 1981, Clarke began to work with nondance material in two one-act monologue plays written by Sam Shepard and performed by Joseph Chaikin. *Savage Love* (1981) and *Tongues* (1982) destroy the notion of stage space and speeches as the basic content of a theatrical performance. They instead emphasize the act of vocal articulation itself, gesture, and the human figure as the material for choreographically styled performance. Images are processed through a variety of special effects that slow down, repeat, and stretch phonetic articulation and gesture. Abstract formal qualities within the individual actor's performance are themselves the expressive elements.

Between 1975 and 1985, Clarke was a professor of film and video at the University of California at Los Angeles. Like so many other independent filmmakers, Clarke relied upon the university system as a means of economic support and base for artisanal activities. But in the middle 1980s, she quit California and returned to New York City. Since then, she has resumed filmmaking and has been a recipient of the American Film Institute's newly created Maya Deren Award in Independent Filmmaking. But, like Wieland, Clarke began a new film with old footage and aesthetic strategies from past decades. Clarke's *Ornette: Made in America* (1985) is a feature-length, vérité-styled documentary about jazz musician Ornette Coleman. It balances footage that Clarke shot in the late 1960s when she first started this documentary with current material and interviews.

In a similar vein, movie footage that Deren shot in the 1940s and 1950s has been reworked and released in two separate films. *The Witch's Cradle*, the unfinished film that Deren started on the Surrealist "Art of This Century" Gallery, is now available as unedited rolls put together end to end. In the late 1970s, Deren's widower Teiji Ito and his wife Cherel edited Deren's old Haitian footage into a documentary, *The Divine Horsemen: The Living Gods of Haiti* (1977). Their chronology tries to be faithful to the sequence in which Deren shot film and the ideas that she expressed in her book on Haiti. The movie, a linkage of shots for realistic illusion, is not organized according to the purpose that Deren originally intended since she had hoped to make an experimental dance film with the material. Instead, *The Divine Horsemen* is an anthropological document of Haitian culture. But because it is comprised entirely of Deren's point of view, the film encourages one to identify with Deren as a seeing subject; Deren's eye is the camera eye. The film's primary interest within cinema studies, therefore, has been the way that it cinematically activates Deren as a historical figure and "preserves" her way of seeing as the film's subject.

Wieland, Clarke, and Deren have all been recent authors of "new" work that has (perhaps ironically) contributed to their feminist inscription as "old" subjects. The critical reception for these films has depended heavily on the filmmakers' associations with past cinema movements and the obvious use of old footage in the films, as well as cinematic strategies that do not engage current critical practice but reenforce their current relevancy as historical figures. Their dominant position in contemporary discourse has become one of female role models: exceptional women who were successful in male-oriented worlds.

Deren, Clarke, and Wieland, however, are less interesting as simple auteur studies than as subjects of significant cultural formations in cinema and the arts. The woman artist has long been a threat to unified discourse in the avant-garde because she categorically challenges ideological effects of sexual difference in patriarchy. Inasmuch as Deren, Clarke, and Wieland lived and worked in avant-gardes that attempted to contain and recuperate them, the results of such attempts were more a series of conflicts over the meanings of their work and power roles. Their positions were constituted by complex interrelationships among gender values, the existing forms and structures of cultural resistance, and the discursive interplay that contains any social resistance. Their lives, labor, and artistic production were crisscrossed by circumstances that necessitated they oppose contemporary avant-garde practices.

It may be inevitable that each succeeding generation of historians and critics as well as filmmakers will recast and remap the activities of past avant-gardes. But it is not inevitable, once women's presence in the arts institutions of the past has been detected, that it will be welcomed in the present and in the future. Because the New York avant-garde cinema has been so narrowly constructed within film history as interlocking aesthetic, patriarchal structures, it has generally been overlooked or dismissed as a site for women's political struggles and expression.[10] At the heart of the matter lies the question of whether or not independent cinema in North America can function as a site for radical film practices (feminist and otherwise), whether a system that allows for and contains opposition along its margins can truly empower radical critique and change.

Current feminist critical categories suggest a framework for rethinking the functions and values of the postwar New York cinema and these women's places within it. They offer a means for constructing competing discourses in which to read past artistic activity against the grain of traditional or established categories. Within feminist discourse, films such as *Meshes of the Afternoon, The Cool World,* or *The Far Shore* may assume new significance for their gender-identified critiques of cinematic representation, for their advocacy of a politics of representation, and for their involvement in processes of alternative cinemas. The fact that these features were often the least understood or most suppressed in competing and dominant discourses does not diminish the importance of their place within women's discourses.

The significance of Deren's, Clarke's, and Wieland's positions is that they demonstrate not only how women artists are constructed within patriarchy but what constitutes women's past struggles for power. Such a project is neither a simple reclamation of female heroines nor an attempt to perpetuate history writing as the framework for individual adventurers who are the subjects of dramatically styled narratives of action, opposition, and victory. It is not a history of victims or villains. What is important is the role that gender plays in constructing the past as well as the present meanings and values of art and cinema. The relationship of gender to discursive interplay can neither be fixed nor attached to any individual heroes, heroines, or villains.

But the role of gender in language and textual meaning is also tied to the ways that social institutions participate in discourse and patriarchy. When women participate in these institutions, their individual actions assume significance within larger political struggles. While arguing for a politics of history that looks at cultural practice and language, one can still maintain a commitment to biography as a political site for feminist practice.

The struggles of Deren, Clarke, and Wieland over power relations, social and artistic practice, and the ways that cinema conveys meanings offer evidence that the meaning of art is itself not fixed. It is, rather, culturally circumscribed and a site for active conflict within society. The history of individual women in the American avant-garde cinema, filtered through the historiographic activity of analyzing how cultural practices construct power relations and textual meanings, then becomes a narrative of sexual difference, power, and politics.

The value of this enterprise is to suggest a means by which we can recover women's artistic production for feminist goals. Bertolt Brecht once said that the avant-garde apparatus will go on fulfilling its (inherently conservative) functions with or without the products that artists freely invent.[11] But a history organized by women's desires necessarily recognizes that the positions of women's activities, meanings, and values in the avant-garde cinema apparatus are subversive. It argues for the ways that artists have changed or attempted to change the apparatus, the only viable means that Brecht recognized for a radical avant-garde. The project of feminist history is to arrange radical discursive purpose for the present and to name the potential for political configurations in the future.

NOTES

1. Joyce Wieland, as quoted in Marie Fleming, "Joyce Wieland: A Perspective," in *Joyce Wieland*, ed. Philip Monk (Toronto: Key Porter Books, 1987), 93.

2. In particular, see Carole Corbeil, "Joyce Wieland Finds Room to Bloom," *Toronto Globe and Mail*, 2 Mar. 1981.

3. Fleming, "Joyce Wieland," 108.

4. Joyce Wieland, as quoted in *In Search of the Far Shore: The Films of Joyce Wieland,* ed. Simon Field (London: Canada House, 1988).

5. Jay Scott, "Full Circle: True, Patriot Womanhood, The 30-Year Passage of Joyce Wieland," *Canadian Art* 4, no. 1 (Spring 1987): 63.

6. Christopher Hume, "Wieland Tells AGO the Show Must Go On," *Toronto Star,* 10 Apr. 1987, D3.

7. Kass Banning, "The Mummification of Mommy: Joyce Wieland as the AGO's First Living Other," *C Magazine,* no. 13 (Mar. 1987), 32.

8. Banning is referring largely to essays written by Lucy Lippard and myself for the retrospective catalogue, *Joyce Wieland,* ed. Philip Monk.

9. Banning, "The Mummification of Mommy," 32; Scott, "Full Circle," 63.

10. Two recent books, Lucy Fischer's *Shot/Countershot: Film Tradition and Women's Cinema* (Princeton, N.J.: Princeton University Press, 1989) and David E. James's *Allegories of Cinema: American Film in the Sixties* (Princeton, N.J.: Princeton University Press, 1989), offer new consideration of this topic.

11. Bertolt Brecht, *Brecht on Theatre,* trans. John Willett (London: Methuen, 1964), 34–35.

Filmography

Maya Deren (1917–61)

1943—*Meshes of the Afternoon,* codirected with Alexander Hammid.
1944—*The Witch's Cradle*
1944—*At Land*
1945—*A Study in Choreography for the Camera*
1946—*Ritual in Transfigured Time*
1948—*Meditation on Violence*
1955—*The Very Eye of Night*
1977—*The Divine Horsemen: The Living Gods of Haiti,* footage shot by Deren, compiled and edited by Teiji and Cherel Ito

Shirley Clarke (1919–)

1953—*Dance in the Sun*
1954—*In Paris Parks*
1955—*Bullfight*
1957—*A Moment in Love*
1958—*Brussels Film Loops*
      Bridges-go-round
1959—*Skyscraper*
1960—*A Scary Time*
1961—*The Connection*
1963—*The Cool World*
1964—*Robert Frost: A Lover's Quarrel with the World*
1967—*Portrait of Jason*
1985—*Ornette: Made in America*

Joyce Wieland (1931–)

1958—*Tea in the Garden,* codirected with Warren Collins
1959—*A Salt in the Park,* codirected with Michael Snow

1963—*Larry's Recent Behavior*
1964—*Peggy's Blue Skylight*
    Patriotism, Part I
    Patriotism, Part II
1965—*Water Sark*
    Barbara's Blindness, codirected with Betty Ferguson
1967—*Sailboat*
    Hand Tinting
    1933
1968—*Catfood*
    Rat Life and Diet in North America
1969—*Reason over Passion*
    Dripping Water, codirected with Michael Snow
1972—*Pierre Vallières*
1973—*Solidarity*
1976—*The Far Shore*
1984—*A & B in Ontario,* codirected with Hollis Frampton
1985—*Birds at Sunrise*

Selected Bibliography

General Works

Abel, Richard. *French Cinema: The First Wave, 1915–1929.* Princeton, N.J.: Princeton University Press, 1984.

Alexander, William. *Film on the Left: American Documentary Film from 1931 to 1942.* Princeton, N.J.: Princeton University Press, 1981.

Allen, Jeanne. "Self-reflexivity in Documentary." *Cine-tracts* 1, no. 2 (Summer 1977): 37–43.

Allen, Robert C., and Douglas Gomery. *Film History: Theory and Practice.* New York: Alfred A. Knopf, 1985.

Barry, Judith, and Sandy Flitterman. "Textual Strategies: The Politics of Art-making." *Screen* 21, no. 2 (1980): 35–48.

Battcock, Gregory, ed. *The New American Cinema: A Critical Anthology.* New York: E. P. Dutton, 1967.

Becker, Howard S. *Art Worlds.* Berkeley: University of California Press, 1982.

Benjamin, Walter. "The Author as Producer." In *Reflections: Essays, Aphorisms, Autobiographical Writings,* edited by Peter Demetz, translated by Edmund Jephcott. New York: Harcourt Brace Jovanovich, 1978.

Bordwell, David, Janet Staiger, and Kristin Thompson. *The Classical Hollywood Cinema: Film Style and Mode of Production to 1960.* New York: Columbia University Press, 1985.

Bruno, Giuliana. "Women in Avant-garde Film: An Interview with Annette Michelson." *Millennium Film Journal* 16–18 (Fall–Winter 1986–87): 141–51.

Brunsdon, Charlotte, ed. *Films for Women.* London: British Film Institute, 1986.

Bürger, Peter. *Theory of the Avant-garde.* Translated by Michael Shaw. Minneapolis: University of Minnesota Press, 1984.

Campbell, Russell. *Cinema Strikes Back: Radical Filmmaking in the United States, 1930–1942.* Ann Arbor, Mich.: UMI Research Press, 1982.

———. "Eight Notes on the Underground." *The Velvet Light Trap,* no. 13 (Fall 1974): 45–46.

Carroll, Noël. "Avant-garde Film and Film Theory." *Millennium Film Journal,* nos. 4–5 (Fall 1979): 135–43.

Caughie, John, ed. *Theories of Authorship: A Reader*. Boston: Routledge and Kegan Paul, 1981.

Chodorow, Nancy. *The Reproduction of Mothering: Psychoanalysis and the Sociology of Gender*. Berkeley: University of California Press, 1978.

Coe, Robert. *Dance in America*. New York: E. P. Dutton, 1985.

Cornwell, Regina. "Some Formalist Tendencies in the Current American Avant-garde Film." *Studio International* 184 (Oct. 1972): 110–14.

Coward, Rosalind. *Patriarchal Precedents: Sexuality and Social Relations*. Boston: Routledge and Kegan Paul, 1983.

Crane, Diana. *The Transformation of the Avant-garde: The New York Art World, 1940–1985*. Chicago: University of Chicago Press, 1987.

Curtis, David. *Experimental Cinema*. New York: Universe Books, 1971.

De Lauretis, Teresa. *Alice Doesn't: Feminism, Semiotics, Cinema*. Bloomington: Indiana University Press, 1984.

Delphy, Christine. *Close to Home: Materialist Analysis of Women's Oppression*. Translated and edited by Diana Leonard. London: Hutchinson, 1984.

Doane, Mary Ann. *The Desire to Desire: The Woman's Film of the 1940s*. Bloomington: Indiana University Press, 1987.

———. "Woman's Stake: Filming the Female Body." *October*, no. 17 (Summer 1981): 23–36.

Dozoretz, Wendy. "Dulac versus Artaud." *Wide Angle* 3, no. 1 (1979): 46–53.

Edinburgh '76 Magazine. *Psychoanalysis/Cinema/Avant-garde*. Edinburgh, Scotland: Edinburgh Film Festival, 1976.

Erens, Patricia, ed. *Sexual Strategems: The World of Women in Film*. New York: Horizon Press, 1979.

Falk, Lorne, and Barbara Fischer, eds. *The Event Horizon: Essays on Hope, Sexuality, Social Space and Media(tion) in Art*. Toronto: Coach House Press and Walter Phillips Gallery, 1987.

"Feminism and Film: Critical Approaches." *Camera Obscura*, no. 1 (Fall 1976): 3–10.

Field, Simon. "Underground 1: Re-viewing the Avant-garde." *Monthly Film Bulletin* 50 (Aug. 1983): 204–6.

———. "Underground 2: Re-viewing the Avant-garde." *Monthly Film Bulletin* 50 (Sept. 1983): 234–36.

Film-Makers' Cooperative. *Film-Makers' Cooperative Catalogue No. 6*. New York: Film-Makers' Cooperative, 1975.

Fischer, Lucy. *Shot/Countershot: Film Tradition and Women's Cinema*. Princeton, N.J.: Princeton University Press, 1989.

Flitterman, Sandy. "Montage/Discourse: Germaine Dulac's *The Smiling Madame Beudet*." *Wide Angle* 4, no. 3 (1980): 54–59.

Foucault, Michel. "What Is an Author?" In *Language, Counter-memory, Practice*, edited by Donald F. Bouchard, translated by Donald F. Bouchard and Sherry Simon. Ithaca, N.Y.: Cornell University Press, 1977.

Frascina, Francis, ed. *Pollock and After: The Critical Debate*. New York: Harper and Row, 1985.

Frascina, Francis, and Charles Harrison, with Deirdre Paul, eds. *Modern Art and Modernism: A Critical Anthology.* New York: Harper and Row, 1982.

Freyer, Ellen. "Formalist Cinema: Artistic Suicide in the Avant-garde." *The Velvet Light Trap,* no. 13 (Fall 1974): 47–49.

Friedberg, Anne. "And I Myself Have Learned to Use the Small Projector: On H. D., Woman, History, Recognition." *Wide Angle* 5, no. 2 (1982): 26–31.

Gablik, Suzi. *Has Modernism Failed?* New York: Thames and Hudson, 1984.

Gidal, Peter, ed. *Structural Film Anthology.* London: British Film Institute, 1978.

Gledhill, Christine, ed. *Home Is Where the Heart Is: Studies in Melodrama and the Woman's Film.* London: British Film Institute, 1987.

———. "Recent Developments in Feminist Criticism." *Quarterly Review of Film Studies* 3, no. 4 (1978): 457–93.

Guilbaut, Serge. *How New York Stole the Idea of Modern Art: Abstract Expressionism, Freedom, and the Cold War.* Translated by Arthur Goldhammer. Chicago: University of Chicago Press, 1983.

Hanhardt, John G., ed. *A History of the American Avant-garde Cinema.* New York: American Federation of the Arts, 1976.

Heck-Rabi, Louise. *Women Filmmakers: A Critical Reception.* Metuchen, N.J.: Scarecrow Press, 1984.

Hoberman, J. "Three Myths of Avant-garde Film." *Film Comment* 17, no. 3 (May–June 1981): 34–35.

———. "Where Is the Avant-garde Going?" *American Film* 5 (Nov. 1979): 36–40.

———, and Jonathan Rosenbaum. *Midnight Movies.* New York: Harper and Row, 1983.

James, David E. *Allegories of Cinema: American Film in the Sixties.* Princeton, N.J.: Princeton University Press, 1989.

Johnston, Claire. "The Subject of Feminist Film Theory/Practice." *Screen* 21, no. 2 (1980): 27–34.

———. "Women's Cinema as Counter-cinema," in *Notes on Women's Cinema,* edited by Claire Johnston. London: SEFT, 1974. Reprinted in *Sexual Strategems: The World of Women in Film,* edited by Patricia Erens. New York: Horizon Press, 1979.

Kamuf, Peggy. "Dialogue: Replacing Feminist Criticism." *Diacritics* 12 (Summer 1982): 42–47.

———. *Signature Pieces: On the Institution of Authorship.* Ithaca, N.Y.: Cornell University Press, 1988.

Kaplan, E. Ann. "Integrating Marxist and Psychoanalytic Approaches in Feminist Film Criticism." *Millennium Film Journal,* no. 6 (Spring 1980): 8–17.

———. *Women and Film: Both Sides of the Camera.* New York: Methuen, 1983.

———, ed. *Women in Film Noir.* London: British Film Institute, 1978.

Kay, Karyn, and Gerald Peary, eds. *Women and the Cinema: A Critical Anthology.* New York: E. P. Dutton, 1977.

Kuhn, Annette. "The Camera I: Observations on Documentary." *Screen* 19, no. 2 (Summer 1978): 71–83.

———. *Women's Pictures: Feminism and Cinema.* Boston: Routledge and Kegan Paul, 1982.

———, and Ann Marie Wolpe, eds. *Feminism and Materialism: Women and Modes of Production.* Boston: Routledge and Kegan Paul, 1978.

LeGrice, Malcolm. *Abstract Film and Beyond.* Cambridge, Mass.: MIT Press, 1977.

Lehmann, Peter. "The Avant-garde: Power, Change, and the Power to Change." In *Cinema Histories, Cinema Practices,* edited by Patricia Mellencamp and Philip Rosen. Frederick, Md.: University Publications of America, 1984.

———. "For Whom Does the Light Shine?" *Wide Angle* 7, nos. 1–2 (1985): 68–73.

Lesage, Julia. "The Political Aesthetics of the Feminist Documentary Film." *Quarterly Review of Film Studies* 3, no. 4 (1978): 507–23.

Levin, G. Roy. *Documentary Explorations: 15 Interviews with Film-makers.* Garden City, N.Y.: Doubleday, 1971.

Lippard, Lucy. *From the Center: Feminist Essays on Women's Art.* New York: E. P. Dutton, 1976.

MacDonald, Scott. "Amos Vogel and Cinema 16." *Wide Angle* 9, no. 3 (1987): 38–51.

———. *A Critical Cinema: Interviews with Independent Filmmakers.* Berkeley: University of California Press, 1988.

Mamber, Stephen. *Cinema Verite in America: Studies in Uncontrolled Documentary.* Cambridge, Mass.: MIT Press, 1974.

Mayne, Judith. "Feminist Film Theory and Criticism." *Signs: Journal of Women in Culture and Society* 11, no. 1 (1985): 81–100.

———. "The Woman at the Keyhole: Women's Cinema and Feminist Criticism." In *Re-vision: Essays in Feminist Film Criticism,* edited by Mary Ann Doane, Patricia Mellencamp, and Linda Williams. Frederick, Md.: University Publications of America, 1984.

Mekas, Jonas. *Movie Journal: The Rise of the New American Cinema, 1959–1971.* New York: Collier Books, 1972.

Mellencamp, Patricia. "Receivable Texts: U.S. Avant-garde Cinema, 1960–1980." *Wide Angle* 7, nos. 1–2 (1985): 74–91.

Michelson, Annette, ed. *New Forms in Film.* Montreux, Switzerland, 1974.

Miller, Nancy K. "The Text's Heroine: A Feminist Critic and Her Fictions." *Diacritics* 12 (Summer 1982): 48–53.

Moi, Toril. *Sexual/Textual Politics: Feminist Literary Theory.* New York: Methuen, 1985.

Mulvey, Laura. *Visual and Other Pleasures.* Bloomington: Indiana University Press, 1989.

Nichols, Bill. "Documentary Theory and Practice." *Screen,* 17, no. 4 (Winter 1976–77): 34–48.

———, ed. *Movies and Methods.* Berkeley: University of California Press, 1976.

Parker, Rozsika, and Griselda Pollock. *Old Mistresses: Women, Art and Ideology.* New York: Pantheon, 1981.

Penley, Constance. "The Avant-garde and Its Imaginary." *Camera Obscura*, no. 2 (1977): 3–33.

———, and Janet Bergstrom. "The Avant-garde: Histories and Theories." *Screen* 19, no. 3 (Autumn 1978): 113–27. Reprinted in *Movies and Methods, Volume Two*, edited by Bill Nichols. Berkeley: University of California Press, 1985.

Petro, Patrice. "Reception Theory and the Avant-garde." *Wide Angle* 8, no. 1 (1986): 11–17.

Polan, Dana B. *The Political Language of Film and the Avant-garde.* Ann Arbor, Mich.: UMI Research Press, 1985.

Poggioli, Renato. *The Theory of Avant-garde.* Translated by Gerald Fitzgerald. Cambridge, Mass.: Belknap Press, 1968.

Renan, Sheldon. *An Introduction to the American Underground Film.* New York: E. P. Dutton, 1967.

Rich, B. Ruby, et al. "Women and Film: A Discussion of Feminist Aesthetics." *New German Critique* 13 (1978): 83–107.

Rosenberg, Jan. *Women's Reflections: The Feminist Film Movement.* Ann Arbor, Mich.: UMI Research Press, 1983.

Rosenthal, Alan. *The New Documentary in Action: A Casebook in Film Making.* Berkeley: University of California Press, 1971.

Sandler, Irving. *The Triumph of American Painting: A History of Abstract Expressionism.* New York: Harper and Row, 1977.

Silverman, Kaja. *The Acoustic Mirror: The Female Voice in Psychoanalysis and Cinema.* Bloomington: Indiana University Press, 1988.

———. *The Subject of Semiotics.* New York: Oxford University Press, 1983.

Sitney, P. Adams. *Visionary Film: The American Avant-garde, 1943–1978,* 2d ed. New York: Oxford University Press, 1979.

———, ed. *The Essential Cinema: Essays on the Films in the Collection of Anthology Film Archives.* New York: New York University Press and Anthology Film Archives, 1975.

———, ed. *Film Culture Reader.* New York: Praeger, 1970.

Smith, Sharon. *Women Who Make Movies.* New York: Hopkinson and Blake, 1975.

Sobchack, Vivian. " 'No Lies': Direct Cinema as Rape." *Journal of the University Film Association* 29, no. 4 (1977): 13–18.

Stauffacher, Frank, ed. *Art in Cinema.* San Francisco: Art in Cinema Society, San Francisco Museum of Art, 1947.

Stern, Lesley. "Feminism and Cinema: Exchanges." *Screen* 20, nos. 3–4 (1979–80): 89–105.

———. "Point of View: The Blind Spot." *Film Reader* 4 (1980): 214–36.

Tyler, Parker. *Underground Film: A Critical History.* New York: Grove Press, 1969.

Vogel, Amos. *Film as a Subversive Art.* New York: Random House, 1974.

Wallis, Brian, ed. *Art after Modernism: Rethinking Representation.* New York: New Museum of Contemporary Art, 1984.

Weedon, Chris. *Feminist Practice and Poststructuralist Theory.* New York: Methuen, 1987.

Wheeler, Dennis, ed. *Form and Structure in Recent Film.* Vancouver: Vancouver Art Gallery/Talon Books, 1972.

Wollen, Peter. "The Avant-gardes: Europe and America." *Framework,* no. 14 (1981): 9–10.

———. "Popular Culture and Avant-garde." *Wide Angle* 7, nos. 1–2 (1985): 102–4.

———. *Readings and Writings: Semiotic Counter-strategies.* London: New Left Books, 1982.

Woolf, Virginia. *A Room of One's Own.* New York: Harcourt, Brace and World, 1957.

Maya Deren

Extensive materials on Maya Deren are held in the Maya Deren papers, Mugar Memorial Library Special Collections, Boston University.

A special issue of *Film Culture,* no. 39 (Winter 1965) is devoted to a selection of Maya Deren's writings. *Filmwise,* no. 2 (1962) is a collection of essays on Maya Deren.

Works by Maya Deren

Deren, Eleanora [Maya]. "Religious Possession in Dancing." *Educational Dance* (Mar.–Apr. 1942).

Deren, Maya. *An Anagram of Ideas on Art, Form and Film.* Yonkers, N.Y.: Alicat Book Shop Press, 1946.

———. "Cinema as an Art Form." *New Directions,* no. 9 (Fall 1946): 111–20.

———. "Cinematography: The Creative Use of Reality." *Daedalus* 89, no. 1 (Winter 1960): 150–67. Reprinted in *The Avant-garde Film: A Reader of Theory and Criticism,* edited by P. Adams Sitney. New York: New York University Press, 1978.

———. "Creative Cutting." *Movie Makers Magazine* (May–June 1947).

———. "Creative Movies with a New Dimension—Time." *Popular Photography* 19, no. 6 (Dec. 1946): 130–32.

———. *Divine Horsemen: The Voodoo Gods of Haiti.* New York: Dell Publishing, 1970.

———. "From the Notebook of 1947." *October,* no. 14 (Fall 1980): 21–46.

———. "A Letter to James Card." *Film Culture,* no. 39 (Winter 1965): 29–33.

———. "Magic Is New." *Mademoiselle* 22, no. 3 (Jan. 1946).

———. "Movie Journal." *Village Voice* 5, no. 44 (25 Aug. 1960): 6, 8. Reprinted in *Film Culture,* no. 39 (Winter 1965): 49–55.

———. "New Directions in Film Art." *Film Culture,* no. 29 (Summer 1963): 64–68.

———. "Of Critics and Creators." *Village Voice* 5, no. 38 (14 July 1960): 10.

———. "Ritual in Transfigured Time." *Dance Magazine* 20, no. 12 (Dec. 1946): 9–13.

———. "Some Metaphors for the Creative Process." *Village Voice* 5, no. 39 (21 July 1960).

———, and Gregory Bateson. "An Exchange of Letters." *October,* no. 14 (Fall 1980): 16–20.

"Interview with Maya Deren," WGXR-Radio, New York City, 1947, Audio tape collection, School of the Art Institute of Chicago.

"Meditation on Violence." *Film Culture,* no. 39 (Winter 1965): 18–21.

"Poetry and the Film: A Symposium." *Film Culture,* no. 29 (Summer 1963): 55–63. Reprinted in *Film Culture Reader,* edited by P. Adams Sitney. New York: Praeger, 1970, 171–86.

Works about Maya Deren

Brakhage, Stan. "An Open Letter to Maya Deren." *Filmwise,* no. 2 (1962): 13–15.

The Camera Obscura Collective. "Excerpts from an Interview with *The Legend of Maya Deren* Project." *Camera Obscura,* nos. 3–4 (Summer 1979): 177–91.

Clark, VèVè A., Millicent Hodson, and Catrina Neiman. *The Legend of Maya Deren: A Documentary Biography and Collected Works. Volume I, Part One: Signatures (1917–1942).* New York: Anthology Film Archives/Film Culture, 1984.

———. *The Legend of Maya Deren: A Documentary Biography and Collected Works. Volume I, Part Two: Chambers (1942–1947).* New York: Anthology Film Archives/Film Culture, 1988.

Cornwell, Regina. "Maya Deren and Germaine Dulac: Activists of the Avant-garde." *Film Library Quarterly* 5, no. 1 (Winter 1971–72): 29–38. Reprinted in *Sexual Strategems: The World of Women in Film,* edited by Patricia Erens. New York: Horizon Press, 1979.

"The Film That Dreams Are Made On." *Esquire,* Dec. 1946, 187.

Hoberman, J. "The Maya Mystique." *Village Voice* 23, no. 20 (15 May 1978): 54.

Kelman, Ken. "Widow into Bride." *Filmwise,* no. 2 (1962): 20–23.

Krevitsky, Nik. "Maya Deren and Dance in the Filmic Medium." *Impulse: The Annual of Contemporary Dance* (1960): 48–49.

Maas, Willard. "Memories of My Maya." *Filmwise,* no. 2 (1962): 23–29.

Mekas, Jonas. "The Experimental Film in America." *Film Culture,* no. 3 (May–June 1955): 15–20. Reprinted in *Film Culture Reader,* edited by P. Adams Sitney. New York: Praeger, 1970, 21–26.

———. "Maya Deren and the Film Poem." *Movie Journal: The Rise of a New American Cinema, 1959–1971.* New York: Collier Books, 1972, 1–3.

Michelson, Annette. "Camera Lucida/Camera Obscura." *Artforum* 11, no. 5 (Jan. 1973): 30–37.

———. "On Reading Deren's Notebook." *October*, no. 14 (Fall 1980): 47–54.

Neiman, Catrina. "An Introduction to the Notebook of Maya Deren, 1947." *October*, no. 14 (Fall 1980): 3–15.

Nin, Anaïs. *The Diary of Anaïs Nin, Volume Four: 1944–1947*. Edited by Gunther Stuhlmann. New York: Harcourt Brace Jovanovich, 1971.

———. *The Diary of Anaïs Nin, Volume Six: 1955–1966*. Edited by Gunther Stuhlmann. New York: Harcourt Brace Jovanovich, 1976.

Tallmer, Jerry. "For Maya Deren—In the Midst of Life." *Filmwise*, no. 2 (1962): 7–9.

Tyler, Parker. "Maya Deren as Filmmaker." *Filmwise*, no. 2 (1962): 3–6.

Valasek, Thomas E. "Alexander Hammid: A Survey of His Filmmaking Career." *Film Culture*, nos. 67–69 (1979): 250–322.

Shirley Clarke

Materials on Shirley Clarke are held principally in the Shirley Clarke papers, Wisconsin Center for Film and Theater Research, University of Wisconsin–Madison and the State Historical Society of Wisconsin.

Interviews with Shirley Clarke in Chicago, on 23, 24, and 26 Sept. 1981, supplement primary and secondary sources.

Works by Shirley Clarke

Clarke, Shirley. "Cine-dance: A Statement on Dance and Film." *Dance Perspectives* 30 (Summer 1967): 2–23.

———. "A Conversation—Shirley Clarke and Storm De Hirsch." *Film Culture*, no. 46 (1967): 44. Reprinted in *Women and the Cinema: A Critical Anthology*, edited by Karyn Kay and Gerald Peary. New York: E. P. Dutton 1977.

———. "The Cool World." *Films and Filming* 10, no. 3 (Dec. 1963): 7–8.

———. "Maya Deren." TS, Nov. 1966. Shirley Clarke papers.

———, and Storm De Hirsch. "Female Filmmaking." *Arts* 41 (Apr. 1967): 23–24.

"The Expensive Arts: A Discussion of Film Distribution and Exhibition in the U.S." *Film Quarterly* 13, no. 4 (Summer 1960): 19–34.

Works about Shirley Clarke

Archer, Eugene. "Woman Director Makes the Scene." *New York Times Magazine*, 26 Aug. 1962.

Bachmann, Gideon. "Shirley Clarke." *Film Quarterly* 14, no. 3 (1961): 13–14.

Bebb, Bruce. "The Cool Medium of Shirley Clarke." *L.A. Reader* 4, no. 18 (26 Feb. 1982).

Berg, Gretchen. "Interview with Shirley Clarke." *Film Culture*, no. 44 (Spring 1967): 52–55.

Bermel, Albert. "Young Lady with a Camera." *Escapade* 10, no. 5 (May 1967): 78.

Biró, Yvette. "Medium Hot." *Village Voice* 29, no. 10 (6 Mar. 1984): 43.

Breitrose, Henry. "Films of Shirley Clarke." *Film Quarterly* 13, no. 4 (Summer 1960): 57–58.

Crowther, Bosley. "Choice of Words: Let the Film-makers Pick Their Own." *New York Times*, 11 Feb. 1962, sec. 2, p. 1.

Delahaye, Michael, and Jacques Rivette. "Entretiens—Le depart pour mars." *Cahiers du cinema* 205 (Oct. 1968): 20–33.

"Film Unions and the Low Budget Independent Film Production—An Exploratory Discussion." *Film Culture*, nos. 22–23 (Summer 1961): 134–50.

Gilliatt, Penelope. "The Connection." *Sight and Sound* 30, no. 3 (Summer 1961): 145–46.

"How to Get a Free Hand in American Film-making." *London Times*, 17 June 1961, C5.

Lithgow, James. "Filmmakers' Distribution Center." *Filmmakers Newsletter* (Apr. 1969).

Madsen, Axel. "Recontre avec Shirley Clarke." *Cahiers du cinema*, no. 153 (Mar. 1964): 20–26.

Mekas, Jonas. "Movie Journal: Open Letter to the New York Daily Movie Critics." *Village Voice* 7, no. 51 (11 Oct. 1962): 13.

———. "Shirley Clarke: Retrospective at the Museum of Modern Art, New York." *Village Voice* 16, no. 20 (20 May 1971): 63.

Miller, Warren. *The Cool World*. Boston: Little, Brown, 1959.

New York State Board of Regents v. *The Connection* Company, 12 NY2d 779 (New York State Court of Appeals, 1962).

Polt, Harriet. "Interview with Shirley Clarke." *Film Comment* 2, no. 2 (Spring 1964): 31–32.

Rabinovitz, Lauren. "Choreography of Cinema: An Interview with Shirley Clarke." *Afterimage* 11, no. 5 (Dec. 1983): 8–11.

Rice, Susan. "Shirley Clarke: Image and Images." *Take One* 3, no. 2 (Nov.–Dec. 1970): 20–22.

Richie, Donald. "Letter from Cannes." *The Nation* 192, no. 24 (17 June 1961): 526–27.

Rosen, Marjorie. "Shirley Clarke: Videospace Explorer." *Ms.* 3, no. 10 (Apr. 1975): 107–10.

"The Sad Boppers." *Newsweek* 63, no. 16 (20 Apr. 1964): 114.

Taylor, Nora E. "Finding a Market for 'Personal Cinema.' " *Christian Science Monitor*, 14 Sept. 1968, 10.

Thompson, Howard. "Big Country in 'Loops.' " *New York Times*, 20 Apr. 1958, sec. 2, p. 7.

———. "Shirley Clarke: Lady with a Lens." *New York Times*, 4 Sept. 1955.

————. "The 16mm Honor Roll." *New York Times,* 29 Dec. 1957, sec. 2, p. 5.

Tomkins, Calvin. "All Pockets Open." *New Yorker* 48, no. 46 (6 Jan. 1973): 31–49.

Vogel, Amos. "Brakhage, Brecht, Berlin, Eden West and East." *Village Voice* 10, no. 10 (23 Dec. 1965).

Ward, Melinda, and Bruce Jenkins, eds. *The American New Wave: 1958–1967.* Minneapolis and Buffalo: Walker Art Center and Media Study, 1982.

Wright, Basil, and Arlene Croce. " 'The Connection'—Pro and Con." *Film Quarterly* 15, no. 4 (Summer 1962): 41–45.

Young, Colin, and Gideon Bachmann. "New Wave—or Gesture?" *Film Quarterly* 14, no. 3 (Spring 1961): 6–14.

Joyce Wieland

Materials on Joyce Wieland are held in several locations. The National Gallery of Canada, Ottawa, Ontario, has a file of published articles on Joyce Wieland as well as all records of her relationship with the National Gallery. The materials contained here include detailed correspondence, financial arrangements, and all other records pertaining to her 1971 National Gallery of Canada show, *True Patriot Love/Véritable amour patriotique.*

The Isaacs Gallery, Toronto, Ontario, also keeps a file on record of published materials on Joyce Wieland. Most of the materials here pertain to her work as a visual artist and document her professional career.

The Midwest Film Center, School of the Art Institute of Chicago, has materials relating to *The Far Shore.* Because the Film Center held the United States premiere of the film, it received and has preserved a full package of all published and publicity materials relating to the film's history and reception.

In 1988–89, Joyce Wieland donated her personal papers to York University Library, Special Collections, Toronto, Canada.

Interviews with Joyce Wieland in Toronto, Canada, on 14, 15 and 16 Nov. 1979, and 11 Mar., 1980, supplement other materials.

Works by Joyce Wieland

Wieland, Joyce. "A qui nada 1970." *Canadian Forum* 50 (June 1971): 19–22.

————. "Artist Wieland Finds Maturity." *Toronto Star,* 27 Apr. 1980, D10.

————. "Jigs and Reels." In *Form and Structure in Recent Film,* edited by Dennis Wheeler. Vancouver: Vancouver Art Gallery/Talon Books, 1972.

————. "North America's Second All-woman Film Crew." *Take One* 1, no. 8 (1967–68): 14–15.

————. " 'Pierre Vallières?': Notes from the Film-makers." In *New Forms in Film,* edited by Annette Michelson. Montreux, Switzerland, 1974, 117.

————. "True Patriot Love: A Canadian Love, Technology, Leadership and Art Story." *Film Culture,* no. 52 (Spring 1971): 64–73.

——. *True Patriot Love/Véritable amour patriotique.* Ottawa: National Gallery of Canada, 1971.

——, and Hollis Frampton. "I Don't Even Know about the Second Stanza." TS, New York City, May 1971. National Gallery of Canada.

Works about Joyce Wieland

Armatage, Kay, director. *Artist on Fire.* 1987.

——. "The Feminine Body: Joyce Wieland's *Water Sark.*" *Canadian Woman Studies* 8, no. 1 (Spring 1987): 84–88.

——, and Linda Beath. "Canadian Women's Cinema." In *Women and Film Festival Notes.* Toronto: Toronto Women and Film Festival, 1973, 5–6.

Auchterlonie, Bill. "Joyce Wieland Filmmaker—*The Far Shore* in Progress." *Art Magazine* 7, no. 24 (Jan. 1976): 6–11.

Balkind, Alvin. *17 Canadian Artists: A Protean View.* Vancouver: Vancouver Art Gallery, 1976.

Banning, Kass. "The Mummification of Mommy: Joyce Wieland as the AGO's First Living Other." *C Magazine,* no. 13 (Mar. 1987): 32–38.

——. "Textual Excess in Joyce Wieland's *Handtinting.*" *CineAction!* no. 5 (Spring 1986): 12–14.

Beattie, Eleanor. *The Handbook of Canadian Film,* 2d ed. Toronto: Peter Martin Associates, 1977.

Bowser, Sara. "Art: Joyce Wieland." *Canadian Architect* 5, no. 10 (Oct. 1960): 69–71.

Burnett, David. *Toronto Painting '84.* Toronto: Art Gallery of Ontario, 1984.

Cameron, Janice, ed. *Eclectic Eve.* Toronto: Woman's Press, 1974.

Camper, Fred. "Avant-garding the Future." *Chicago Reader,* 3 Mar. 1978, 16.

Chandler, John. "Drawing Reconsidered." *Artscanada* 27, no. 5 (Oct. 1970): 19–56.

Cornwell, Regina. *Snow Seen: The Films and Photographs of Michael Snow.* Toronto: Peter Martin Associates, 1979.

——. "True Patriot Love: The Films of Joyce Wieland." *Artforum* 10, no. 1 (Sept. 1971): 36–40.

Cowan, Bob. "Letter from New York City." *Take One* 2, no. 6 (July 1969): 25–26.

——. "New York Letter." *Take One* 1, no. 10 (July 1968): 29.

Crean, Susan M. "Notes from the Language of Emotion: A Conversation with Joyce Wieland." *Canadian Art* 4, no. 1 (Spring 1987): 64–65.

Dault, Gary Michael. "Bill's Hat." *Artscanada* 25, no. 2 (Apr. 1968): 42.

"Debby Magidson and Judy Wright Interview Joyce Wieland." *Canadian Forum* 54 (May–June 1974).

Delaney, Marshall. "Wielandism: A Personal Style in Full Bloom." *Saturday Night* 91, no. 3 (May 1976): 76–77.

Donnell, David. "Joyce Wieland at the Isaacs Gallery, Toronto." *Canadian Art* 21, no. 2 (Mar.–Apr. 1964): 64.

Farber, Manny. "Film." *Artforum* 8, no. 5 (Jan: 1970): 28–29.

———. "Films at Canadian Artists '68." *Artscanada* 26, no. 1 (Feb. 1969): 28–29.

———. "La raison avant passion." *Artscanada* 26, no. 4 (Aug. 1969): 45–46.

Farr, Dorothy, and Natalie Luckyj. *From Women's Eyes: Women Painters in Canada*. Kingston: Agnes Etherington Art Centre, 1975.

"The Far Shore." *Variety*, 18 Aug. 1976.

Feldman, Seth, and Joyce Nelson. *Canadian Film Reader*. Toronto: Peter Martins Associates, 1977.

Fetherling, Doug. "Wieland's Vision." *Canadian Forum* 56 (May 1976): 40–41.

Foreman, Richard. "New Cinema Festival at Jewish Museum." *Artscanada* 24, no. 2 (Apr. 1967): 9–10.

Freedman, Adele. "Joyce Wieland's Re-emergence: The Arctic Light at the End of *The Far Shore*." *Toronto Life*, June 1980, 184–85.

Fulford, Robert. *Marshall Delaney at the Movies: The Contemporary World as Seen on Film*. Toronto: Peter Martins Associates, 1974.

Gow, Gordon. "Underground Patriotism." *Films and Filming* 19, no. 5 (Feb. 1973): 65–66.

Graham, Mayo. *Some Canadian Women Artists*. Ottawa: National Gallery of Canada, 1975.

Gronau, Anna. "Avant-garde Film by Women: To Conceive a New Language of Desire." In *The Event Horizon: Essays on Hope, Sexuality, Social Space and Media(tion) in Art*, edited by Lorne Falk and Barbara Fischer. Toronto: Coach House Press and Walter Phillips Gallery, 1987, 159–76.

Hale, Barrie. "Son of Toronto Painting 1953–1965." *Artscanada* 30, no. 1 (Feb.–Mar. 1973): 56–64.

———. "The Vanguard of Vision: Notes on Snow and Wieland." *Saturday Night* (June 1974): 21–23.

Harcourt, P. "The Far Shore." *Take One* 5, no. 2 (May 1976).

Holstein, J. "New York's Vitality Tonic for Canadian Artists." *Canadian Art* 21, no. 5 (Sept.–Oct. 1964): 270–79.

Hume, Christopher. "Art of the Matter." *Flare* 9, no. 4 (Apr. 1987): 65.

"Kay Armatage Interviews Joyce Wieland." *Take One* 3, no. 2 (Nov.–Dec. 1970): 23–25. Reprinted in *Women and the Cinema*, edited by Karyn Kay and Gerald Peary. New York: E. P. Dutton, 1977.

Kome, Penney. "Joyce Wieland: Artist and Filmmaker." *Chatelaine* 49, no. 4 (Apr. 1976).

Landsberg, Michelle. "Joyce Wieland: Artist in Movieland." *Chatelaine* 49, no. 10 (Oct. 1976).

Lippard, Lucy. *Pop Art*. New York: Praeger, 1966.

Lord, Barry. *The History of Painting in Canada: Towards a People's Art*. Toronto: N. C. Press, 1974.

McLarty, Lianne M. "The Experimental Films of Joyce Wieland." *Cine-tracts* 5, no. 1 (Summer-Fall 1982): 51–63.

McPherson, Hugo. "Toronto's New Art Scene." *Canadian Art* 22, no. 1 (Jan.–Feb. 1965): 8–23.

———. "Wieland: An Epiphany of North." *Artscanada* 28, no. 4 (Aug.–Sept. 1971): 17–27.

Magidson, Debbie. "Joyce Wieland's Vision." *Canadian Forum* 55 (Sept. 1975): 70–71.

———. "True Patriot Love." *Art and Artists* 8 (Oct. 1973): 38–41.

Malcolmson, Harry. "True Patriot Love—Joyce Wieland's New Show." *Canadian Forum* 50 (June 1971): 17–18.

Martineau, Barbara Halpern. "The Far Shore." *Cinema Canada* 27 (Apr. 1976): 20–23.

Mekas, Jonas. "Movie Journal." *Village Voice* 13, no. 37 (27 June 1968): 41.

———. "Movie Journal." *Village Voice* 14, no. 25 (3 Apr. 1969): 53.

———. "Movie Journal." *Village Voice* 14, no. 58 (20 Nov. 1969): 57.

———. "Movie Journal. *Village Voice* 17, no. 28 (13 July 1972): 57.

Mendes, Ross. "Light: 24 Frames per Second." *Canadian Forum* 49 (Sept. 1969): 135–36.

Monk, Philip, ed. *Joyce Wieland.* Toronto: Key Porter Books, 1987.

Montagnes, Anne. "Myth in Many Media: Joyce Wieland." *Communique,* no. 8 (May 1975): 36–39.

Moses, Michele. "A Glimpse of 'The Far Shore.' " *Cinema Canada,* no. 23 (Nov. 1975): 41–43.

Murray, Joan. "A Lusty Salute to the Erotic." *Macleans* (9 Mar. 1981): 70–71.

Paikowsky, Sandra. *Joyce Wieland: A Decade of Painting.* Montreal: Concordia University and Concordia Art Gallery, 1985.

Pinney, Marguerite. "Joyce Wieland Retrospective, Vancouver Art Gallery." *Artscanada* 25, no. 3 (June 1968): 41.

Porter, John. "Artists Discovering Film, Post-war Toronto." *Vanguard* 13, nos. 5–6 (Summer 1984): 24–26.

———. "Consolidating Film Activity: Toronto in the 60s." *Vanguard* 13, no. 9 (Nov. 1984): 26–29.

Pringle, Douglas. "La raison avant la passion." *Artscanada* 26, no. 4 (Aug. 1969): 45–46.

Rabinovitz, Lauren. "The Development of Feminist Aesthetics in the Films of Joyce Wieland." *Film Reader* 5 (1982): 132–40.

———. "An Interview with Joyce Wieland." *Afterimage* 8, no. 10 (May 1981): 8–12.

———. "Issues of Feminist Aesthetics: Judy Chicago and Joyce Wieland." *Woman's Art Journal* 1, no. 2 (Fall 1980–Winter 1981): 38–41.

Reid, Alison. *Canadian Women Film Makers.* Ottawa: Canadian Film Institute, 1972.

Reid, Dennis. *A Concise History of Canadian Painting.* Toronto: Oxford University Press, 1973.

———. *Toronto Painting: 1953–1965.* Ottawa: National Gallery of Canada, 1972.

Scott, Jay. "Full Circle: True, Patriot Womanhood, The 30-Year Passage of Joyce Wieland." *Canadian Art* 4, no. 1 (Spring 1987): 56–63.

Silcox, D. P. "Canadian Art in the Sixties." *Canadian Art* 23, no. 1 (Jan.–Feb. 1966): 55–61.

Sitney, P. Adams. "There Is Only One Joyce." *Artscanada* 27, no. 2 (Apr. 1970): 43–45.

Stacey, Robert H. "Joyce Wieland." In *Lives and Works of the Canadian Artists,* vol. 16, edited by Robert H. Stacey. Toronto: Dundurn Press, 1977.

Steed, Judy, director. *A Film about Joyce Wieland.* 1972.

Théberge, Pierre. "Interview with Joyce Wieland, New York, Mar. 28 1971." Translated by Michael Snow. National Gallery of Canada.

————, and Alison Reid. *Joyce Wieland Drawings for 'The Far Shore.'* Ottawa: National Gallery of Canada, 1978.

Wedman, Les. "The Far Shore." *Cinema Canada* 32 (Nov. 1976): 30.

Wilkin, Karen. "The Late-blooming Vitalilty of Toronto Art." *Art News* 79, no. 2 (Feb. 1980): 50–55.

Withrow, William J. *Contemporary Canadian Painting.* Toronto: McClelland and Stewart, 1972.

Wordsworth, Anne. "Interview with Joyce Wieland." *Descant,* nos. 8–9 (Spring-Summer 1974): 108–10.

Index

Note on the Author

Lauren Rabinovitz is an associate professor in American Studies and Communication Studies at the University of Iowa. She received her Ph.D. from the University of Texas at Austin. She has published many articles about experimental cinema, animation, and video, as well as about women and cinema.